REGIMES
of
HISTORICITY

European Perspectives

European Perspectives
A Series in Social Thought and Cultural Criticism
Lawrence D. Kritzman, Editor

European Perspectives presents outstanding books by leading European thinkers. With both classic and contemporary works, the series aims to shape the major intellectual controversies of our day and to facilitate the tasks of historical understanding. For a complete list of books in the series, see pages 261–262.

REGIMES

of

HISTORICITY

PRESENTISM AND EXPERIENCES OF TIME

FRANÇOIS HARTOG

TRANSLATED BY
SASKIA BROWN

COLUMBIA UNIVERSITY PRESS   *New York*

COLUMBIA UNIVERSITY PRESS
PUBLISHERS SINCE 1893
NEW YORK   CHICHESTER, WEST SUSSEX

Copyright © 2003 et 2011 Editions du Seuil pour *Présentisme simple ou par défaut?*
Collection La Librairie du XXIᵉ siècle, sous las direction de Maurice Olender
English translation copyright © 2015 Columbia University Press
Paperback edition, 2017

Cet ouvrage a bénéficié du soutien des Programmes d'aide à la publication de l'Institut français.
This work, published as part of a program of aid for publication,
received support from the Institut Français.

All rights reserved

Library of Congress Cataloging-in-Publication Data
Hartog, François, author.
[Croire en l'Histoire. English]
Regimes of historicity : presentism and experiences of time / François Hartog;
translated by Saskia Brown.
pages cm. — (European perspectives: a series in social thought and cultural criticism)
Includes bibliographical references and index.
ISBN 978-0-231-16376-7 (cloth: alk. paper)—ISBN 978-0-231-16377-4 (pbk. : alk. paper)—
ISBN 978-0-231-53876-3 (e-book)
1. Historiography.   2. History—Philosophy.   I. Brown, Saskia, translator.   II. Title.

D16.8 H37813 2015
907.2—dc23

2014026337

Columbia University Press books are printed on permanent and durable acid-free paper.
Printed in the United States of America

COVER IMAGE: ALESSANDRO RIZZI © GETTYIMAGES
BOOK AND COVER DESIGN: CHANG JAE LEE

*To Jipé Vernant,
by the light of Samzun*

"—in Time"
—MARCEL PROUST

CONTENTS

Presentism: Stopgap or New State? xiii

Introduction: Orders of Time and Regimes of Historicity 1

Gaps 3

From the Pacific to Berlin 7

Universal Histories 11

Regimes of Historicity 15

ORDERS OF TIME 1 21

1. Making History: Sahlins's Islands 23

The Heroic Regime 28

From Myth to Event 32

Working Misunderstandings: From Event to Myth 34

Anthropology and Forms of Temporality 38

2. From Odysseus's Tears to Augustine's Meditations 41

Each Day Is the First Day 41

Odysseus's Tears 46

The Sirens' Call to Oblivion 52

Odysseus Has Not Read Augustine 55

3. Chateaubriand, Between Old and New Regimes of Historicity 65

The Young Chateaubriand's Journey 66

Historia magistra vitae 72

The American Trunk 77

The Experience of Time 79

The Time of Traveling and Time in the *Travels* 81

Ruins 89

ORDERS OF TIME 2 97

4. Memory, History, and the Present 101

The Modern Regime's Crises 104

The Rise of Presentism 107

The Fault Lines of the Present 114

Memory and History 120

National Histories 131

Commemorations 141

The Moment of the *Lieux de mémoire* 143

5. Heritage and the Present   149

A History of the Concept of Heritage   151

Antiquity   155

Rome   162

The French Revolution   170

Toward Universalization   180

The Time of the Environment   186

Our Doubly Indebted Present: The Reign of Presentism   193

Notes   205
Index   247

PRESENTISM

STOPGAP OR NEW STATE?

AT THE TIME THIS BOOK WAS FIRST PUBLISHED, IN 2003, it already talked of a crisis of time, but obviously not of the crisis that has engulfed us since 2008—and I would not go so far as to claim for myself the gift of prophecy (not even with hindsight). However, it is not hard to see that links exist between the crisis, initially financial, which radiated out from the United States, and a world so enslaved to the present that no other viewpoint is considered admissible. What words have we been hearing since 2008? Essentially "crisis," "recession," "depression," but also "(total) transformation" and even "change of era." Some swear by the idea that "nothing will ever be the same again," while others (or the same) just as noisily declare that "the economy is getting back on track" (that is, just like before), that "the green shoots" are visible, that the upturn is just around the corner and we can see the light at the end of the tunnel....

And then no, hopes are dashed again, this recession is still with us—or rather, back it comes—and even more threateningly than before. In any case, "unemployment is due to rise" (again), and the only business plans anyone still dares to make are redundancy lists. In Europe it is now all the fault of certain countries' public deficits, while financial speculation seems to have been forgotten and, besides, is doing nicely, thank you (and what more presentist phenomenon than this speculation?). The split-second time of the markets can be accommodated neither by the economy nor by politics, which itself obeys several times: the imperious time of the electoral calendar, the age-old idea of "saving time" (by deciding to defer decisions till later), and, last but not least, the time of the spin doctors (whose unit of measurement is media time). And so political leaders are required to "rescue" the euro, for instance—or the whole financial system, for that matter—every month or so, or at least to declare they are doing so. And this raises an even more fundamental problem: our old representative democracies are beginning to realize that they don't really know how to adapt their methods and rhythms of decision making to this tyranny of the immediate without sacrificing precisely what made them democratic in the first place.

We have heard over and over again that there is a big, bad, short-termist financial capitalism, to be contrasted with a good old industrial capitalism and its managers of yesteryear, or only yesterday. But ever since historians started taking an interest in the history of capitalism, they have noted its malleability, and if there is any unity to the concept, in its path from thirteenth-century Italy to the whole of the Western world today, it resides first and foremost, as Fernand Braudel has argued, in its seemingly limitless plasticity, its capacity to mutate and adapt. Capitalism, which Braudel distinguished from the market economy, always goes where there are profits to be made: "It represents the high-profit zone." The Belgian historian Henri Pirenne was also struck by the "truly surprising regularity with which phases of economic freedom and of economic regulation have succeeded each other" in capitalism's history since the Middle Ages. And Marc Bloch pointed out, in a lecture given in 1937, that ever since Solon canceled all debts in sixth-century B.C. Athens, "economic progress has consisted of a series of bankruptcies."

Without wishing to transform this preface into a commentary on our present crisis, I think it needs to be said that once the 2008 financial collapse had been dealt with *in extremis*, it seemed—and it still seems—extremely difficult to see beyond it. Reactions were legion, and actions few. A mantra such as "the recovery" could suddenly sound reassuring because "recovering" means "getting back to where we were before." It is a candid expression of our collective inability to shake off what is generally called "short-termism" and which I prefer to call "presentism": the sense that only the present exists, a present characterized at once by the tyranny of the instant and by the treadmill of an unending now.

WHAT DOES THE HISTORIAN HAVE TO OFFER? NOT "THE *recovery*," obviously, but perhaps, by taking a step back, the *discovery* of something other than this mesmerizing present. The historian practices viewing from afar. In this book, I shall use and test out the notion of "regime of historicity" as a tool for creating this distance, with a view to having a finer understanding at the end of the process of what is close by. At least, that is my intention and my hope.[1]

My hypothesis (presentism) and my methodological instrument (the regime of historicity) belong together. The notion of a "regime of historicity" helps shape the hypothesis of presentism, and the latter helps flesh out the notion of a "regime of historicity." The two are inseparable, at least in the first instance. Why "regime" rather than "form" (of historicity)? And why "regime of historicity" rather than "regime of temporality"? The term "regime" encompasses the senses of dietary regime (*regimen* in Latin, *diaita* in Greek), of political regime (*politeia*), of the regime of the winds, and in French the term extends to an engine's speed (*le régime d'un moteur*), its revs per minute. What these relatively disparate domains have in common is the idea of degrees, of more or less, of mixtures and composites, and an always provisional or unstable equilibrium. Speaking of a "regime of historicity" is thus simply a way of linking together past, present, and future, or of mixing the three categories, in the same way that one talks of a "mixed constitution" in Greek political theory (combining elements of aristocracy, oligarchy, and democracy, one of which was always dominant in practice).

And why "historicity"? This is a weighty philosophical term, with a long history behind it, extending from Hegel to Ricoeur, via Dilthey and Heidegger. Whatever the emphasis given—on the human being's self-awareness as a historical being, on his finitude, or on his openness toward the future (in Heidegger's "being-for-death")—the term essentially refers to how individuals or groups situate themselves and develop in time, that is, the forms taken by their historical condition. But, you may ask, can one legitimately talk of "historicity" before even the advent of the modern concept of history (between the end of the eighteenth and the beginning of the nineteenth century)? Yes, if by "historicity" we mean this primary experience of *estrangement*, of distance between self and self, to which the categories of past, present, and future give order and meaning, enabling it to be grasped and expressed. For example, going way back to Homer, one could cite the scene in which Odysseus hears his own exploits sung by the Phaeacian bard. Odysseus is suddenly confronted with his inability to link his previous identity as the glorious victor of Troy to his present one as a shipwrecked and destitute castaway who has lost everything, right down to his own name. What he lacks is precisely the category of the past through which he could recognize himself in that other who is nonetheless himself. A different, but related, experience from the early fifth century this time can be found in Saint Augustine's major meditation on time, in chapter XI of the *Confessions*. At the outset, the problem is not abstract time, but the time he himself experiences, in its three modes of memory (the presence of the past), attention (the presence of the present), and expectation (the presence of the future). Arguably then, the notion of a "regime of historicity" is applicable prior to and independently of the crystallization of the modern concept of history, for example as Reinhart Koselleck has powerfully theorized it.

As for why I have opted for (regimes of) "historicity" rather than of "temporality," the latter has the disadvantage of referring to an external standard of time, such as can still be found in Braudel, where the different *durées* are all measured against an "exogenous," mathematical, or astronomical time (which Braudel himself calls the "imperious time of the world").

So what is a regime of historicity, and what is it not? It is not a factual given. It cannot be observed directly, nor found in today's almanacs. It is constructed by the historian. Regimes do not come in a series, one mechanically following another, whether these are understood as sent from heaven or emanating from the earth. They are not the same as Bossuet's or Condorcet's "stages" and are not remotely related to those vast and vague approximations we call civilizations. A regime of historicity is, rather, an artificial construct whose value lies in its heuristic potential. And it should be classed alongside Weber's ideal type, as a formal category. Depending on whether the category of the past, the future, or the present is dominant, the order of time derived from it will obviously not be the same. Hence certain behaviors, certain actions, and certain forms of historiography are more possible than others, more—or less—in tune with the times, untimely or seemingly perfectly timed. A regime of historicity is a category (without content), which can elucidate our experiences of time, and nothing restricts it to the European or Western world alone. On the contrary, in its very conception it is intended as a tool for comparative study.

I will use "regime of historicity" sometimes in a broad, macrohistorical sense, and sometimes in a narrow, microhistorical one. It can help us understand the biography of an ordinary person or equally of a historical figure like Napoleon, caught between the modern regime introduced by the Revolution and the old regime symbolized by the Empire and his marriage to Marie Louise of Austria. With it, we can delve into a major work (whether literary or not), for instance Chateaubriand's *Memoirs*, in which the author characterizes himself as "a swimmer who has plunged into the river of time, struggling between its two banks." It can equally be used to examine a city's architecture, past and present, or to compare the dominant rhythms and changing relations to time of different societies, near and far. Whatever the particular focus, I hope to generate new insights through close attention to moments of crisis of time and how these are expressed.

LET ME ATTEMPT AT THE OUTSET TO DISPEL SOME misunderstandings, first and foremost the possible confusion of "presentism" with "the present." My hypothesis of presentism does not automatically imply that I condemn or am hostile to the present. My position is neither nostalgic (in relation to another, better regime) nor accusatory, but it also rejects any uncritical acceptance of the present order of time as it stands. Evoking an omnipresent present in no way exempts us from exploring ways out of it but quite the contrary: in a world in which presentism reigns supreme, the historian's place is more than ever among those who "vigilantly watch over the present [*les guetteurs du présent*]," in Charles Péguy's words.

The French neologism *le présentisme* [presentism] was first coined by analogy with *le futurisme* [futurism], in which the future laid down the law. For me "presentism" was initially a hypothesis, which came with a series of questions: does our way of articulating past, present, and future have something specific to it, something which makes today's present, here and now, different from previous presents? Convinced that yes, there is something specific about our present, I was led to a further question not yet formulated in those terms in the book's first edition: is our presentism a *stopgap* or a new *state*? Is it simply a pause, a moment of stasis before we move on again to a more or less "radiant" future, a futurist type of future (given that we are unlikely to turn to a past-oriented regime)? Or is this omnipresent present ("omnipresent" like "omnivorous") a substantial state? In which case it might indicate a new experience of time and a new regime of historicity, all the more distinctive for the fact that the West has spent the last two hundred years dancing to the tune of the future—and making others do likewise. It is too early to tell. This presentist present is by no means uniform or clear-cut, and it is experienced very differently, depending on one's position in society. On the one hand there is the time of flows and acceleration, and of a valued and valorizing mobility, and on the other what the sociologist Robert Castel calls the "status of casual workers [*le précariat*]," whose present is languishing before their very eyes, who have no past except in a complicated way (especially in the case of immigrants, exiles, and migrants), and no real future either (the temporality of plans and projects is denied them). Today's presentism can thus be experienced as emancipation or enclosure: ever greater speed and mobility or living from hand to mouth in a stagnating present. Not to forget a further aspect of our present: that the future is perceived as a threat not a promise. The future is a time of disasters, and ones we have, moreover, brought upon ourselves.

It becomes clear, therefore, that a lot more thought is needed to understand this crisis through which we are struggling somewhat blindly. The concept of presentism alone cannot explain it (and makes no pretence to, either), but perhaps it can highlight the risks and consequences of living in a world governed solely by an omnipresent and omnipotent present, in which immediacy alone has value. What I am endeavoring to do in this context is, as previously, to understand our present conjuncture through the questions I ask as a historian, working alongside others, and steering clear of any nostalgic outpourings or dogmatic pronouncements. In order that, in Michel de Certeau's resonant words, we may move from "the uncanniness of 'what happens' today" to "the discursivity of 'understanding.'"

People in search of a presentist experience need only look around them at certain cityscapes, replicated across the globe, for which the Dutch architect Rem Koolhaas has invented the concept "Generic City," associated with the notion of "Junkspace." This is where presentism is really at home, eating up space and reducing or banishing time. The Generic City, freed from its enslavement to the center, is without history, even if it goes to great lengths to advertise its pseudo-historical district, where history is a service provided, complete with quaint trains and horse-drawn carriages. And if, despite everything, a center survives, it has to be at once "the most old and the most new," "the most fixed and the most dynamic." As the product of "an encounter between escalator and air-conditioning, conceived in an incubator of Sheetrock," Junkspace never ages: it knows only self-destruction and on-site rebuilding or else almost instantaneous dilapidation. Airports, completed or (constantly) under construction (the ubiquitous *"Work in progress. We apologize for the temporary inconvenience caused"*) have become emblematic of the Generic City. They are forever transforming and mutating, while imposing ever more complex trajectories on their temporary inhabitants. As bubbles of expanding, transformable space, they epitomize Junkspace, and are its principle producers. Such space leaves no trace in our memories, because "its refusal to freeze ensures instant amnesia."[2] But can one actually *live* in a presentist city?

REGIMES
of
HISTORICITY

INTRODUCTION
ORDERS OF TIME AND
REGIMES OF HISTORICITY

NO ONE DOUBTS THAT AN ORDER OF TIME EXISTS—OR RATHER, that orders of time exist which vary with time and place. These orders are, in any event, so imperious and apparently so self-evident that we bow to them without even realizing it, without meaning to or wanting to, and whether we are aware of it or not. All resistance is in vain. For a society's relations to time hardly seem open to discussion or negotiation. The term "order" implies at once succession and command: the times (in the plural) *dictate* or *defy*, time *avenges* wrongs, it *restores* order following a disruption, or *sees justice done*. "Order of time" can thus immediately shed light on another expression that might initially seem a little enigmatic, "regimes of historicity."

As early as the fifth century B.C. the Greek philosopher Anaximander used the expression "order of time" to suggest, precisely, that things "suffer punishment and give satisfaction to one another for injustice according to the order of time."[1] For Herodotus, history was essentially the interval, calculated in generations, between an injustice and its punishment or redress. The historian's task was to study the delays of divine vengeance, with a view to using this knowledge to identify and link up the two ends of the chain.

For example, the true meaning behind the reversal of fortune suffered by King Croesus was that at four generations' remove he was paying for the misdeeds of his ancestor Gyges.[2] This link between history and justice will not, however, be the path I follow here.

The expression "order of time" might also evoke Michel Foucault's *Order of Discourse*, a short and engaging programmatic text, given as his Inaugural Lecture at the Collège de France in 1971. It still speaks to us, inviting us to take his work further, elsewhere, in different ways, and with different questions.[3] I would thus be doing for time what Foucault previously did for discourse, or would at least draw my inspiration from this. Lastly, *The Order of Time* is actually the title of the historian Krzysztof Pomian's important work on time, which he described as a history of "time itself," a "philosophical" history of time, "approached from an encyclopaedic perspective."[4]

Time has recently become something of an obsession. It is the subject of books, journals, and conferences, more or less everywhere. Literature too is dealing with it, in its own way. An attack of "time-itis" was what our doctors of the intellect instantly diagnosed. Indeed—meaning . . . ? At best, this label suggests "Watch out—problem area."[5] The work of Paul Ricoeur, from *Time and Narrative* (1983) to *Memory, History, Forgetting* (2000), conveniently frames the period in question. It shows how a philosopher who had always sought to be the contemporary of his contemporaries was drawn to reflect on the aporias in the experience of time, before turning later to issues around "a policy of the just allotment of memory." In *Time and Narrative* Ricoeur linked up "temporal experience and the narrative operation" directly, but at the price of "an impasse in respect to memory," as he himself acknowledged. *Memory, History, Forgetting* was an attempt to remedy this omission by investigating the "median levels" between time and narrative,[6] moving from the truth of history to the faithfulness of memory, while keeping both in play.

A few years earlier, Michel de Certeau had remarked, as though in passing, that "for three centuries maybe the objectification of the past has made of time the unreflected category of a discipline that never ceases to use it as an instrument of classification."[7] It was a thought-provoking statement, and these pages can be read as my attempt to follow it through, starting from an assessment of where we are today.

Gaps

Our relations to time were suddenly and irreversibly shattered and confounded by certain events of the recent past: the fall of the Berlin Wall in 1989, the collapse of the communist ideal as the future of the revolution, and the simultaneous rise of a number of fundamentalist movements.[8] Everywhere the order of time ceased to be self-evident. Fundamentalisms, with their mixture of archaic and modern features, grapple in part with a crisis of the future. Since the traditions they turn to in order to remedy the ills of the present are incapable of opening onto a future, they are largely "invented."[9] How, in such conditions, can past, present, and future be articulated? In 1995 François Furet wrote that history had once again become

> a tunnel that we enter in darkness, not knowing where our actions will lead, uncertain of our destiny, stripped of the illusory security of a science of what we do. At the end of the twentieth century, deprived of God, we have seen the foundations of deified history crumbling—a disaster that must somehow be averted. To add to this threat of uncertainty, there is the shock of a closed future.[10]

In Europe, deep rifts had already begun to appear many years previously, in the aftermath of the First World War and, differently, after 1945. Paul Valéry's writings provide a sensitive seismograph of the former. In 1919 he wrote of "our Hamlet of Europe," gazing out "on an immense sort of terrace of Elsinore" at "millions of ghosts." "He broods on the tedium of rehearsing the past and the folly of always trying to innovate. He staggers between two abysses." And, in a lecture from 1935, Valéry drew an even sharper picture of this experience of broken continuity, where "each person" feels he belongs to "two eras." "On the one hand," he continued, "there is the past that can neither be abolished nor forgotten, but from which we can derive almost nothing that will orient us in the present or help us to imagine the future. On the other hand, there is the future without the least shape."[11] So Valéry's experience of time, which he returned to again and again, was an experience of its disorientation, in which the "today" of his *Reflections on the World Today* was situated between two *abysses* or two *eras*. In 1920s Germany, a similar experience of time informed the writings of Franz Rosenzweig, Walter Benjamin, and Gershom Scholem, who each cast around for a new vision of history in which continuity and progress would be abandoned in favor of discontinuities and breaks.[12]

Stefan Zweig's *The World of Yesterday*, published in the same year as his suicide, also bore witness to such breaks: "All the bridges between our today and our yesterday and our yesteryear have been burnt."[13] That was in 1942, yet already in 1946 Lucien Febvre was exhorting all readers of the *Annales*, in an eloquently entitled editorial, "Facing Into the Wind," to "do history" in the knowledge that they had entered a world "in a state of irreversible instability," everywhere in ruins. But in this world there were "a lot more than ruins, and worse still: an extraordinary acceleration which, in telescoping continents, erasing oceans, and eradicating deserts, suddenly brings into contact human groups of opposite electrical charge." If we wished to understand tomorrow's—no, already today's—globalized world, we should, as a matter of urgency, look ahead, in front of us, and not backward at what had already taken place: "Yesterday's world is over. Over forever. If we French have a chance of pulling through, it is by grasping this obvious truth quicker and better than others. By not hanging onto the wreckage, but taking the plunge. In you go, I say, and keep your head above water." Explaining "the world to the world," and addressing the questions people ask themselves today—that is the task of the historian who faces into the wind. The point is not to wipe the slate of the past clean, but to "understand fully how it differs from the present,"[14] and so in what ways it is past. From everything in the few pages of this manifesto—its content, tone, and rhythm—the reader senses that there is no time to lose, and that the present dictates.[15]

Hannah Arendt was keenly aware of breaks in time as early as the 1950s, but that aspect of her work passed relatively unnoticed at the time. The poet René Char's assertion that "our heritage was not preceded by any *testament*," an aphorism published in his collection *Leaves of Hypnos* in 1946,[16] was an attempt to make sense of the strange experience of the French Resistance as an in-between time, in which a "treasure" had been discovered and fleetingly possessed, but which no one knew how to name or transmit. In Arendt's terms, this treasure was the ability to establish "a common world."[17] Just when Europe was at last enjoying liberation, the Resistance proved incapable of drawing up a "testament" to enshrine ways of preserving and, if possible, extending the public space it had begun to construct and in which "freedom could appear." Significantly, insofar as a testament "telling the heir what will rightfully be his, wills past possessions for a future," it is, from a temporal viewpoint, what "assigns a past to the future."[18]

Hannah Arendt's *Between Past and Future* opens precisely on Char's aphorism, as a way of introducing the concept of a "gap between past and future" around which the rest of the book is organized. This "gap" was an "odd in-between period . . . in historical time, during which one becomes aware of an interval in time which is entirely determined by things that are no longer and by things that are not yet."[19] Historical time appears to have come to a standstill. And in her pioneering work *On the Origins of Totalitarianism*, Arendt had come to the conclusion that "Western culture's innermost structure, with all its beliefs, had collapsed about our ears," in particular the modern concept of history, based on the notion of process.[20] Here again there was an experience of disorientated time.

In 1968 the Western and Westernized world was convulsed by a movement of contestation targeting, among other things, capitalist progress. It gave expression to a loss of faith in time itself as progress, that is, as an agent moving to overturn the present. The words "rift" and "breach" were used by contemporary observers to define this moment, even while they also noted the extensive use of images drawn from the glorious revolutions of the past.[21] The young rebels of the time, for the most part born after 1940, could, at least in France, turn to the great figures of the Resistance, as well as to the teachings of Mao's *Little Red Book* or to the example of the Vietnamese communists, who had beaten the former colonial ruler at Diên Biên Phù and would soon be claiming victory over America. Yet in a recent novel by Olivier Rolin the narrator describes his own origins to his much younger companion in the following terms: "It's from there [the years 1940–1945] you come, my friend, from this enormous disaster, without having been part of it. Your generation is born of an event it never knew."[22] The crisis of the 1970s (not least the oil crisis) seemed momentarily to confirm the challenges to the status quo. Some people even sang the praises of "zero growth"! France's postwar boom years had just come to an end, those three decades of reconstruction and rapid modernization when East and West competed over their achievements against the background of the Cold War and the nascent nuclear arms race.

The theme of "returns to" was soon to enjoy great success (becoming something of a prepackaged formula and a commercial product). Returns to Freud or Marx were subversive, but then came the returns to Kant or God, and many other fleeting "back to"'s which vanished no sooner than declared. Meanwhile, technological progress kept forging ahead, and the consumer society grew and grew, and with it the category of the present, which this society targeted and, to an extent, appropriated as its particular trademark. The products of the digital revolution, the much-vaunted information society, as well as advances in biotechnology, began to trickle down to the general public. Soon came the supremely imperious time of globalization in the form of a *world economy*, which pushed for ever greater mobility and referred increasingly to "real time." But it also came in the form of a *world heritage*, as codified in UNESCO's charters, such as the 1972 "Convention Concerning the Protection of the World Cultural and Natural Heritage."

The 1980s saw the idea of memory unfurl like a giant wave, accompanied by its more visible and tangible alter ego, heritage, and the issue of protecting, cataloguing, promoting, and rethinking it. Memorials were erected, museums of all sizes built, others renovated, and a nonspecialist public, concerned or curious about genealogy, began visiting the archives. The memory attached to places became important, and in 1984 a historian, Pierre Nora, introduced the idea of a "site of memory" (*lieu de mémoire*). The notion emerged from his assessment of France's present, and gave its title to his vast editorial project, the *Lieux de mémoire*.

At around the same time, Claude Lanzmann's *Shoah* (1985) was released, an extraordinarily powerful film on testimony and the "non-sites" of memory. In presenting the spectator with "people coming into their own as witnesses,"[23] the film aimed at abolishing the distance between past and present, making the past spring out from the present. A few years previously, in 1982, the American historian Yosef Yerushalmi had published *Zakhor*, which was an immediate success on both sides of the Atlantic. It launched the debates on history and memory. "Why is it," asked Yerushalmi, "that although Judaism throughout the ages was absorbed with the meaning of history, historiography itself played at best an ancillary role among the Jews, and often no role at all; and, concomitantly, that while memory of the past was always a central component of Jewish experience, the historian was not its primary custodian."²⁴

Here a little earlier, and there a little later, this groundswell touched the shores of almost all countries, if not all milieus. The wave broke first over Old Europe, and then swept across the United States, postdictatorship South America, the Russia of *glasnost*, the former Eastern block countries, and South Africa as it emerged from apartheid. The rest of Africa, Asia, and the Middle East remained relatively untouched (with the notable exception of Israeli society). After peaking in the mid-1990s, this phenomenon of memory developed in different directions depending on the particular context. But there can be no doubt that the crimes of the twentieth century, its mass murders and monstrous industry of death, were at the origin of these shock waves of memory, which finally caught up with our contemporary societies and shook them in their blast. The past just would not go away, and at the second or third generation it began to be questioned. Other, more recent tides of memory, such as those of communism, still have a long path ahead of them, and will advance at different speeds and rhythms.²⁵

At all events, "memory" became an all-embracing term, a metahistorical and even at times a theological category. It seemed that everything had the makings of memory, and in the duel between memory and history, the former quickly won the day, spearheaded by a figure who has come to occupy a central position in our public space: the witness.²⁶ We turned our attention to the issue of forgetting, and endorsed and promoted the "duty to remember"; we even began, at times, to condemn certain excesses of memory or heritage.²⁷

From the Pacific to Berlin

I did not focus directly on any of these large-scale movements. Being neither a historian of the contemporary world nor an analyst of current events, I pursued my research along other paths. Theorizing history is not immediately my field either, although I attempt wherever possible to reflect on history while doing history. So my intention here is not to add a better and broader explanation of these contemporary historical phenomena to the general ones already in existence. My approach is different, as is my aim. I address these phenomena obliquely, asking what temporalities structure and govern them. What order of time makes them possible? And of what order of time are they the symptoms or the messengers? What crisis of time do they signal?

To follow this up, I needed to find a specific angle of attack. As a historian of history, understood as a form of intellectual history, I have gradually come round to Michel de Certeau's idea that time has become so everyday for historians that they have naturalized or instrumentalized it. Time is an unthought, not because it is unthinkable, but because it is not thought or, more simply, no one gives it a thought. As a historian who tries to be attentive to his time, I have, like many others, observed how the category of the present has taken hold to such an extent that one can really talk of an omnipresent present.[28] This is what I call "presentism" here.

Can this phenomenon be more closely defined? How significant is it, and what does it mean? One can note, for example, that there emerged in the 1980s among French historians a "History of the present time." In the words of one of its most faithful advocates, René Rémond, "a history of the present is a good antidote to *a posteriori* rationalization, to the optical illusions that spatial and temporal distance can bring with them."[29] Professional historians were requested, and sometimes required, to respond to a plethora of demands for contemporary or very contemporary history. This history developed on various fronts, and came under the spotlight particularly in connection with crimes against humanity, which are characterized by their utterly novel temporality: for such crimes, statutory time limitations are not applicable.[30]

The notion of "regime of historicity" seemed particularly useful for my research. It had made a first unobtrusive appearance in my work in 1983, to account for what I considered the most interesting aspect of the American anthropologist Marshall Sahlins's thought. But no one paid it much attention at the time, I no more than others.[31] Times would have to change! Sahlins had been trying to determine the historical form characterizing the Pacific Islands by going back to Claude Lévi-Strauss's notions of "hot" and "cold" societies. I then left the expression alone, so to speak, without working on it further, until it re-emerged for me, not in relation to so-called savages in the past, but right next door and in the present. After 1989, the notion suddenly seemed self-evidently relevant, as the prism through which to examine a particular conjuncture in which the question of time had become an important stake and also a problem, occasionally to the point of obsession.

Meanwhile, I had become acquainted with the meta-historical categories of "experience" and "expectation," as defined by the German historian Reinhart Koselleck in his work on the semantics of historical time. He explored experiences of history through the question "how, in a given present, are the temporal dimensions of past and future related?"[32] Koselleck had hit upon a most interesting area, in which he was attentive to the tensions between the space of experience and the horizon of expectation, and to how the past, the present, and the future were articulated. The notion of regime of historicity could thus be enriched by a conversation struck up—even if only through my agency—between Sahlins and Koselleck, that is, between anthropology and history.

I took up the notion again and worked on it with an anthropologist, Gérard Lenclud, for a conference devised by the Hellenist Marcel Detienne, a fervent advocate of comparative study. It was a way of continuing, while also displacing somewhat, another dialogue between anthropology and history, the one which Lévi-Strauss had begun in 1949, and which had resurfaced from time to time, stagnated along the way, but never disappeared. At the time, I defined "regime of historicity" in two ways: in a restricted sense, as the way in which a given society approaches its past and reflects upon it; and in a broader sense, as "the modalities of self-consciousness that each and every society adopts in its constructions of time and its perceptions."[33] To borrow Lévi-Strauss's terms (which I return to below), the notion refers to how a particular human community "reacts" to a "degree of historicity" which is the same in all societies. More specifically, it is a tool for comparing different types of history, and also (or above all, I would now say) for highlighting modes of relation to time, and exploring forms of temporal experience here and elsewhere, today and in the past—in short, it serves to explore ways of being in time. Whereas Paul Ricoeur traced the *philosophical* concept of historicity from Hegel to Heidegger, defining it as "the historical condition,"[34] or "man present to himself as a being in history,"[35] I will focus rather on the *diversity* of regimes of historicity.

Lastly, the notion accompanied me during a fellowship at the Wissenschaftskolleg in Berlin in 1994, at a time when the traces of the Wall had not yet disappeared, when the city center was one huge building site of work in progress or still to come, when arguments already raged about the project to rebuild the City Palace, and when the huge, dilapidated buildings in the East, their façades riddled with bullet holes, made visible a time which, over there, had passed differently. It would be wrong, of course, to say that time had stood still. But, with its vast empty expanses, its cleared spaces, and its "shades," Berlin seemed a perfect city for historians, where more than elsewhere the unthought of time—and not only its forgetting, repression, or denial—could come to the surface.

All through the 1990s, Berlin, more than any other city in Europe and perhaps in the world, put thousands of people to work, from immigrant laborers to major international architects. It was manna from heaven for town planners and journalists, and became a mandatory and fashionable reference, a "good subject," a laboratory, and a space of "critical reflection." It generated countless commentaries and as many controversies, prodigious quantities of images, words, and texts, and in all likelihood a few great books as well.[36] And the city also experienced the suffering and disillusion these upheavals carried in their wake. In Berlin more than elsewhere time was a visible and a tangible problem that could not be eluded. What should the relations with the past be, or rather with pasts in the plural, but also, and no less importantly, with the future? Not forgetting the present, while also avoiding the other extreme, that of being blind to anything beyond it. In other words: how to inhabit the present, in the most literal sense? What should be destroyed, preserved, reconstructed, or built, and how? For any decisions and actions to be taken, relations to time had first to be clarified. Was the sheer obviousness of this fact behind our many efforts to evade it?

For on both sides of the Wall—which would gradually become a wall of time—the first step taken was to erase the past. Hans Scharoun's statement could be applied to both West and East: "One cannot hope at the same time to build a new society and to rebuild old buildings."[37] Scharoun, who is best known for building the Berlin Philharmonic concert hall, was a well-known architect who had presided over Berlin's planning and architecture commission immediately after the war. Now, as the twenty-first century has dawned, Berlin is an emblematic city, a site of memory for the whole of Europe, caught as it is between, broadly, amnesia and the duty to remember. There, the *flâneur*-historian can still come across fragments, signs, and traces of different orders of time (in the sense we give to orders of architecture).

Thus the notion of regime of historicity, which had first emerged for me on the shores of the Pacific Islands, ended up alighting at the heart of modern European history, in Berlin. That is where it took shape for me, in its reworked form. In the first section of this book, entitled "Orders of Time 1," I shall move from the Fiji Islands to Scheria—from the Pacific Ocean of Sahlins's research to the seas crossed by Homer's hero Odysseus—to test out the notion and practice of a twofold "view from afar." Then, in the course of a long voyage that will take us almost directly to late eighteenth-century Europe, I shall make a short stop under the heading "Odysseus Has Not Read Augustine." There I shall envisage a Christian experience of time, a Christian order of time, and even a Christian regime of historicity.

Thereafter, for Europe's most momentous crisis of time, in the years preceding and following the French Revolution, Chateaubriand will be our main guide. He will lead us from the Old World to the New, from France to America and back. A tireless traveler and a "swimmer" placed "at the confluence of two rivers," as he describes himself at the end of his memoirs, the *Mémoires d'outre-tombe*, Chateaubriand seems caught between two orders of time, and torn between two regimes of historicity: the old and the new—or modern—regime. Over and over again his writing starts from and returns to this change of regime, this rift in time which was the French Revolution.

In "Orders of Time 2," I shall focus on the contemporary period directly, guided by two watchwords: memory and heritage. These key terms, which have been put to all sorts of uses, abundantly glossed and interpreted in all sorts of ways, will not be broached for themselves, but treated exclusively as signs and symptoms of our relation to time: as different ways of translating, refracting, obeying, or obstructing the order of time. As such, they will testify to the uncertainties in, or the crisis of, the present order of time. This second section could be framed by the following question: is a new regime of historicity centered on the present taking shape today?[38]

Universal Histories

Every historical period has had its great "chronosophy"—a mixture of prophecy and periodization—or, later, its universal history, from Bossuet to Marx, via Voltaire, Hegel and Comte, Spengler and Toynbee.[39] These constructions, however varied their presuppositions (whether their vision was, broadly, linear or cyclical), were essentially concerned to grasp the relations between the past and the future, and to discover, define, and master these in order to understand and predict. As we enter this long gallery which has lain in ruins for many a year, let us first pause before the statue which appeared in a dream to the king of Babylon, Nebuchadnezzar.

This statue is described as gigantic, his "head was of fine gold, his breast and his arms of silver, his belly and his thighs of brass, his legs of iron, his feet part of iron and part of clay." But a stone falling out of nowhere smashed the statue to smithereens. The prophet Daniel, who alone can interpret the dream, is brought before the king, and begins by declaring that "there is a God in heaven that revealeth secrets, and maketh known to the king Nebuchadnezzar what shall be in the latter days." Every metal, and every part, he explains, corresponds to the reign of a monarchy: a first monarchy will be succeeded by a second one, then by a third and a fourth, until the advent of the fifth and final one, which will be for all eternity the reign of the Kingdom of God.[40] That is what the king's dream vision means.

The Book of Daniel, which dates from 164–163 B.C., was referring to the Babylonian, Median, Persian, and Macedonian kingdoms, with Alexander and his successors. Its authors combined in an original way the paradigm of metals with that of imperial succession—used by Greek historians since Herodotus—and gave this schema a completely new twist by placing it within an apocalyptic perspective.[41] Later scholars would argue over the identity of the kingdoms, with the Medians sometimes bowing out and the Romans bringing up the rear for a long time, but the prophetic value of the general schema remained intact.

Another highly influential paradigm was that of the ages of the world. In the fifth century A.D., Saint Augustine lent such lasting prestige to the model of the Seven Ages of the World that it could still serve as the backbone of Bossuet's *Discourse on Universal History* in the late seventeenth century. The "order of times" which Bossuet expounded for the benefit of the young heir to the throne was, he declared, derived from "that famous division of world history [into seven ages] made by the chronologists."[42] The first order began with Adam, and the sixth with Jesus. The latter corresponded to the sixth day, was also the time of old age, and was to last until the end of the world.[43] But this "intermediate time" was one both of old age and of renewal in anticipation of the sabbath on the seventh day, which would bring eternal rest in the vision of God.

These models—the ages of the world and the succession of empires, to which was later added the notion of transfer of rule [*translatio imperii*]— were an active, operative matrix in Western history for a very long time. Humanism brought with it a first set of divisions, into "Ancient Times," "Middle Ages [*Media Aetas*]," and "Modern Times." Thereafter, as the ideal of perfection became temporalized, the idea of the future and of progress, and the openness they represented, began gradually but increasingly to split off from the promise incarnated by the end.[44] Perfection then gave way so completely to perfectibility and progress that not only the past—considered outmoded—but also the present were devalorized in the name of the future. The present, as nothing but the eve of a better if not a radiant morrow, could, and indeed should, be sacrificed.

Nineteenth-century evolutionary theory naturalized time, while humanity's past kept stretching ever further back. The six thousand years since the Creation, as Genesis would have it, was a fairytale compared with the progress of Reason, the stages of evolution, or the succession of modes of production, not to mention the whole temporal arsenal contained in philosophies of history. For this was the Golden Age of the great philosophies of history, before the 1920s brought with them meditations on civilizations' decadence and death, for example in Spengler's *The Decline of the West*, or Valéry, whom we mentioned above, "despairing" of history and coming to the realization that civilizations were mortal.[45] Triumphant and forward-looking universal histories seemed to have run their course. Entropy was gaining ground and would end up carrying the day.

During those same years, historians, or at least those who aspired to see history become a social science, began seriously looking for other, more deep-rooted temporalities, slower and more concretely powerful ones. Their explorations of cycles, phases, and crises gave rise to a "history of price."[46] This was the first stage in the development of an economic and social history centered around the first *Annales* school in France. For the period after the Second World War, three features of time stand out. New findings in archaeology and physical anthropology kept placing the emergence of the first hominids at a different point, and in an increasingly distant past. Time was henceforth measured in millions of years, and since on that scale the "Neolithic Revolution" was only yesterday, what of the Industrial Revolution?! Among the historians, Fernand Braudel advocated the *longue durée* to all social scientists and encouraged attention to the "plurality of social time."[47] History itself became a dialectic of *durées*, in which structures, levels, and registers were carefully differentiated, each with its own temporality. No longer was there a single time, and if time was an agent, it had many and mutable forms, and was anonymous, as suggested by Braudel's description of the *longue durée* as an "immense surface of almost stagnant water" which irresistibly "draws everything onto itself."

Lastly, and most importantly for us here, there was the theorization of cultural diversity. Lévi-Strauss's *Race and History*, commissioned and published by UNESCO in 1952, is the authoritative work in this domain.[48] Lévi-Strauss began by criticizing "false evolutionism," as displayed by Western travelers believing they have "found," for example, the Stone Age among the indigenous populations of Australia or Papua New Guinea. Next, the idea of progress was sharply reframed. Forms of civilization which we tended to imagine as "succeeding one another in time" should rather be seen as "spread out in space." Humanity's progress "can hardly be likened to a person climbing stairs and, with each movement, adding a new step to all those he has already mounted; a more accurate metaphor would be that of a gambler who has staked his money on several dice … it is only occasionally that history is 'cumulative,' that is to say, that the scores add up to a lucky combination."[49]

In addition to this relativization on a theoretical level, Lévi-Strauss introduced a relativization linked to the position of the observer, which he explained by reference to the theory of relativity: "In order to show that the dimensions and the speed of displacement of a body are not absolute values but depend on the position of the observer, it is pointed out that, to a traveler sitting at the window of a train, the speed and length of other trains vary according to whether they are moving in the same or the contrary direction. Any member of a civilization is as closely associated with it as this hypothetical traveler is with his train."[50]

Lastly, and in apparent contradiction with the preceding point, Lévi-Strauss argued that "no society is therefore essentially and intrinsically cumulative." The most cumulative forms of history have never been attained by isolated cultures but only by those which have, voluntarily or involuntarily, "combined their play." This led to the work's final argument, that a culture's "true contribution" down the ages is not to be found in the "the list of inventions which it has personally produced," but in the *differential gap* between itself and other cultures.[51] Having now entered a world civilization, we should try to preserve diversity, but understood as form rather than content; the "fact" of diversity matters much more than "the outward and visible form in which each period has clothed that diversity."[52] UNESCO has at least partially responded to Lévi-Strauss's call, through its Charters and Conventions, especially in its work toward an international convention on cultural diversity. These, then, are the main points of a text which was hailed as "the last of the great discourses on universal history."[53]

But universal history was suddenly thrust into the limelight again, precisely in 1989, with Francis Fukuyama's "The End of History?," as though for a new, but maybe also a last, flowering of the genre. Fukuyama's argument, first published in article form to worldwide acclaim before becoming a book, was that liberal democracy might well be "the final form of all human government," and hence, in that sense, "the end of History." "The appearance of democratic forces in parts of the world where we never expected to see them, the instability of authoritarian forms of government and the complete absence of coherent *theoretical* alternatives to liberal democracy force us to ask the old question anew: from a much more 'cosmopolitan' point of view than was possible in Kant's time, can a universal history of humankind exist?"[54] Fukuyama's answer was yes. But he immediately added: and it's over.[55]

Regimes of Historicity

Where are we to situate the notion of regime of historicity within this gallery of famous landmarks we have been sweeping through at such speed? The claims we make for it are infinitely more modest, and its scope, to the extent that it has one, is considerably smaller. A regime of historicity is simply a tool. It does not presume to decide upon the history of the world as it was, and even less as it will be. It is neither a chronosophy nor a discourse on history, and its function is not to denounce or deplore the present times, but at best to shed light on them. Historians have learned by now not to claim any superior vantage point. That does not mean, however, that they must live with their heads in the sand or in the depths of the archives, deaf to anything outside *their* period. Nor does it force them to revive a notion of history driven by a single time, whether this is the *staccato* of the event or, at the other extreme, the immobility of the long or very long *durée*. And there is no reason for historians to forfeit the wealth of insights afforded by the discovery of the multiplicity of social times: the many-layered, overlapping, and desynchronized times, each with its own rhythm, which Braudel so passionately explored, and many others in his wake. The social sciences were immeasurably enriched by these discoveries, and their questions gained in complexity and subtlety as a result.

What the notion of regime of historicity can do, however, is help us examine our relations to time historically. Historically, that is, moving across several times at once, putting into play the present and the past, or rather pasts in the plural, however far apart they may be in space and time. The sole specificity of this notion, which was developed in response to our present situation and to the diversity of experiences of time, is its mobility. It is a heuristic tool which can help us reach a better understanding not of time itself—of all times or the whole of time—but principally of moments of crisis of time, as they have arisen whenever the way in which past, present, and future are articulated no longer seems self-evident. After all, is that not what we mean when we talk of a "crisis of time"? The notion of regime of historicity is thus a way of shedding light, almost from the inside, on today's questioning of time and particularly on the uncertainty of the categories at stake: are we dealing with a past which has been forgotten or which is too insistently recalled? A future which has almost disappeared from our horizon or which hangs over us as an imminent threat? Does our present no sooner arrive than it is consumed, or is it almost static and unending, eternal even? The notion of "regime of historicity" also sheds light on the much-discussed issues of memory and history, memory versus history, and the "never enough" or "already too much" of cultural heritage.

Within its field of operation as outlined above, the notion of "regime of historicity" is only meaningful in its movement between times. However, I do not aim to encompass time as it has always been lived, from the most immediate to the most mediated experience, from the most idiomatic to the most common, and from the most organic to the most abstract.[56] Again, my focus is first and foremost on the categories that organize these experiences and allow them to be spoken; and more precisely, on the ways in which these universal categories or forms we call "the past," "the present," and "the future" are articulated.[57] How are these categories, which partake both of thought and of action, actualized at different times, and in different places and societies, and how do they make possible and perceptible a particular order of time? What present are we dealing with in different places and at different times, and to what past and future is it linked? These questions concern something that is not yet history (as a genre or a discipline), but at the same time every history, however it is expressed, ultimately presupposes, refers to, translates, betrays, magnifies, or contradicts an experience or experiences of time. We are thus able to grasp, through the notion of "regime of historicity," one of the conditions of possibility of historical writing: how, depending on the way relations between the past, the present, and the future are configured, certain types of history are possible and others are not.

If, following Reinhart Koselleck, we posit that a sense of historical time is generated by the distance, and tension, between the space of experience and the horizon of expectation, then we can say that what the regime of historicity, and this book itself, seek to explore, are precisely the distance and tension between the two; more precisely, the types of distance and the modes of tension.[58] For Koselleck, the temporal structure of the modern period is characterized by an asymmetry between experience and expectation that is produced by the idea of progress and the opening of time onto a future. This asymmetry grew ever more extreme from the end of the eighteenth century, as time speeded up. The history of modernity could thus be summarized in the words "The lesser the experience, the greater the expectation." In 1975, Koselleck tried to formulate what an "end" or "exit" from modern times might look like. Maybe, he suggested, it could be captured in a formula such as "The greater the experience, the more cautious one is, but also the more open is the future."[59]

Has a somewhat different configuration not taken over since then, in which the distance between the space of experience and the horizon of expectation has been stretched to its limit, to breaking point? With the result that the production of historical time seems to be suspended. Perhaps this is what generates today's sense of a permanent, elusive, and almost immobile present, which nevertheless attempts to create its own historical time. It is as though there were nothing but the present, like an immense stretch of water restlessly rippling. So should we talk of an end of, or an exit from, modernity, from that particular temporal structure we call the modern regime of historicity? It is too early to tell. But we can certainly talk of a crisis. "Presentism" is the name I have given to this moment and to today's experience of time.

This book is neither a discourse on universal history, nor a history of time, nor even a treatise on the notion of regime of historicity. It focuses on certain historical moments, and on certain words of the moment, on a selection of famous characters and a range of familiar and less familiar texts. All of these are examined through the prism of the forms of experience of time constituting or inhabiting them, sometimes in unacknowledged ways. I do not intend to enumerate all the regimes of historicity that have appeared in the long history of human society. Although my starting point is our contemporary situation today, I constantly de-familiarize this context by moving far back in time, in order better to return to the present, yet without ever entertaining the illusion of an all-embracing viewpoint. As previously, my intellectual convictions and leanings draw me to a "movement which breaks up the lines," in which I privilege limits and thresholds, moments of modulation and reversal, and phenomena of dissonance.

This was how my earlier *Mirror of Herodotus* was also organized. Was Herodotus, I asked, before or beyond the limit which brought Western History into being? Was he already a historian, or not yet? The father of history—or a liar? Similar questions emerged in my exploration of a century of French historiography, a narrower and more restricted field through which I was guided by Fustel de Coulanges, who, born in 1830, died in the centenary year of the French Revolution. He was nothing if not a historian, almost to excess, yet he was always working against the grain. He was at odds with history's scientific methodology, while at the same time being one of its particularly uncompromising advocates; and he was also in conflict with the newly reformed Sorbonne, despite its creation of the first Chair in Medieval History—for him. These dissonances, which outlived him, enabled me to construct the *case* of Fustel. Later, Odysseus came to epitomize this dissonant perspective, which I explored in *Memories of Odysseus* through the question of cultural borders in the ancient world. As the very first traveler and frontiersman, Odysseus was forever drawing boundaries and crossing them, at the risk of getting lost and losing himself also. He traced the outlines of something like a Greek identity, along with all those who came after him and who, on some pretext or other, traveled through the space of Greek culture. In the space and *longue durée* of this culture, Greek *itineraries* were thus marked out. They were sensitive to moments of crisis, moments when perceptions became blurred, or changed focus, or were reformulated.

Although this work on regimes of historicity is likewise concerned with itineraries, it has a different focus, and the context is different too. I will be tracing a new itinerary, between experiences of time and histories, one which has developed at a moment of crisis of time. Compared to my previous work, the canvas is broader, and the present is more immediately present. But how I proceed, the way I see and do things, has remained the same: it is what I like to call my way of working.

*

My thanks to Jean-Pierre Vernant, who encouraged me to write this book and who was its first reader. Thanks also to Maurice Olender, who commissioned it, and to Gérard Lenclud, Éric Michaud, Jacques Revel, and Michael Werner. Lastly, a thank you to all who attended my seminar, and endured these "regimes."

ORDERS
of
TIME 1

1
MAKING HISTORY
SAHLINS'S ISLANDS

IN A LECTURE SIGNIFICANTLY ENTITLED "OTHER TIMES, Other Customs: The Anthropology of History," Marshall Sahlins evoked Jean-Paul Sartre's question of whether we are yet able "to constitute a structural, historical anthropology." Sahlins's response was unequivocal: "Yes, I have tried to suggest here, *le jour est arrivé*" (in French in Sahlins). In other words, the day had dawned when one could "explode the concept of history through the anthropological experience of culture."[1] Taking my cue from this, I will start with this anthropological experience of culture, guided by Sahlins, whose lecture sought to bring that "day" into being, or at least see it break, with all the promises it held. What interests me here is the anticipated or desired *explosion* of the concept of history, and with it the assertion that "the heretofore obscure histories of remote islands deserve a place alongside the self-contemplation of the European past."[2] And not only as parallel histories, but as a contribution from the margins to our thinking about history and historical time.

That was in 1982, which was—already—another time, if not other customs. What were the issues back then? Sahlins had developed his historical anthropology on the basis of the ethnographic, historical, and archival work he had carried out on the distant islands of the Pacific Ocean. Over the years, his fieldwork and tireless archival research had made these islands into something to be reckoned with in any work on anthropology and history, and particularly on forms of history. Hawaii was particularly important for him, and especially the emblematic figure of Captain Cook (whose twofold apotheosis Sahlins describes).[3] Time and again, in article after article—and supplement after supplement—this Sherlock Holmes of the South Pacific called his historian and anthropologist colleagues to account,[4] with a *Supplement to the Voyage of Cook* and even eventually a *Supplement* to Claude Lévi-Strauss's *The Savage Mind*,[5] whose thought had initially so inspired him. Sahlins's body of work marked the beginning of another time, which sought to consecrate at long last the marriage of structural method and history through a structuralism informed by language pragmatics. The first imperative was to undo the plethora of false binary oppositions structuralism had spawned, and particularly the opposition of history and structure, for which Sahlins proposed the alternative of "structure of the conjuncture."[6]

What were the influences on Sahlins? In 1960 Lévi-Strauss had made a distinction between "cold" and "hot" societies. It met with immediate success, but was also the object of fierce debate and to this day is poorly understood.[7] "Cold" societies border on "the zero [of] historical temperature" and seem to be predominantly concerned with "preserving their existence." "Hot" societies, on the other hand, exist at a higher temperature or, more precisely, experience internal differences in temperature within the system, from which they "extract change and energy." They "interiorize history, as it were, and turn it into the motive power of their development."[8] Such are, preeminently, European societies. Lévi-Strauss's metaphors are clearly drawn from the model of the steam or internal combustion engine, even though, as we have seen, he attributed the first period of "warming up" to the Neolithic revolution, of which the Industrial Revolution was but a distant copy.

Importantly, when Lévi-Strauss returned to this distinction some twenty years later, he stressed that it should be taken for what it was, namely, a model. His aim in presenting two states which, like the state of nature in Rousseau "do not exist, have never existed, and will never exist," and yet which must be "[understood] correctly," was above all "heuristic." "All societies," he went on,

> are equally historical, but some of them admit it openly whereas others resist the idea and prefer to ignore it. So if we can legitimately place societies on an ideal scale not according to their *degree of historicity*, which is the same for all, but according to the way they experience it, it is important to identify and analyze the borderline cases: under what conditions and in what forms does a community's way of thinking and the individuals who constitute it open up to the idea of history? When and how do they come to view it as a tool by means of which they can act on the present and transform it, rather than as a disorder and a threat?[9]

In Lévi-Strauss's terms, one could say that all societies have the same degree of historicity, but that "the subjective image they have of themselves" and "the way they experience it" vary. Their awareness of history and the uses they put it to are not the same. That is, societies differ in their modes of historical consciousness, and their ways of living, thinking, and exploiting it, in other words, in the ways they articulate past, present, and future. It is their regimes of historicity, therefore, which differ.

Later still, in 1998, Lévi-Strauss again felt obliged to clarify his position, which was still being misunderstood. He again stressed the point that at issue were only a society's "subjective" attitudes toward history, which is why "if it is not *our* history, we fail to perceive them." He then made a new point, which reflected the decade of the 1990s: "I have been wondering, as this century draws to a close, whether there are not perceptible signs that our own societies are cooling down." He went on to explain:

> Our societies, which are the perpetrators or victims of such ghastly tragedies, which are frightened by the consequences of demographic expansion, of wars and other scourges, have rediscovered an attachment to heritage and the importance of roots . . . , which is their way of living the illusion, as it is for other countries which feel under threat, that they can—symbolically only, of course—move against the course of history and suspend time.[10]

For Lévi-Strauss, "cooling down" was thus another name for the crisis of the future.

Yet Lévi-Strauss had not always approached history through this kind of subjective comparison of historicities. In his original article on ethnology and history, published in 1949, his argument had taken a different turn, and centered on each discipline's relation to the object. The two disciplines differed, in his view, not in the nature of their object, aim, or method, but solely in the perspective adopted, since "history organizes its data in relation to conscious expressions of social life, while anthropology proceeds by examining its unconscious foundations."[11] Historicity, or rather its different modes, was not Lévi-Strauss's main concern at this point.

In 1952, however, when commissioned by UNESCO to write *Race and History*, he could no longer ignore the issue, but he chose a different focus.[12] As we saw in the prior chapter, in order to establish the idea of the diversity of cultures, he introduced the notions of "stationary" and "cumulative" history, while immediately adding that the processes of accumulation were neither continuous nor the privilege of a single civilization, and that the difference between "stationary" and "cumulative" history was a function of the observer's viewpoint, such that phenomena that seemed to the observer to be developing in the same direction as his or her civilization tended to be regarded as "cumulative," whereas those which lay outside the civilization's frame of reference, as "stationary." If we reckon with the "ethnocentric point of view which we always adopt in assessing the value of a different culture," then historicity, "or, to use a more accurate term, [a culture's] *eventfulness*, thus depends not on its intrinsic qualities but on our situation with regard to it and on the number and variety of our interests involved."[13] Or, in another wording, "the contrast between progressive and stagnant cultures would thus appear to result, in the first place, from a difference of focus."[14]

This conclusion prompted Lévi-Strauss to call for a general theory of relativity that could embrace both the physical and the social sciences. *Race and History* was a wide-ranging meditation on the diversity of cultures, published at a time when a global civilization was appearing for the first time. He stressed the "fact" of diversity, but the analysis of different cultures' forms or regimes of historicity evidently lay beyond the book's scope. Nevertheless, he gestured toward these ideas through ill-fitting notions such as "eventfulness," which is dependent upon a culture's "intrinsic qualities." With hindsight, we can interpret this slightly hesitant or clumsy vocabulary as the sign of a difficulty in defining what was being referred to. But no precise terms seemed available, and historians certainly had nothing better to offer. With *Race and History*, Lévi-Strauss had established a framework or, better, opened up an approach based on the idea of relativity.[15] It was, after all, the era of decolonization.

In the very same year, 1952, and likewise exploring the notion of historicity, Claude Lefort's somewhat overlooked article "*Société 'sans histoire' et historicité*" ("Societies 'without history' and historicity") also broke new ground. It went back to Hegel's great divide between societies with and without history, and tried to move beyond it by placing the question of historicity squarely in the center.[16] "What is proper to *historical* societies," Lefort maintained, "is that they contain the principle of the event within themselves and have the capacity to convert it into the dimension of an experience, such that it may figure as an element in an on-going debate."[17] When Lefort referred to an "event," he clearly had in mind an event like the French Revolution, whereas Lévi-Strauss in his speculations on the emergence of "hot" societies was thinking, rather, of the Neolithic revolution. The time—and temperature!—scales were clearly not the same. For Lefort, "historical" societies were based on the "principle of the event," whereas the principle of "primitive" societies had yet to be defined. Far from separating the two or treating them as opposites, Lefort wanted to make them comparable, precisely by "distinguishing two modes of historicity." His introduction of the notions of "principle" (the principle of the event) and of "modes of historicity" provided a way out of the vagueness of the historical categories used hitherto, and enabled the question of forms of historicity to be addressed more subtly.

Lefort's question was thus: "How does primitive society close off its own future, how does it develop without being aware that it is changing and, as it were, establish itself in view of its own replication?" In short, what is its historical principle, "what genre of *historicity*" does it have, "by which we mean the general relation which people entertain with the past and the future"?[18] This was a definition of historicity we could already work with, except for the omission of any explicit consideration of the present. Although Lefort was well-read in anthropology, he wrote as a philosopher, mindful of preserving differences without reducing them to a lack that would reactivate the old Hegelian divide between societies with and without history. Exploring this "genre of historicity" further, through fieldwork, lay beyond Lefort's scope.

This is where Marshall Sahlins came in. Although with Sahlins the key issue—the type of historicity—remained unchanged, the terms used to address it were no longer the same. Structuralism had left its mark, first on anthropology, and then on the study of history.[19] It was something one supported, opposed, or wanted to improve. The whole field of the humanities and social sciences was bristling with binary oppositions, not least myth and history, which would be the object of fierce debate, along with event and structure. The terms of the discussion were to change yet again, with the various moves out of structuralism. But let us simply explore for the moment the context of Sahlins's work, its methods, and its concerns.

The Heroic Regime

Sahlins starts by transporting his reader to Fiji. Through a series of microanalyses he depicts how the history, or rather mode of historical consciousness, of these islands is experienced, constructed, and narrated. In a short introduction, he reminds the reader that Western history itself has a history and that its modern forms, concerned with quantifiable data, cycles, and structures, are inseparable from the forms of our modernity. But this word of caution, which seems so very obvious to us today, is immediately overlaid or relativized by another one, to the effect that a history in which numerical importance and the idea of collective values counted emerged long before the market economy and modern democracies. For with the rise of the Greek city-state (for which Sahlins refers to Jean-Pierre Vernant's *Origins of Greek Thought*[20]), a new history had gained currency in which the *agora* replaced the royal palace and the majority principle won out over the appropriation of power by a single person. In other words, in ancient Greece, a new mode of historical existence had arisen, as well as a new historical consciousness (which would soon lead to this history being written down, becoming what the Western tradition would thereafter precisely call "History").[21]

Sahlins's double detour, however schematic or approximate it may appear, had the propaedeutic virtue of injecting a dose of relativism into Western observers, prompting them from the outset to question their own traditions: "*Other times, other customs,*" to be sure, but also *other histories*. However, these histories were not like the islands on which Odysseus set foot, self-enclosed and scattered across the vast ocean, such that no historian's or anthropologist's craft could ever reach them or relate them to each other. On the contrary, Sahlins was adamant that a comparable structure implied a comparable historicity, by which he clearly wished to intervene in the debate on the divine nature of kingship precisely in terms of its specific mode of historicity, which he called "heroic." Sahlins's analysis thus never loses sight of a broader comparative dimension. At this point, in order to arrest the giddying movement of the term "history," which Sahlins uses in a different sense every time, let us at least provisionally call the mode of historical existence Sahlins describes the "heroic regime of historicity."

FOR SAHLINS, HEROIC HISTORY'S THEORIZATION DESCRIBES AN arc in time with, at one end, Giambattista Vico (the heroic age, situated between those of the gods and of men), and, at the other end, Louis Dumont and his concept of hierarchy, with Frazer's and Hocart's analyses of archaic royalty in between. Since the king is the very condition of possibility of the society, it follows that "if I eat, it is the King; if I sleep, it is the King; if I drink, it is the King," as everyday parlance has it. Here "history is anthropomorphic in principle, which is to say in structure."[22] It is like Fenimore Cooper's Mohicans walking in single file, one behind the other, giving the impression of being just one giant Indian. A historiography based on sampling and statistics cannot but miss the mark, since this is not a world in which "Every man counts as 'one' (vote)," but rather a world in which "one alone counts": this would be the first rule of "heroic statistics." In Fiji, for example, Christianity was long referred to as "the religion of Thakombau," Thakombau being the leader of the main Fijian federation. Although in 1852 a missionary survey registered only 850 converts, once Thakombau had declared his allegiance to the Christian God, in 1854, there suddenly appeared the admirable figure of 8,870—from which it can be deduced that

8,870–850 = 1, with Thakombau making up the statistical difference.[23] Although quantitative historical research might still have been fair game at the beginning of the 1980s, the charge still seems a little facile; after all, not all historians walked in single file like those Mohicans. . . . But let us get back to Sahlins.

There is more to say about this adoption of Christianity: the circumstances of the conversion must also be taken into account. Acknowledging the truth of Christianity is one thing, and conversion is another, for, as Thakombau said to a missionary, "everything is true that comes from the white man's country; muskets and gunpowder are true, and your religion must be true."[24] The extra-ordinary presence of Europeans was a "total social fact" for the Fijians, inseparably religious, political, and economic. So why did they not convert immediately? Because the population waited for a cue from its chiefs, each chief watched the next, and the last chief waited for the right moment. That is exactly what Thakombau did, encountering "the true God" at a time when he had suffered serious military setbacks. In opting to convert to Christianity, he made it impossible for his enemies to do likewise, while at the same time securing the assistance of missionaries and the support of the king of Tonga, who was already a Christian. In short, he won—and "was saved." Could we not see in Thakombau a distant cousin of Constantine?

It should be added that the sudden death of the enemy chief in the preceding weeks left the enemy coalition in total disarray. But one way or another, the Fijians became Christian by fighting, as they were obliged to, for their chief and for Christianity, that is, for "the religion of Thakombau." Heroic history really *is* a history of kings and battles, but only because in that particular culture the social system is an echo chamber for the actions of the king, which consequently have "a disproportionate historical effect."[25] It is a history which, structurally, "produces great men" and seems, at first sight, to oscillate between the stroke of genius (conversion) and the stroke of (good) fortune (the sudden death of Thakombau's opponent). These sudden reversals are precisely one of its characteristics.

One could point out in passing that the world of Plutarch's *Lives* functioned in a similar way, with human destiny being woven out of an ongoing confrontation between *Tukhe* (Fortune) and *Arete* (Excellence).[26] Reversals of fortune—or *peripeties*, to give them their Greek name—also organized the lives of the heroes of antiquity. Moreover, the notion of peripety comes from Greek tragedy, which is not to suggest that such lives were in themselves tragic, but that the tragic schema can enable a person's life be understood and narrated in the form of one of the *Lives*. It should be said that Sahlins was not very forthcoming about the origins or construction of the categories he employed in his heroic history.

Be that as it may, Sahlins's heroic regime should prompt us to question the separation we blithely make between ritual and history. When a king dies, there ensues a period of chaos we call ritual, until the heir reinstates the taboos and restores order on all levels. However, when an army suddenly loses its leader, breaks ranks, and scatters, we talk of a battle and a defeat. In so doing we are insidiously introducing our own distinctions as to what is real and what is symbolic, what is history (history as kings, queens, and battles) and what is ritual. Yet, says Sahlins, these two moments of collapse are essentially the same, and both confirm the same hierarchical system.

Of course, heroic history is not simply borne on the breeze. It is subtended by a number of "social forms." These are "a system of heroic segmentation" (which, for Sahlins, develops from top to bottom, unlike the classical lineage system, which develops from the bottom up), with at its pinnacle "the privileges of authority," which take precedence over the "principles of descent"; a "solidarity" which is less "mechanical" or "organic" than "hierarchical"; forms of succession and kinship systems; a sort of "division of labor as regards historical consciousness"; and "annals" filled with byzantine intrigues punctuated by fratricides and parricides.

The king's actions are the temporal yardstick: the royal traditions, whose experts cleverly manipulate cultural categories, function as reference points and even as history for the elite. Researchers investigating how the king's subjects fitted into this general framework often observed that when asked about "custom" or "history," the subjects were unable to answer, as though they had not yet attained historical consciousness. But, Sahlins argues, their culture is above all something they experience; it is part of their *habitus*. Also, they express their knowledge and grasp of cultural codes differently, not through lengthy genealogies, cosmic myths, and royal legends, but through items of news exchanged, and all the little stories (and tales) one tells and is told—obeying certain rules, of course—about different people, relatives, and acquaintances. These are the ordinary annals of the poor.

The king alone can proclaim heroic history, but instead of the "royal we" familiar to Europeans, there is a "heroic I." This "I" is "even more radical," however, because it implies not only the speaker but also those no longer living, the past generations who "weigh like a nightmare on the brain of the living."[27] "'I' have done" can thus mean "this was performed by an ancestor, who died long before I was born." If one can say that every cultural order has its own historicity, or even its own regime of historicity, then Fiji can be said to represent "the paradigm of heroic history." It comes complete with its conditions of possibility, and its forms of "historical consciousness," divided between the "annals of the poor," which are to do with *habitus* and "talk story," and its "heroic annals," which are a combination of myth and history or, more precisely, "explicitly organize historical action as the projection of mythical relations."[28]

From Myth to Event

After characterizing the nature of the heroic regime, as though in reply to Lefort's question on primitive societies' operative "principle," Sahlins turns to the relations between myth and event. Again, he starts with a reference to the Greeks, returning to his recurrent comparison of the "Savages" with the "Ancients," and citing Thucydides's *History of the Peloponnesian War*. Thucydides declares in the book's opening pages that he intends to eliminate any trace of *muthos* from his account (pejoratively calling it *muthôdes*, a sort of poetic exaggeration, as alluring as it is empty). In so doing, he says, he seeks to ensure that the work may be "profitable" to those who, now and in the future, wish to understand the present time and its crises.[29] After Thucydides, history would thus involve pursuing and examining the truth of what had occurred. At this point Sahlins shifts again, not back to the Greeks this time, but over to the Maori. Now it so happened, says Sahlins, that when the new governor, Sir George Grey, took up office in 1844, he landed in the midst of a Maori uprising. In order to understand what people around him were talking about, and above all, what on earth was going on, he had been obliged, he explained, to set about gathering and deciphering indigenous myths and proverbs. The moral of the story was that it was impossible to write a history of the Polynesian wars without including precisely what the history of the Peloponnesian war *excluded* from the outset, namely *muthos:* no history without *muthos*, but at the same time no "true" history with it. Sahlins simply reveled in this dissonance. It should be pointed out, however, that Thucydides was native to the culture, whereas Sir George was not, and that in order to break with the myths of the tribe one has first to know them!

The Maori think that "the future [is] behind them."[30] The past is a vast reservoir of models of action, from which the mythical tradition which best gives form and expression to the concrete "interests" of the moment is skillfully extracted. This reservoir contains everything from myths of origin to recent memories, from the separation of Earth and Heaven to the tracing of the group's frontiers, from the divine to the human, the abstract to the concrete, and the universal to the particular. There are no breaks between these "stages" or "epochs," and they all have the same degree of existence (they are all real life). The Maori can move between them all the more smoothly because they are structurally similar: each is basically an episode which, in its own way, tells the same story, and even if there are variations, the overall framework remains the same. As a result, cosmic myth ends up inhabiting "current events," such that events really *are* myths.

But by the same token, the event is no event at all. It is not an event as modern European history construes it, that is, as so unique and novel that it can only be apprehended (and contained) by assigning it a teleological orientation by virtue of which "if it didn't have a past, it would have a future,"[31] courtesy of process and progress. Nor is it an event in the terms of what for a time was called "non-events-based" history, in which the event was essentially unimportant, barely the frothy mark left by the receding wave (and counting bubbles tells us nothing of the movement of the seas). For the Maori, events are immediately perceived "in the received order of structure, as identical with their original."[32] Events do not occur, they recur; they are not unique, they are repetitions.

In examining this more closely, we find two symmetrical and opposite strategies for accommodating the event. For how are we to understand that in this world which knows no future, where nothing "occurs," the present reproduces the past? Through the mediation of descent, says Sahlins, since ancestors' characteristics reappear in their descendants. "The whole universe is for the Maori a comprehensive kindred of common ancestry."[33] "It is a source of pure, unadulterated joy for the old Maori to be able to say to an enemy 'I ate your father' or 'your ancestor,' although the occurrence may have occurred ten generations before his time."[34] From this we can see how the heroic "I" functions: the past can only be experienced in the present, or rather, the divide between the two which inaugurates modern Western history does not exist.[35] It would be better to say that past and present coexist, and that the "past" is "reabsorbed" into the "present."[36]

Working Misunderstandings: From Event to Myth

Sahlins analyzes with brio the tragic interferences between two cultural orders and two regimes of historicity in his writings on the Hone Heke uprising of 1844–1846, which precisely brought Sir George Grey to New Zealand in the first place (and gave us his collection of Maori myths). In tracing the fate of the "working misunderstanding" (Sahlins), or parallel encoding, of what should have been an identical event for all the protagonists, he demonstrates that there are not only "other times, other customs," but also other forms of history. Or, to use a different set of concepts, the protagonists experience the simultaneity of the nonsimultaneous.[37] The emblematic focus of the revolt was the flagpole on which, as one might expect, the British colors were flying. Four times it was chopped down by the Maori, and four times the British put it back up. For the rebel chief, the flagpole was, in his own words "the root cause of the war."[38] For the British, "flying the British colors" was an imperious (and imperial) necessity, on which any concession was unthinkable. So after each attack, the British sent for reinforcements and better security for their flag, eventually surrounding the pole with a stockade and blockhouse.

But there was a "misunderstanding." The priority for the Maori was to hack down the pole on which the flag was flying, and the priority for the British was to protect the flag flying on the pole. Flagpole on the one hand, and Union Jack on the other; therein lay the discrepancy, even if what both sides basically wanted was territorial control. When the British finally put up fortifications to protect the flag, they confirmed the Maori's initial hypothesis: the whole thing began to look more and more like a *tuahu*, a fortified altar—on which one or several poles were erected—and at the end it looked almost identical to the ones built by their ancestors when they first came to the island, to signify that the *mana* of the land was theirs. Boas's words are borne out once again: the seeing eye is truly the organ of tradition. Moreover, building these sacred compounds mimetically re-enacted the originary separation of Earth and Heaven by Tane, and thus repeated the act through which human beings inherited the earth. And Tane was, of course, a tree. The link between the flagpole and possession of the land was thus more than simply symbolic: the flagpole was, literally, "the root" of war.

The misunderstanding also revealed other aspects of heroic history. Although Heke's rebellion appeared to respond to a radically new situation, he explained one day to the governor that he was only an heir who had inherited rebellion and usurpation. His ancestral forbears forced him to wage war. The course of his life had been fixed long ago, with or without the Union Jack!

And to those trying to explain away the revolt by an economic crisis, Sahlins has no difficulty demonstrating that what this crisis, although real enough, represented for the Maori was the concrete consequence of a previous, unresolved episode. In 1840, the treaty "signed" by Maori chiefs confirmed their "ownership" of the land in return for acknowledging British "sovereignty." However, as the Colonial Office well knew, these concepts did not exist in Maori. The meaning of the treaty remained open-ended. A first interpretation concluded, "The shadow of the land goes to Queen Victoria, but the substance remains to us," but later the reverse seemed more accurate, "The substance of the land goes to the Europeans, the shadow only will be our portion."[39]

It became clear, in any case, that the real issue was the *mana*. In toppling the flagpole, Hone Heke was being perfectly consistent with himself and the whole of his history. His "demystification" was absolutely correct, revealing as it did what the "Whites" "were prepared to conceal sometimes even from themselves." He was re-enacting what the founding chiefs from distant Hawaiki did when they landed and took control of the country so many years previously. A myth was thus "decoded" by another myth, since the treaty was indeed a myth, even in the European sense of the term (something designed to deceive ignorant "savages").

Sahlins applied similar frames of analysis to the sorry tale of Captain Cook. By dissecting the Hawaiian and the English parallel encoding of the same event (the sacrifice of Cook-Lono on 14 February 1779), he exposed how the "working misunderstanding" was active from the very beginning, starting before Cook's death, culminating with it, and continuing afterward. Cook became a cult figure for both the British and the Hawaiians, and underwent a kind of double apotheosis. The British, for their part, generally "entered into the role the Hawaiians cast for them," albeit "unwittingly," not least Cook in his "passive acceptance of the dignities of his installation as Lono."[40] The outcome was that, "by virtue of Cook's sacrifice, the *mana* of the Hawaiian kingship was itself British," since any ruler now had to ensure Cook's support. This did not escape Kamehameha, who, after killing the legitimate heir and seizing power, also seized Cook's bones. Contrary to certain reductive explanations, Cook was considered to be a god not

> because of empirical resemblances between the events of his voyage and the details of the Makahiki rites; rather, these rites were latterly elaborated, primarily by Kamehameha, *as an iconic representation of Cook's voyage*. The Makahiki as we have come to know it is testimony to Cook's sacrifice as a source of legitimacy of that chieftainship, and at the same time of the transformation of that chieftainship into statehood.[41]

That is how the tale of Cook came to underlie a powerful Hawaiian political myth. The Hawaiians' decoding of Cook's arrival as the return of Lono generated a whole series of exchanges between event and system, history and structure, and present and past, bringing countless misunderstandings in its wake.

As well as outlining his concept of *heroic history*, Sahlins suggested a particular approach: an *anthropology of history*. He did not simply want to do historical research in Fiji, but also to show how Fiji or Hawaii were themselves sources of history and in all senses *Islands of History*: islands in history, which have a history, but which are also productive of history, according to a specific, if by no means unique, order of time and regime of historicity. This specificity can best be grasped when interference between systems gives rise to discrepancies. A genuinely experimental situation is created, in which misunderstandings can bring into particularly sharp focus the different forms of temporality and the different regimes of historicity at work. A new perspective no longer centered on Western modes of historicity is introduced, and it provides, as Sahlins wished, "all kinds of new things to consider."

To make Sahlins's approach even clearer, we could compare his minutely detailed reconstructions of Hone Heke's battles with medievalist Georges Duby's analysis of the Battle of Bouvines. Both accounts were written around the same time, and both were concerned with rethinking the *event*. Duby set out "to look at this battle and the memory it has left us from the perspective of an anthropologist; in other words, to attempt to perceive both the battle and the memory as wrapped up in a cultural whole different from the one which at present molds our own relationship with the world."[42] He wanted his historical research to mirror the anthropologist's attention to differences between cultural spheres. Mobilizing the whole range of his knowledge as a medievalist, he sought to produce an exhaustive interpretation of the traces left by the event, and managed to transform the few hours of the Battle of Bouvines into a way of shedding light on how a whole society acted and thought. As for the event itself, it "is nothing," Duby maintained, outside of the traces it leaves. Once the cardinal transgression of engaging battle on a Sunday had been duly noted, Duby could explore the notion of "other times, other customs" to the full, but he never directly addressed the forms of temporal experience at stake, or their impact on the perception and construction of the event.[43] Sahlins, by contrast, working as an anthropologist attentive to forms of history and the categories and conditions of production of history, added a third term: "other histories." To which I, going one step further, have added: "other regimes of historicity."

THIS FIRST EXERCISE IN "VIEWING FROM AFAR" CONNECTS WITH a particular debate, active from the 1950s to the 1980s, insofar as Sahlins's work was also a kind of reply to Lefort's question and enriched Lévi-Strauss's theoretical reflections through concrete analyses (no, differences are not only on the side of the observer). By accompanying Sahlins across the Pacific, too rapidly no doubt, I have been able to extend my own field of inquiry or, more precisely, to delve into it more deeply. I have used Sahlins both as a reference point (on the question of forms of history) and as an interpreter (since I myself have no access to the Polynesian material). What emerges is that the notion of "regime of historicity" is relevant outside of European historiography (and is thus not simply a product of Europe's self-contemplation); and, above all, that exploring the forms of history characterizing the societies of the Pacific Islands can actually help delineate the notion more closely. Heroic history, in Sahlins's sense, is something of a touchstone.

Anthropology and Forms of Temporality

A last word before moving on: a historian might regret that Sahlins compared the heroic regime of history not with the European form most closely resembling it, namely *historia magistra vitae*, but with the modern regime. His own reference to Vico might have inspired him to do otherwise. Was the Homeric epic already a form of heroic history? Europe's great historiographic model, *historia magistra*, served for many centuries—until the end of the eighteenth century—to make the present intelligible through the past and the force of the exemplary. I shall come back to this in greater detail.[44] But to what extent, precisely, were the Polynesian and European forms of history comparable? How were the categories of present, past, and future articulated in each case? What about Cook and his crew—how did they experience their order of time, and what regime of historicity organized their thinking? Sahlins counterpoints heroic history only with modern historiography, which he treats at times with a certain irony, whereas this historiography has precisely abandoned the exemplary for the unique—as though he had forgotten that this history also has a history, which itself presupposes another order of time. Two requirements had to be met for the (modern) event to appear: the future had to be "in front" (whereas in Fiji it was "behind," and people had their backs to it); and the separation between past and present had to be in place.

Since the publication of *Islands of History*, anthropologists have continued discussing both the history of anthropology and the history of the societies anthropologists study. Johannes Fabian has argued that "anthropology emerged and established itself as an allochronic discourse; it is a science of other men in another Time," or even outside of time.[45] Anthropology's object was constructed by situating it in another time. Since evolutionism, functionalism, and structuralism simply incorporated this premise uncritically, each in its own way, time never had the place it should have had in anthropology. Anthropology must henceforth be set upon firmer foundations, Fabian declared, by positing "coevalness" from the start: we and the other are "of the same age." Although this radical critique of the discipline's presuppositions seeks to introduce or reintroduce time, it has very little to say on the question of history: on the links between relations to time and forms of history (before, during, and after colonial imperialism, from the perspective of both the colonized and the colonizer). Recognition of the coevalness of the interlocutors is not the answer to everything and throws hardly any light on the temporality of this co-presence.[46] Might, then, the notion of the simultaneity of the nonsimultaneous, as Koselleck used it, be a satisfactory tool, or should it be rejected as setting too European a standard?

A collective volume, entitled *Time*, likewise focused on time, and usefully brought together anthropologists and historians writing about different places and periods. The book addressed the experience of time in different geographical, cultural, and historical contexts, from clocks in the European Renaissance to the pasts of an Indian village.[47] From the outset it rejected any sort of "great divide," and instead sought to address different temporalities and highlight the complexity of each. In viewing these societies not as outside time but, on the contrary, as participating in the same "turbulent stream of time," the book could present different but comparable historicities. Yet however valuable the research areas opened up by pooling and diversifying histories, anthropological data, and temporalities, the issue of the types of history involved and their articulation with forms of temporality was not broached directly. It lay beyond the volume's scope.

Nicholas Thomas, whose concerns were with "the incorporation of ... temporal processes in general in anthropological thought," took up Fabian's argument that history had been excluded from anthropology, because the latter's object "was and is essentially a social or cultural system or structure out of time."[48] Time can be integrated into anthropology, he argued, only if the object of study changed from "the system" to "the systemic process." Failing this, any attempt to integrate time into anthropology, as Sahlins does, would inevitably miss the mark. When we read Sahlins, we have no idea how "change" was conceived in Hawaii before the arrival of the Europeans: "The analysis of history developed by Sahlins and some of his associates is thus a very limited theory, which says nothing about the historical processes which actually make the conditions of life and culture variable across time and space."[49]

Although Sahlins's theory is undoubtedly limited—but also, I tend to think, deliberately so—it throws into sharp relief a particular moment, the liminal moment of the encounter. Sahlins analyzes how the interpretative logics of the two protagonists differ, and the interferences, misunderstandings, and discrepancies arising. In short, he shows how the parties construe events in terms of their own experience and expectations. Through such events, understood as "interpreted instances," a crisis of time becomes visible. On both sides, an order of time is at least momentarily revealed and disturbed. Sahlins's contribution to our inquiry is therefore doubly precious. Was the heroic regime the "historical principle," in Lefort's sense, of these societies? And was it the only one, and at what point in time? All these questions are open to further debate. Our detour via the Pacific has in any case enabled us to confirm the purchase of the notion of regime of historicity beyond the frontiers of Europe, and also to define more closely Sahlins's and, before him, Lévi-Strauss's conception of history. Moreover, Sahlins's notion of "structure of the conjuncture" is itself a way of describing how past, present, and future may be articulated. If in turn we historicized this structure, might we not discover that each great regime of historicity has a "structure of the conjuncture" proper to it?[50]

2

FROM ODYSSEUS'S TEARS TO AUGUSTINE'S MEDITATIONS

ANYONE TRANSPORTED DIRECTLY FROM THE PACIFIC TO THE AEGEAN, from the world of royal kingship to the "world of Odysseus," moving simultaneously through space and back in time, would have no difficulty recognizing in the Homeric hero certain characteristics of the heroic regime of history. But it would be a different type of heroic regime, one incarnated by Achilles and Odysseus, as Vico describes them. Anyway, I do not intend to compare Thakombau or Hone Heke with Agamemnon or Nestor, and list similarities and differences, but rather focus on one figure in particular, Odysseus. He who, to quote the Russian poet Ossip Mandelstam, returned "full of space and time." I shall leave aside the question of space, and concentrate on time, even if the two are obviously linked.[1] In the course of this second exercise in viewing from afar, Odysseus will also encounter Augustine.

Each Day Is the First Day

On his return, was Odysseus "full of time"? We are going to catch up with him a little earlier, just before the Phaeacians, those unrivaled seamen with their magical boats, transported him from Scheria to Ithaca and, after his ten long years of wandering, his trials and tribulations, delivered him onto home ground. After what was to be his last shipwreck, Odysseus was welcomed as a distinguished guest by King Alcinous and his wife, and celebrated at length. During the banquet in his honor, a remarkable encounter took place between him, the hero, and the Phaeacian bard who, as befitted solemn occasions, was in attendance. The apparently simple words of their brief exchange are worth dwelling upon, since in that crucial scene we are given a fleeting but vividly revealing glimpse of a prehistory of history (understood as the narrative of things that have occurred). The issue of historicity itself arises, in Lefort's sense of the articulation of the past with the future, and even that of historicity's prehistory, insofar as the real problem here is the past itself, as a category of experience. Thakombau was about to convert to the Promises of Christ, and so was about to enter a completely different economy of time, incompatible with the heroic regime. Not so for the Homeric hero, who is and remains forever untouched by Revelation, and can no more conceive of a covenant between a single and unique God, Creator of all things, and an elect people than he can conceive of a savior, a son of God made man, who would suddenly, and quite literally, give meaning to time. Homer's world can never enter the order of time, which is why for us it can feel doubly distant.

For Marcel Detienne, "Homer offered his audience no incentive to separate 'what has been' from 'what is.' . . . By fabricating continuity by means of tradition and memory, [he] obstructed the creation of a new consciousness of the past."[2] This unwavering judgment concurs with the fundamental categories sketched earlier by Erich Auerbach when, employing a different method and from a different perspective, he opposed the Homeric style to that of the Old Testament, in the opening pages of his masterly work, *Mimesis*. Comparing the Bible story of the sacrifice of Isaac with the scene of recognition of Odysseus by his old nursemaid Euryclea on his return to Ithaca (due to the scar left by the wild boar), Auerbach characterizes Homer's style as a "perpetual foreground" which, despite many anticipatory gestures and flashbacks, always presents what is being narrated as a pure present, without temporal perspective, in which there is "no development, and [their] life-histories are clearly set forth once and for all."[3] By contrast with the Old Testament figures, who are so much "more fraught with their own biographical past," and constantly "worked upon" by the hand of God, Homer's heroes have clearly defined destinies and "wake every morning as if it were the first day of their lives."[4] So, for Auerbach, Homer's epics have the character of legends, with one-dimensional characters, whereas in the Old Testament historicity is present, shaping lives and organizing narratives. And history itself is already there or just emerging.[5]

Achilles, destined to a brief life of glory, seems to fit this definition of the hero perfectly: each day is for him the first day of his life. Only the present exists, even if he knows, or all the more so since he knows, that sometime soon will come a day, a morning, noon, or night, which will be his last. He finally escapes from time and can—for ever after—be celebrated in song as the "best of the Achaeans," the epic hero par excellence. Odysseus may return, but Achilles cannot. On three occasions, however, Achilles uses an expression suggesting that he wants to break with what went before. He declares, first to Patroclus, then to his mother, and lastly to Agamemnon: "these things will we let be past and done [*alla ta men protetuchtai easomen*]." Paul Mazon's French translation poetically renders the phrase as "Laissons le passé être le passé" ("Let bygones be bygones")—but in so doing Mazon resolves—in other words, glosses over—what is at stake. When the hero Achilles states that "these things will we let be as past and done, for all our pain, curbing the heart [*thumos*] in our breasts, because we must,"[6] he is referring to the pain caused by Agamemnon's insult, which he must put behind him every time, despite himself. Without the break it represents in this enduring present, no action would be possible. Nothing would move. Patroclus would not borrow Achilles's armor, Achilles would not return to battle, and the *Iliad* would never come to a close.

Is Achilles's decision enough to make what "has been done" into a past, into a present time which must pass? Clearly not, because what Achilles has to master are his anger and his pain, which, as Homer makes clear, remain unchanged and ready to surface at any moment, as present as ever. He has no distance from them. Rather, Achilles's heroic resolve produces a *new* or, better, a *reactivated* present, a new dawning day, and yet the *preceding* present does not shift as a result into the past, especially since the whole drama unfolds under the all-seeing eyes of Zeus, whose "designs" prevail.

The question of the *past* and of mourning emerges again, from a different angle, in a magnificent scene just prior to Patroclus's burial. Hector is already dead, and Achilles is at last weary of slaughter. As night falls, he can be found on the seashore, alone and shaken by sobs. No sooner has he sunk at last into sleep than Patroclus appears to him in a dream. "Thou sleepest, and hast forgotten me, Achilles. Not in my life wast thou unmindful of me, but now in my death! Bury me with all speed."[7] Then, before evoking the period of their life together, he asks Achilles to place his (Achilles's) ashes alongside his own, as though he saw Achilles's death, and in the present. Patroclus seems, in death, to be able to view the whole of his own life and that of Achilles in a single glance and in the present moment. His reproach that Achilles has forgotten him is clearly groundless, since Achilles was still crying over Patroclus when he was overcome by sleep.[8] The exact contrary holds: Achilles is unable to relegate Patroclus to the past. He has no words to express that Patroclus was—and no longer is. But as soon as he crosses the frontier between waking and sleep, Patroclus is immediately there again: his "spirit," his "phantom," which in every respect resembles Patroclus as he was alive, stands before him. When Achilles tries to embrace it, it dissolves like vapor, and he seizes nothing but a void: Patroclus has passed over.[9]

Only a seer can know the present, the past, and the future. Such a one is Calchas, whose gifts come from Apollo,[10] or blind Tiresias, whom Odysseus has to consult in Hades to find out how to return to Ithaca, and who also informs him of the ordeals he will suffer up to the day of his death.[11] The seer is a trusted figure whose knowledge is much sought after. Likewise the bard's knowledge, which is inspired by the Muse or Apollo. Ever-present and all-knowing, the Muses, says Hesiod, voice what is, what will be, and what was, whereas the bard sings (only?) of what will be and what was.[12] But this divinatory knowledge is always voiced or sung in the present, regardless of whether the content refers to the present, the past, or the future. Calchas can see what angers Apollo in the present moment, Tiresias foresees the course of Odysseus's life to the end of his days, and at the request of the suitors Phemios sings the "heart-breaking" tale of the Achaeans' homecoming. The time of the events described—past, present, or future—is itself unimportant. The elements of knowledge imparted by the seer are situated on an identical plane, and it matters little that some are marked as past and others as yet to come. He simply brings forth or reveals one sequence rather than another, according to the counsel sought and thanks to his divine gift of synoptic vision. There is no question of historicity.

So Achilles is enshrined forever in the perpetual present of epic time as "the best of the Achaeans," because he has exchanged living (and returning) for renown. Yet Odysseus, who at length returns, and precisely because he does so, also merits undying fame, and is also called "the best of the Achaeans."[13] His return is what mobilizes the entire narrative of the *Odyssey*, from past departures (leaving Greece twenty years previously, and Troy, ten years thereafter) to the future of this homecoming, which is always envisaged and always deferred. The tension between the two (which is a narrative prefiguration of the categories of experience and expectation) raises the question of the status of the years which have passed and yet weigh ("like a nightmare") on the characters' present.

For even if one does return, can one just take up where one left off? The old hound Argos, lying on a pile of dung on which he has been abandoned, dies on recognizing his master disguised as a beggar. Time catches up only with this faithful old animal, and after twenty years' waiting, this new day will be its last.[14] Also, before Odysseus can fully regain his old self, he must win back his throne and his wife, with the help of his son.[15] Singled out throughout the *Odyssey* as the one who, unlike his companions, refuses to lose sight of his return, he cannot simply reappear for the twenty years of his absence to vanish as though by enchantment. Even if Athena gives him back his former appearance, he still has to prove he is really Odysseus.

From a broader perspective, we can also make the obvious point that the *Odyssey* comes after the *Iliad*; it was called an "epilogue" already in the time of Pseudo-Longinus.[16] In the *Iliad*, Troy has not yet been captured, and Achilles is still alive: we are in a time of *before*, anticipating events we know have to happen. But although the *Iliad*'s future may be described as "a suitable past for the *Odyssey*,"[17] there is a shift in perspective from the first to the second poem. In the *Odyssey*, we are immediately in an *afterward*, in the position of remembering events and the grief and suffering endured. The Trojan War remained an "axial" event right up to the modern age, a reference point initially shared and later contested, in relation to which the *Odyssey*'s narrated episodes of the war could be construed as *history*.[18] Accordingly, we are plunged from the start into the time of memory, and shadowed by the possibility of forgetting, which is sometimes feared and sometimes desired. In the *Odyssey*, the memory of those who have died and disappeared haunts the living.

Thus, for example, Penelope weeps. She cannot bear to hear the Ithacan bard, Phemios, sing of the return from Troy and the misfortunes of the Achaeans, when she herself is still mourning her absent husband: she suffers from *pothos*, that unending sorrow for the lost person whose memory preys on one.[19] Likewise Menelaus, when he tells his guest Telemachus that despite retrieving both his kingdom and his wife on his return from years of wandering, he no longer takes any joy in ruling. He mourns all those who fell at Troy. And one person in particular, who haunts his memory beyond all others, whether he sleeps or wakes: Odysseus.[20] When Telemachus, who has not yet introduced himself to his hosts, hears his father's name mentioned, he bursts into tears. Whereupon Helen arrives, Telemachus is recognized, and all weep again.

Helen finally intervenes to calm the distress of the banquet guests, and dry their tears. She starts by pouring into the wine a drug (*pharmakon*) that works as an "anti-affliction" (*nepenthês*), alleviating all pain, anger, and memory of ills. She then calls upon all those present to give themselves over to feasting and to take pleasure (*terpsis*) in listening to the tales. She herself recounts an episode of Odysseus's exploits at Troy, just as a bard might. Menelaus takes up the tale with a different episode, describing what happened inside the Trojan horse. This is the first direct mention of the fall of Troy. Then Telemachus briefly evokes Odysseus's cruel fate, and asks to be allowed to retire.[21] The evening has been saved, and Helen's drug has enabled the guests to go through a process which the solitary Penelope never manages to complete. The distance introduced has made the guests listen to the exploits of Odysseus as though it were not Helen, but Homer himself speaking, as though they were not contemporaries of the events, but rather belonged to the future generations to whom the bard's song is precisely destined. The *pharmakon* briefly transformed an *absence* into a *past*, and the hero into one of those "men of former times" whom the epic is there to celebrate.

Odysseus's Tears

Odysseus also weeps, and not once but twice, as he listens to the blind bard Demodocus at Alcinous's banquet. No Helen comes to the rescue with her "anti-affliction." The king, as a solicitous host, has no choice but to interrupt the bard's song. When the bard first comes forward and happens to sing of the quarrel between Odysseus and Achilles, Odysseus at once draws his purple robe across his face to hide his tears.[22] On the bard's second appearance, in the open air, he sings of the love between Ares and Aphrodite.[23] Odysseus is pleased this time, and Homer even adds that the pleasure (*terpsis*) he derives from listening to how Hephaestus takes revenge on the lovers who tricked him is as great as that of the other listeners. When Demodocus steps forward a third time, we have the most important episode. Odysseus will shortly set sail, and the Phaeacian leaders are gathered round for a last banquet with their guest. The bard has been summoned, as befits the occasion, and before he begins Odysseus honors him by having a portion of meat brought to him and praising his skill.

Then, almost as though he were issuing a challenge, Odysseus asks the bard to recount the episode of the Trojan Horse. Demodocus immediately does so, and whereas the Phaeacians are delighted, Odysseus is unable to hold back his tears. How can he weep at a tale which he himself has asked to hear?[24] Alcinous at once silences the bard, since he precisely wants the pleasure of the occasion to be shared by all equally (*homôs terpômetha pantes*):[25]

> And tell me why thou dost weep and wail in spirit as thou hearest the doom of the Argive Danaans and of Ilios. This the gods wrought, and spun the skein of ruin for men, that there might be a song for those yet to be born. Did some kinsman of thine fall before Ilios, some good, true man, thy daughter's husband or thy wife's father, such as are nearest to one after one's own kin and blood? Or was it haply some comrade dear to thy heart, some good, true man? For no whit worse than a brother is a comrade who has an understanding heart.[26]

With the *Odyssey* we seem to have entered a time where the pleasure (*terpsis*) generally anticipated and derived from the bard's song is, on several occasions, blighted or ruined by the pain, grief, and regret it generates or awakens in some of the listeners. As though an untrammeled pleasure were no longer possible, except in an exceptional society such as that of the Phaeacians (who have remained close to a golden age). And as though the epic poem were no longer equal to the task of preserving the glorious memory of heroes.

Before we come back to Odysseus's tears, it is worth noting what Odysseus says to the bard: "Demodocus, verily above all mortal men do I praise thee, whether it was the Muse, the daughter of Zeus, that taught thee, or Apollo." This reminder of the close link between the poet and the Muse remains within the sphere of a conventional and unexceptional expression of praise: the bard, inspired, is a seer. But what follows is more surprising: "for too perfectly [*liên kata kosmon*] dost thou sing of the fate of the Achaeans, all that they wrought and suffered, and all the toils they endured, as though [*hôs*] haply thou hadst thyself been present [*pareôn*], or hadst heard the tale from another [*akousas*]."[27] There is a change of register here: the seer is also a "voyeur," or rather his description is so precise, too (*liên*) precise even, that Odysseus is tempted to believe that the seer actually saw what he sings, although he knows this cannot possibly be true. Demodocus, the blind bard, can in no sense be considered a witness. If witness there was, it is Odysseus, and Odysseus alone.

Odysseus seems to be saying that Demodocus's tale is too lifelike not to be that of an eyewitness. The ability to describe everything down to the very last detail is, for Odysseus the witness and protagonist, the surest sign of the song's truthfulness.[28] And for the Muse, of course, seeing, knowing, and saying go together, and are indeed one and the same operation. In these few lines, however, Odysseus curiously inverts the perspective and takes human vision as the standard against which the accuracy of divine vision is to be measured. It is as though "Demodocus the bard" and "Demodocus the historian" were momentarily juxtaposed, even if "the historian" appears only long enough to "authenticate" the other figure, "the bard." Unsurprisingly, Demodocus does not respond to Odysseus's challenge, and the latter does not insist. It is the Muse who has the last word—and how could it be otherwise? Yet this change of register or splitting of Demodocus into "bard" and "historian," however briefly it occurs, is a significant moment for the poetics of knowledge, and particularly significant is the fact that Odysseus singles it out. His words afford us a momentary glimpse of another possible configuration of knowledge, one which as yet has no name, but which points toward the historiographical move Herodotus would later make. Odysseus's words make this move neither necessary nor probable, but simply possible.

Hannah Arendt interprets this scene, in which the hero listens to the tale of his own actions recounted to him by the bard, as the beginning, at least in a literary register, of the category of history, since it is the first narrativization of an event: "What had been sheer occurrence now became 'history.'" What distinguished this "history" was that Odysseus's presence both there (at Troy) and here (at the banquet) proved that it really took place. An absolutely novel configuration was produced, an "anomaly," since in the epic poem the bard's speech is normally wholly dependent on the authority of the Muse, who is both its source of inspiration and the guarantor of its truthfulness. Arendt went still further, considering this scene to be "paradigmatic" for history and poetry since, as she says in her very condensed style, "the 'reconciliation with reality,' the *catharsis*, which, according to Aristotle, was the essence of tragedy and, according to Hegel, was the ultimate purpose of history, came about through the tears of remembrance."[29]

But can this episode really be called a "first" historical narrative? For whom? Perhaps for us, but if so, then as something like a primal scene. The individual for whom the question really arises is Odysseus, since he is the only person to know from experience that this history is inseparably his history and history itself. And his reaction is—to weep.[30] But are his tears really "tears of remembrance"? Is he, like Penelope or Menelaus, overcome by grief on hearing the misfortunes of the Achaeans? Is he tormented by an unfinished or impossible work of mourning? This is in fact the question Alcinous asks Odysseus on noticing his tears: has he lost a relative or a close comrade at Troy?[31] Odysseus does not reply at once.

However, even before Alcinous's question, the exceptional nature and the importance of these tears are suggested by a striking comparison, which draws attention to the presence of the narrator-poet:

> And as a woman wails and flings herself about her dear husband, who has fallen in front of his city and his people, seeking to ward off from his city and his children the pitiless day; and as she beholds him dying and gasping for breath, she clings to him and shrieks aloud, while the foe behind her smite her back and shoulders with their spears, and lead her away to captivity to bear toil and woe, while with most pitiful grief her cheeks are wasted: even so did Odysseus let fall pitiful tears from beneath his brows.[32]

That Odysseus should weep may be comprehensible—but why "like a wife"? For whom does he shed these "pitiful tears"? We have the grief-stricken wife mourning the loss of her husband—and that is Penelope. We have the wife who, seized as a slave, had previously witnessed her husband's death before the walls of his own city and under the eyes of his own people—and that is Andromache.[33] We can note in passing that the evocative power of this comparison, its capacity to condense or universalize a condition (Odysseus's suffering is that of all victims of war), illustrates the "art of allusion," which Pietro Pucci identifies as one of the *Odyssey*'s narrative devices.[34] We find an echo, or a modern deployment, of it in Baudelaire's *The Swan*, with its opening "Andromache, I think of you!," leading to a final generalization, in which the poet thinks "of whoever has lost that which is never found / Again! Never! . . . /—Of the captives, of the vanquished! . . . of many others too!" Homer's use of comparison at all events gives the *Odyssey*'s narrative a depth of field that arguably exceeds the "foreground" of pure present to which Auerbach wishes to reduce it.

Odysseus cries over himself: he is mourning his own loss. After all, who is he? Since the storm at Cape Malea and his wanderings adrift in the world of the nonhuman, Odysseus has gone missing: neither alive nor dead, he no longer even has a name.[35] In this sense he is like a wife who, on the death of her husband, no longer has anything or is anyone. The heroic, masculine part of himself, to which he owes his fame, has, so to speak, been left behind on the shores of Troy. And when he lands among the Phaeacians, a people adept at frontier-crossings and at mediating at the margins, he hears his own exploits and his own heroic name being celebrated by the bard Demodocus. At that moment the husband becomes the weeping wife. But immediately afterward he explicitly manages to link the two parts of his existence, Odysseus at Troy and Odysseus wandering the seas, when he finally declares, in reply to Alcinous's questions, "I am Odysseus, son of Laertes."[36] Although he states that his suffering can only be increased by recounting the tale of his misfortunes, once having launched into his story he takes the listener without a break from Troy to his last shipwreck, including each passage ashore and all his dashed hopes and hardships.

But before we get to this point, there is one last ordeal Odysseus has to endure. When Demodocus sings his praises, Odysseus finds himself in the painful position of having to listen to the tale of his own deeds, in the third person, as though he were absent or no longer alive, or as though the song concerned somebody else. Moreover, for the Phaeacians listening to their bard, "Odysseus" is of course just the name of one of those heroes whose skein of ruin the gods have spun in order to ensure songs for future generations.[37] Listening to Demodocus's words, Odysseus is wrenched out of himself and forced to adopt the position which would later, in historical narrative, be that of the dead.[38] He is a survivor—but is he alive or dead? What he is hearing is what no living person should normally hear. In a certain sense this experience is even more radical than the episode of his descent to the house of Hades to question Tiresias. In it he had approached the ultimate limit between the living and the dead, but had remained squarely on the side of the living.[39]

Despite having consulted Tiresias and knowing what lies ahead of him and that he will return home, Odysseus nevertheless sheds tears for himself at Alcinous's banquet. These tears are not for the death that will come to him; he never rebels against his mortal condition. But when Demodocus's words conjure up for him what he once was, he feels no pleasure of recognition (that was me, it was like that).[40] On the contrary, he is shaken by sobs. He cannot yet link the present which is no more to today's present, by means of a history—his own—which would transform the former present into a past. He is exiled from that former present, which is why he is so shaken when Demodocus depicts it. It is as though he were dreaming of himself, while fully aware that he is awake. Or as though a dead person appeared to him in his sleep, like Patroclus to Achilles, except that this dead person is none other than himself. In a sense, Odysseus has survived his own death, and is no more able to seize hold of himself than Achilles was able to embrace the soul of his companion—hence his tears.

As the bard's song unfolds, Odysseus is thus led to experience a painful lack of self-coincidence. It cannot yet be expressed in words, but Homer makes it visible, and almost palpable, through Odysseus's tears, which are then "explained" by the comparison. He inhabits an intermediary zone in which he is no longer and not yet Odysseus, not yet capable of declaring "I am Odysseus." And what emerges in this gap opened up between alterity and identity is indeed an experience of time. Not, as we have stressed, the anguished experience of finitude, since Odysseus knows he is mortal and would not wish it otherwise. Nor is it an experience of time as flux. Rather, this experience of self-estrangement can be called an encounter with historicity. Unable to grasp this past, his own past, as precisely past, Odysseus at first seems overwhelmed—and he weeps.

Then, as soon as he has reclaimed and voiced his proper name, he is able to recover through narrating his adventures. By stringing together incident after incident, the Odysseus who set sail from Troy can eventually link up with the shipwrecked wayfarer in the midst of his Phaeacian hosts. Episodes ashore follow one another, each recounted as a past-present, and gradually a chronological mechanism is established in which imperceptibly the narrative form gives shape to time: narrative order becomes an order of time. This order is also triggered by Alcinous's question "Who are you?" It requires a reply, at least so that the king may know whom he is dealing with and, as nobles, each may thereafter become the other's guest, but, more essentially, also because it is not enough simply to give one's name. A real reply involves recounting what has happened, and thus forging the kind of "narrative identity" to which Paul Ricoeur has drawn our attention in some comments on Arendt.[41] Meanwhile the Phaeacians perceive none of the stakes involved in this crucial scene, and simply listen spellbound to the tale as though it were being sung by a bard.[42] But Odysseus, despite appearances, is no bard. He has suffered in the flesh what the bard, who celebrates illustrious heroes and the dead, has only ever sung: at one remove, from afar.

The Sirens' Call to Oblivion

Let us turn now to the enigmatic Sirens, whom Odysseus encounters after his descent into Hades. They are certainly Muses, or at least possess the Muses' attributes (they are ever-present and all-knowing). But they should more accurately be described as counter-Muses, since they undermine and destroy the economy of *kleos*.[43] Whoever approaches them will experience a pleasure (*terpsamenos*) similar to that procured by the bard's song, as they say to Odysseus: "For we know [*idmen*] all the toils that in wide Troy the Argives and Trojans endured through the will of the gods, and we know all things that come to pass upon the fruitful earth."[44] However, as Circe warns, imprudent travelers seduced by their sweet song forfeit everything: for them there can be no return and no renown. They are lost forever, their bones lie bleaching on the Sirens' shores, and their flesh decays. Their names are destined not for undying fame but for oblivion. In epic poetry, the "price" paid for the listener's pleasure is actually the death of others; Alcinous's statement that others die in order to provide pleasure for generations yet unborn is simply the epic's logic taken to its limit.[45] For this logic to work, and hence for the epic to function as such, one essential condition must be fulfilled: the "others" must change into "men of former times," that is, a gap must open up between "past" and "future." This is why the *Odyssey*, which is an epic of homecoming—the absent heroes eventually reappear, and Odysseus constantly yearns to return—is an anachronistic epic, or at least one that questions its own mechanisms.

In the case of the Sirens' song, the listener's pleasure is still primary, but the song's hero is also always its only listener—as though the listener had to pay the price of the song with his own death. Since the listener is not a "man yet to be born," he has no choice but to become a "man of former times," and hence disappear, reunited with what he once was. As soon as Odysseus approaches their island, the Sirens call out to him using his heroic name (of former times). They know who he is and use an expression of praise—"Come hither ... renowned Odysseus, great glory [*mega kudos*] of the Achaeans"[46]—which happens to be identical to the expression used by Agamemnon to address Odysseus in the *Iliad*. Once again, the *Iliad* suddenly appears in the *Odyssey*, while at the same time Odysseus is tempted back toward his "past" and the serenity of *kleos*. But reuniting with this past, or yielding to its attraction, would mean bidding farewell to himself forever. The two parts or sides of himself would never be able to link up. The Sirens' only listeners, on their secluded island, are their victims; and since they are immortal, it will ever be so. Never, unlike the bard, will they sing for "men yet to be born": with their song they "bury" not the dead but the living, whom they consign to oblivion in what is effectively a strange funeral ceremony.[47] Whoever hears his glorious deeds praised in the third person pays an exorbitant price for this momentary pleasure. There they stand in a motionless present, all alone on their island in the middle of nowhere, and never will they inspire a bard to glorify their memory in song. They are muses of mourning, or rather of anti-mourning, of disappearance and oblivion.[48] Their effect is quite the opposite of Helen's as she dispenses her *nepenthês* to the guests. Whoever yields to the pleasure of listening to them not only never returns, but will never be transmuted through a bard's song into a "man of former times."

"Past" and "present" are separated in the epic by simple juxtaposition. The contract underlying the epic poem is that as soon as a bard starts singing, a break occurs, and the *klea andrôn* are transformed into the glorious deeds of "men of former times," those who came before (*proteroi*). The dead are present and they speak, as they do in dreams, since the bard is someone who can pass to the other side. The *Odyssey* accordingly seeks to juxtapose times, but since it sings of a return, it cannot do so. Like Odysseus, it comes up against the question of time and of the past, and indeed the past as a question.[49] One can suggest that the *Odyssey* lies between two regimes of utterance: an epic utterance, which it still clings to, and another regime, which has not yet emerged, but which will have to try to take into account if not the fact of time passing and passed, then at least its effects. An echo of this can be found a few centuries later when Herodotus describes the fate of city-states as somewhere between the extremes of large and small: those which were formerly great have become small, and those previously small have grown.[50] The *Odyssey* can no longer simply juxtapose times, but it also cannot yet order them chronologically. Does it hold such fascination for us because it is nostalgic, yearning for an impossible return—to the epic? In other words, to the *Iliad*? But along the way it discovers the past, or rather it keeps coming up against memory, forgetting, mourning, and the pastness of the past: the past as an issue and, above all, as a question.

We have seen that Achilles belongs to the present and the present alone. If he refrains from fighting or refuses to do so, he sacrifices his very essence. At the same time, his *thumos* prevents him from consigning the insult he has suffered to the past, and letting things be "as past and done." That is why he withdraws from battle, paralyzing the action and even risking becoming useless to those "yet to be born," as Patroclus admonishes him.[51] He has to make a heroic decision and put things behind him, which also helps realize Zeus's plans. Thereafter every day can once again be a first day, until his last day dawns. Odysseus's dilemma is more complicated. He has to recognize himself as both identical and different. It was me/it is me; I was/I am Odysseus.

Odysseus's exchange with Demodocus, with its moment of incomprehension, represents an extraordinary situation, in which the bard is confronted with a witness who is also the principal protagonist. What, then, is the status of the bard's song? Normally, as one of those "men of former times," Odysseus should be dead—yet there he stands. We have seen how the *Odyssey*, in its very structure, necessarily confronts the question of the past. It is usually a seer who is called upon to probe the past and the future, since the seer's divinatory powers make everything co-present, embraced within a synoptic vision. By contrast, the bard inspired by the Muse sees into a beyond, and he sees the dealings of gods with men, of heroes rather than men in general, and preferably those who have died a glorious death on the battlefield. His particular task is to celebrate the renown (*kleos*) of those who have died, and in ensuring their *kleos*, to perpetuate their memory. In praising those who have passed on, he fabricates a past, but a past without duration, a past which is simply over. It is a past on demand, generated by the gap introduced by the bard as soon as he breaks into song. But singing of *nostos* disturbs this order. What are heroes who return, who have returned, or who are returning? Unless, like Phemios at Ithaca, he decides to sing only of those who have perished.[52] Returning introduces a dimension of duration. There is a departure, but also a return journey with all its tribulations; there is a before and after the fall of Troy. The fact of returning opens up a gap, creates a tension, and makes a rift in the present. The heroes have not come home. They are absent, but they are not all dead, and indeed several will come back, or have already done so. What is this intervening time, this intermediary period which Odysseus alone is able to traverse, that is, to narrate, thanks to the shock of his encounter with Demodocus? What is it, if not the past? It is a time experienced by Odysseus as painful self-estrangement before he finally discovers that it is the past, and his own.

Odysseus Has Not Read Augustine

My strategy—of selecting instances radically distant in space and time (Fiji and Phaeacia) in order to explore orders of time and regimes of historicity—partakes of a practice of "viewing from afar" which writers from Montaigne to Lévi-Strauss via Rousseau and many others have employed in the search for fresh insights. By decentering our focus we can challenge what we take to be self-evident, and question our own categories. This makes comparative work possible. My own research into regimes of historicity happened to start in the Pacific, through reading Sahlins, and Segalen before that, and of course Lévi-Strauss. But that was just an accident of my own intellectual biography, even if it also reflected a period when anthropology seemed to hold the key to our questions about man and society.

For the Maori in Fiji or Odysseus in Phaeacia, the universe of Jewish and Christian Revelation, which was to alter so radically our forms of experience of time, was inaccessible. Christianity took the biblical economy of time the furthest, and ended up thoroughly and enduringly shaping the West's relations to time. We could not reasonably claim to explore the notion of "regime of historicity" in the modern and contemporary period without testing it against the singular and singularly powerful Christian order of time. But can one identify a properly Christian regime of historicity? This question comes with a secondary one: can the very notion of regime of historicity be dissociated from the experiences of time fashioned by biblical temporalities? But this is not to suggest that such a notion simply repeats or extends these without modification.

Let us start with the statement "Odysseus has not read Augustine." Of course he hasn't, since the *Odyssey* and the *Confessions* were composed some twelve centuries apart! And it is equally obvious that not a few philosophies of time saw the light of day in the intervening period (to mention only Plato, Aristotle, the Stoics, the Epicurians, and Plotinus). Augustine's thought was undoubtedly indebted to this tradition, even if he took it in a different direction and developed something utterly new, a phenomenology of time. So this statement is not to be understood as telescoping the two moments—far from it—but simply as a way of placing the two figures side by side to suggest a kind of intimate snapshot in which Odysseus would be listening to the bard and breaking down in tears while alongside him Augustine would be addressing his questions to God: "What then is time? Provided that no one asks me, I know. If I want to explain it to an inquirer, I do not know."[53] How can I both know and not know? This enigmatic condition is what gives rise to Augustine's meditation, punctuated by prayers and invocations, in book 11 of the *Confessions*. Clearly Odysseus would not only be unable to reply to the question "What is time?," but would not even be able to formulate it in these terms. One could suggest, however, that his tears, and the narrator's comparison that accompanies these, are a substitute reply; indeed, they are his reply or the expression of his inability to reply in his own words.

In particular, Odysseus has not read chapter 28, in which Augustine takes a concrete case through which to test out what his meditations have taught him. Having started with the problem of measuring the passage of time, he has concluded that time is nothing but the mind's "distension." As such, it is measured "in the mind." But how?—by the play of "distension" (*distensio*) and "attention" (*attentio*). "For the mind expects [*expectat*] and attends [*adtendit*] and remembers [*meminit*], so that what it expects passes through what has its attention to what it remembers."[54] This is where Augustine recapitulates his argument, and generalizes it:

> Suppose I am about to repeat a psalm which I know. Before I begin, my expectation is directed towards the whole. But when I have begun, the verses from it which I take into the past become the object of my memory. The life of this act of mine is stretched two ways, into my memory because of the words I have already said and into my expectation because of those which I am about to say. But my attention is on what is present: by that the future is transferred to become the past. As the action advances further and further, the shorter the expectation and the longer the memory, until all expectation is consumed, the entire action is finished, and it has passed into the memory. What occurs in the psalm as a whole occurs in its particular pieces and individual syllables. The same is true of a longer action in which perhaps that psalm is a part. It is also valid of the entire life of an individual person, where all actions are parts of a whole, and of the total history of "the sons of men" (Ps. 30:20) where all human lives are but parts.[55]

So on the smallest as well as the largest scale, whether it is a question of a series of syllables or a sequence of centuries, via an individual's entire life, repeating the psalm remains the paradigm of the to-and-fro constantly occurring between distension and attention, in which attention operates at the very heart of distension.

Now Odysseus is unable to organize the events of his life according to this model, shuttling between memory and expectation. One could say that he has *distensio* but not *attentio*. As Auerbach noted, the Homeric hero, unlike biblical figures, lives each day as though it were his first. I have already mentioned that Achilles can exist only in the present, and he knows no past or future. But even he is obliged to "let [these things] be as past and done," to put behind him the outrage of Agamemnon's insult, to get beyond it: in other words, to consign it to the past, without which he must cease in a certain way to be Achilles. His heroism must include overcoming his *thumos*, so that the action can start up again and he can be wholly himself, Achilles, the "bane of the Trojans," living to the full his brief life in the present.

Odysseus's situation is quite different. His sights are constantly set on his return: he "does not forget" Ithaca. When detained by the goddess Calypso, he unwillingly spends his nights with her and by day "would sit on the rocks and the sands, racking his soul with tears and groans and griefs, and he would look over the unresting sea, shedding tears." And the terms in which he declines her offer of immortality are "I wish and long day by day to reach my home, and to see the day of my return."[56] The tears he sheds are not the same as those he sheds on hearing Demodocus's song. With Calypso, his tears express his longing for Ithaca, and the misery of his prolonged absence. The tears shed at the Phaeacians' banquet are not really tears of remembrance, as Arendt calls them, and the comparison that accompanies them suggests another interpretation. Are they then tears of mourning, as Alcinous assumes? Again, not really, unless by this we mean mourning for oneself.

For it is as though Odysseus were in mourning for that illustrious part of himself which remained at Troy, and was then entrusted to the bards. At all events, in both these scenes, weeping expresses how the (everyday) present of the Homeric hero is torn apart, pulled at once toward the future (the day of homecoming) and toward the past (the fall of Troy). Even the hero of many wiles is at a loss to make sense for himself of this double movement of *distensio*, which is dramatized by the repeated delay in returning from Troy to Ithaca. In Augustinian terms, Odysseus has an experience of time as *distensio*, in the form of his ever-extended journey, but he is unable to grasp and actualize time through *attentio*.[57] As we have stressed, overcoming this last crisis is what will enable Odysseus to declare his name and identify himself in compliance with Alcinous's request. It is through the uninterrupted narrative which he then delivers to the Phaeacians that the Odysseus who set sail from Troy can be reunited with the shipwrecked stranger on the island of Scheria. The narrative identity thus created both illuminates and integrates his shadow side, which until then had been subject only to *dispersio*.[58]

Odysseus has not read Augustine in yet another sense. Augustine's phenomenology of human time is embedded within the structure of an eternal God who has created all times, such that "distension" must additionally be understood as integral to the human condition. Man's lot is dispersion: "I am scattered [*dissilui*] in times whose order I do not understand [*ordinem nescio*]. The storms of incoherent events tear to pieces my thoughts." This order of time which mortal man cannot know is that of a personal God who summons him, so that

> leaving behind the old days I might be gathered [*colligar*] to follow the One, "forgetting the past" and moving not towards those future things which are transitory but to "the things which are before" me, not stretched out in distraction [*distentus*] but extended in reach [*extentus*], not by being pulled apart [*distentio*] but by concentration [*intentio*]. So I "pursue the prize of the high calling" where I "may hear the voice of praise" and "contemplate your delight" (Ps. 25:7; 26:4) which neither comes nor goes.[59]

The Christian order of time to which the believer may aspire thus involves the passage from the mutability of the many to the immutability of God's eternity. The path leads from dispersion to tension, reaching out by means of an effort of intention (and not simply of attention) toward those things that lie before (*ante*) (and not simply toward the future). Augustine is here simply following Saint Paul in his Letter to the Philippians: "Forgetting those things which are behind, and reaching forth unto those things which are before, I press toward the mark for the prize of the high calling of God in Christ Jesus."[60] The image is that of a runner in the stadium. A similar order is suggested at the beginning of *The City of God*, in which the Christian "in this fleeting course of time [*in hoc temporum cursu*]" walks "in the midst of the ungodly [*inter impios peregrinatur*]" and "waits for [*expectat*] the fixed stability of [the City of God's] eternal seat."[61] And Saint Paul once again: "whereto we have already attained, let us walk by the same rule, let us mind the same thing ... for our conversation is in heaven."[62]

It was not Christianity, however, that conceived and experienced time as an expectant tension or an opening of anticipation. This relation to time was already present in Yahweh's promise to Abraham: "Get thee out of thy country, and from thy kindred, and from thy father's house, unto a land that I will shew thee. And I will make of thee a great nation, and I will bless thee, and make thy name great."[63] The Book of Exodus expressed the same idea in richer and more dramatic form: the exodus from Egypt and the journey toward the land of Canaan, guided by Yahweh, fashions a time of expectation in which the Hebrews' constantly deferred arrival is a mainspring of the narrative. This is in fact the root of the interweaving of time and narrative which Ricoeur analyzes in *Saint Augustine and Aristotle*. Moses's task, in Augustinian terms, was to shape deferral and *distensio* into a history, despite the fact that the Hebrews kept losing those members who found the tension intolerable, and who dispersed into the immediacy of the many.[64] On two separate occasions, in Numbers and Deuteronomy, the episodes, stages, and sequence of events leading from the exodus from Egypt to the banks of the Jordan are recounted as the history of the forty years that were to shape Israel as a "kingdom of priests, and an holy nation."[65] The Tables of the Law, engraved not once but twice, and mentioned again in Deuteronomy, were enough to provide the children of Israel with all they needed to remain faithful to the covenant. And when in 100 CE, just thirty years after the destruction of the temple, the rabbis finalized the biblical canon, the picture of what should be known was complete: "For the first time the history of a people became part of its sacred scripture." And since consequently the past was "known" and the future "assured," the time between the biblical era and the coming of the messiah, while it might be "obscure," could bring no "new or useful insights."[66] At all events, with the forward thrust of its strongly linear narrative, the Exodus story came to fashion Jewish and, ultimately, non-Jewish conceptions of time. The narrative's progress through space and time made it possible to conceive and formulate other experiences and to construct other stories. I owe these last remarks to Michael Walzer, who has devoted a whole book to the Exodus story as a revolutionary paradigm in Western history.[67]

As regards relations to time, Christianity's specific contribution was the decisive event of the Incarnation—the birth, death, and resurrection of the Son of God made man—which broke time in two. A new time started, which was to end with a second and last event, the Second Coming of Christ and the Last Judgment. The in-between time was a time of anticipation: a present inhabited by the promise of the end. Jesus himself announced this: "Verily I say unto you, This generation shall not pass, till all these things be fulfilled.... But of that day and hour knoweth no man, no, not the angels of heaven, but my Father only.... Watch therefore: for ye know not what hour your Lord doth come.... Therefore be ye also ready: for in such an hour as ye think not the Son of man cometh."[68] Vigilance is, quite literally, what is required: "Banish slumber," says Saint Luke's gospel.

Besides this eschatological present, what is really new in the New Testament is "the tension between the decisive 'already fulfilled' and the 'not yet completed,' between present and future."[69] On this founding tension is constructed a properly Christian order of time, and history as the history of salvation. But the already does not balance out the not-yet like the two sides of a set of scales: the already carries more weight, since that "decisive point" has irreversibly changed the course of history.[70] The world has already been saved. The present ushered in by this "already" is consequently a privileged time.

It is certainly privileged in relation to the past, which it in no way abolishes but rather reveals as simply prefatory, with a view to fulfilling it. This is apparent in the care taken by the first Christians to prove that the coming of Christ fulfilled scripture, and their insistence on speaking of the Old and the New Covenant, the Old and the New Testament. "Search the scriptures; for in them ye think ye have eternal life: and they are they which testify of me," and "for [Moses] wrote of me,"[71] says Jesus to "the Jews." As for the future, there is initially very little difference between it and this present lived as "anticipation of the end," entirely oriented toward its possibly imminent completion. His kingdom come, and this generation shall not pass, till all these things be fulfilled. As Jesus says to his disciples, "But I tell you of a truth, there be some standing here, which shall not taste of death, till they see the kingdom of God."[72] When this anticipation is fulfilled, nothing more can occur.

Then, with the close of apostolic times, *parousia* seemed to recede, and the in-between time increased with the institutionalization of the Church. This extension of time is reflected in all of Saint Augustine's writings, although the basic tension persists nonetheless. The world had entered its sixth age—old age—since the birth of Christ according to the flesh, and the next age would be the last, the sabbath of the seventh day when the vision of God would be fulfilled.[73] That is when the onward striving would come to an end. Meanwhile, the tension remains, since one should not look behind one to the past, but forward toward Christ; and one should not look to the future (which will likewise vanish), but rather in front of one (*ante*).

Later still, "Rome's political and spiritual heritage passed on to the Christian Church,"[74] and the tension between "already" and "not yet," which had constituted the present as an intermediate time, began to ease. The two poles moved ever further apart, even if there were also periods of sometimes radical revival of this tension. Such periods were expressed in the numerous heresies and reforms proclaimed, abandoned, and repressed throughout Christianity's history, and they had in common the attempt to reinvest the present as a fully messianic time through a return to roots. But the time of the already, enmeshed as it was in a tradition which drew on it and carried it forward, became ever more important. Eusebius, bishop of Caesarea, a contemporary of Constantine, introduced the concept of ecclesiastical history, from the birth of Christ to the present, and fixed the limits of the tradition by citing a series of testimonies which functioned as a system of authoritative sources. Henceforth the believer would be enjoined to look not in front but behind, toward Christ with whom everything began and who is also the ultimate ideal. He is the beacon whose beam reaches into the "before" (from Adam to himself) and into the "after" (from himself to the end of days). "Thanks to the fact that the foundation of the city of Rome was repeated in the foundation of the Catholic Church, though, of course, with a radically different content, the Roman trinity of religion, authority, and tradition could be taken over by the Christian era."[75]

This inflection of the Christian order of time toward the already, toward the past (even if it was a past continually reactivated into the present through the Church's rituals), enabled the Church to rediscover, adopt, and inhabit the classical models of the *mos majorum* and *historia magistra*, and to deploy them to its advantage. But it never identified with them completely. It became a temporal power, while claiming to represent another order of time. All in all, the Christian order of time retained a certain malleability, which allowed present, past, and future to be articulated against a backdrop of eternity. It was not a single regime of historicity, nor can it be reduced to one, not even to its predominant regime of *historia magistra*. Later, Christian time and the time of the world divorced, after going through a whole series of crises. But this in no way implies that nothing passed from one order to another. On the contrary, what the path of progress appropriated, as it gradually replaced the striving for salvation, was the latter's forward-focused tension combined with a "hopeful expectation" oriented toward the future.[76]

3

CHATEAUBRIAND, BETWEEN OLD AND NEW REGIMES OF HISTORICITY

UNLIKE ODYSSEUS, CHATEAUBRIAND *HAD* READ AUGUSTINE. Immersed as he was in a Christian experience of time, his one and only temporal reference was that of the Catholic monarchy. However, since he was born in 1768, he grew up in a period of profound crisis and conflictual relations to time. That is why he will be our guide here, he whose world was utterly shattered by the French Revolution. Yet many other names could rightfully figure between Augustine and Chateaubriand, between Alaric's sack of Rome and the storming of the Bastille, not least Petrarch, Bacon, Montaigne, Perrault, and Rousseau; and several other experiences and crises of time between the fifteenth century and the revolutions of the eighteenth century would deserve analysis.[1]

So why Chateaubriand, the youngest son of a family of Breton noblemen? Because this product and staunch supporter of what was fast transforming under his very eyes into the "ancien régime," this traveler to the New World in search of the timeless age of the savage, this man so squarely on the losing side in the French Revolution nevertheless had a deeper understanding, when all is said and done, of the emergent temporal order of modernity than many of his contemporaries. And he managed to transform his experience of a break, rift, or breach in time into the very mainspring of his writing. Like Augustine before him, he was one of the "vanquished," in Koselleck's sense, for whom "if history is made in the short run by the victors, historical gains in knowledge stem in the long run from the vanquished."[2] Certainly neither Augustine nor Chateaubriand was a historian, but perhaps that was precisely because the genre of history as it existed at the time could not accommodate their experiences in all their radicality.

Toward the end of the preface to his extraordinary *Memoirs*, Chateaubriand wrote: "I found myself between two centuries as at the confluence of two rivers; I plunged into their troubled waters; regretfully leaving the ancient strand where I was born, and swimming hopefully towards the unknown shore."[3] These are the statements of an older man, looking back over his life and encapsulating it in an image he had used several times in his work. It is the start of this adventure that I shall examine first, before the confluence was even on the horizon. Then, through the comparison of two of Chateaubriand's works, his first book, the *Historical Essay* (1797), and his *Travels in America* (1827), I shall delineate a quarter of a century of interaction between three key figures in the Western tradition: the ancients, the moderns, and the savages. I cannot broach their long and rich history here, nor even sketch a brief reminder; I shall simply explore their relations to time, paying particular attention to the temporalities conveyed or produced by the ways in which, during this troubled period, these three figures were linked together.

The Young Chateaubriand's Journey

The *Historical Essay* is part of Chateaubriand's vast body of writings on America. Having left for America in 1791, the young viscount returned to France in 1792, and briefly joined the Army of the Princes before going into exile in London. That was where the *Historical Essay* was written, as he struggled to make ends meet. He returned to London in 1822 as French ambassador, and revisited his old haunts, where he had spent time with his "companions in distress."[4] First published in 1797, the *Historical Essay* was republished in 1826, although Chateaubriand—who was always in dire need of money—was at the time already involved in preparing his *Complete Works*.[5] Between those two dates, this unknown emigré had thus become ambassador in London—as well as in Berlin and Rome—and even minister for foreign affairs. But above all, he had become a famous writer: "Having set out to be a traveller in America, having returned to be a soldier in Europe, I did not follow up either of these careers: an evil genius wrested from me the staff and the sword, and put the pen into my hand."[6] An additional preface and foreword, as well as numerous critical notes, point to the (considerable) distance separating the author of 1826 from his original text, a work he considered to be "one of the most singular monuments" he had ever written.[7] It can be read as a kind of palimpsest.

Unlike the *Historical Essay*, the *Travels in America* did not have a separate first publication, probably because it was not a written text before Chateaubriand started preparing his *Complete Works*. "With his *Complete Works*, Chateaubriand wanted to give the public hitherto unpublished texts. He had amassed citations and analyses over more than a quarter of a century, which constituted a vast reserve of documentation on which he drew for a whole range of works. In 1826, the remainder provided the basis for the penultimate writings on America, since the last word would be reserved for the *Memoirs*."[8] In these penultimate writings a quite different America from the one first visited takes shape before the eyes of the reader, a whole new *journey* to be undertaken.

Western civilization's relation to time was profoundly and lastingly structured by the couple "the ancients" and "the moderns." The many quarrels punctuating its history each time expressed the tension inherent in the pair.[9] The notion of "the savage," which figured already in the first travel writings from the New World, introduced a new term. Arguments no longer hinged on two elements but on three and, most often, on one-plus-two, that is, the moderns versus the ancients/savages. I will select from this long and complex history only two authors, who were important for Chateaubriand.

Rousseau is the first and most obvious figure, the matrix—aporias and all—for Chateaubriand's *Historical Essay* and well beyond, right up to Claude Lévi-Strauss, another fine reader of Chateaubriand, in his *Tristes tropiques*. For Rousseau, the ancients both are and are not models. He holds them in higher esteem than the moderns, viewing them sometimes with nostalgia (as suggested, for example, by his lifelong reading of Plutarch) and sometimes as a utopia. Thus, for his (subsequently abandoned) history of Sparta, he had intended to collect "those precious monuments that teach us what men can be by showing us what they have been."[10] For Rousseau, the movement thus went from the past to the future, or rather toward a future yet to be brought into being, as a goal on which to set one's sights. But even if, in the *Social Contract*, society had something of an ideal Greek *polis* about it, every society (including ancient society) was nonetheless a mutilation compared to the state of nature. Hence the figure of the savage, which the young Chateaubriand invoked and brought to life: "Oh man of nature, you alone make me proud to be a man! Your heart knows no dependence."[11] For Chateaubriand, far from unrest and revolution, the savage resembled an island on which the shipwrecked traveler could find refuge;[12] Rousseau had been left far behind.

Both Chateaubriand and Rousseau were fascinated by the appeal of the savage, appeals to the savage, and the appeal of travel:

> Let us suppose a Montesquieu, a Buffon, a Diderot ... traveling in order to inform their compatriots, observing and describing as they know how to do.... Let us suppose that these new Hercules, back from these memorable treks, then wrote at leisure the natural, moral, and political history of what they would have seen; we ourselves would see a new world traced out by their pen, and we would thus learn to know our own.[13]

This famous scene from the *Discourse on Inequality* reappears almost identically in the *Historical Essay*:

> If he, who has been consumed by a thirst for knowledge, and has torn himself away from the enjoyments of affluence in order to go beyond the seas, to contemplate the grandest spectacle which can be offered to the eye of the philosopher, to meditate on free man in a state of nature and in society, placed near each other on the same soil; ... if such a person, I say, deserves any confidence, readers, you will find him in me.[14]

In Lévi-Strauss's view, Rousseau's ideas here make of him the "founder of the sciences of man,"[15] the first to express what was to be Lévi-Strauss's own theory of "viewing from afar," which I referred to in the last chapter.

The second significant author is Joseph-François Lafitau, whose work is one of the principal sources of the *Travels in America*. Lafitau, a Jesuit missionary in Canada, published *Customs of the American Indians Compared with the Customs of Primitive Times* in 1724. The Homeric flavor of Chateaubriand's savages in the *Travels* largely derives from it. But with Lafitau, the comparison with the ancients served explicitly as a heuristic device, and its ultimate goal was not to develop a comparative anthropology and show, in Arnaldo Momigliano's terms, that the Greeks were also savages, but rather to elucidate common origins. To this end, the savages no less than the ancients were witnesses to be examined and "traces" to be interpreted, in order to shed light on the remotest times of antiquity. The two did not figure for themselves, but rather for what lay beyond them, namely their common origin, which ultimately justifies the comparison between them. Lafitau intended to show atheists and modern skeptics that a primeval religion existed long before the laws of Moses, and that it was everywhere the same.[16] But quite apart from this apologetic framework and its place in the work, Lafitau's method of using parallels effectively "naturalized" the comparison between "the savages" and "the ancients."

THE *HISTORICAL ESSAY* IS A PIECE OF TRAVEL WRITING, THE TALE of a journey to the New World, of course, but the journey is above all internal. For here we have a historical study of revolutions ancient and modern that begins with the question "Who am I?"[17] Who am I indeed, given that the world into which I was born has collapsed? This was a question which Chateaubriand, the fledgling writer, would come back to time and again, pen in hand, on page after page. In the *Notice* to the 1826 edition, placed before the "Introduction," Chateaubriand summarized his book as "a sort of regular diary" of his "mental excursions."[18] When he traveled for the first time alone through the "boundless" American forest, "a strange revolution took place in my sensations"[19]—as though the real revolution were not the one he had fled but the one he had come looking for. And while the reader is led from the ruins of the Old World to the deserts and forests of the New, ending one night in the American forest, the traveler Chateaubriand has in fact gone in exactly the opposite direction, traveling to the New World, and reflecting back on the Old and its history.

To guide him through the world of the ancients, Chateaubriand made extensive use of one of the bestsellers of his day, abbé Jean-Jacques

Barthélemy's *Travels of Anacharsis the Younger in Greece* (1788). The young Anacharsis, "unable to bear longer the wandering life" he had lived until then, had left Scythia to live in Greece, until freedom was dealt a deathblow there (by Philip of Macedonia at Chaeronea in 338 B.C.), and he ended up returning to Scythia;[20] the young Chateaubriand left the Old World (where liberty had breathed its last) in search of the savages and their authentic freedom. But beyond the inverted itineraries of these two travelers, the Scythians occupy an important place in the economy of the *Essay*, to the extent that one can talk of a real Scythian paradigm.

Thus a note in the original version frames the three Scythian chapters as follows: "I am about to present to the reader the savage, pastoral, agricultural, philosophical and corrupted age, and thus [to] give him, without departing from my subject, an index of all societies, and an abridged, but complete history of man."[21] I shall briefly investigate these Scythians, who represent all three ages of civilization, from the state of the savage to that of corruption. They first came on the literary and philosophical scene in book IV of Herodotus's *Histories*, and have attracted countless speculations and comments ever since.[22]

Prior to figuring in Chateaubriand's arguments, the Scythians had surfaced in a play of 1766 by Voltaire called, precisely, *The Scythians* [*Les Scythes*]: "What we have here is, in a sense, the state of nature set in opposition to the state of artificial man, as he is found in the big cities," Voltaire wrote in the preface. And after the play flopped, he bluntly stated, in a letter to the king of Prussia, "*The Scythians* is a work of much mediocrity; it rather depicts the manners of the pretty Swiss cantons, and a French marquis, than the Scythians, and a Persian prince." The *Encyclopédie* article "*Scythe*," written by the indefatigable chevalier de Jaucourt, depicts the Scythians as noble savages. Their desire never went beyond their natural needs. As a consequence they experienced a happiness far greater than the Greeks ever knew. Anacharsis, Toxaris, and Zalmoxis (the trio of famous Scythians, to which one could add Abaris) were, at the end of the day, lawmakers rather than philosophers. Anacharsis, the most famous of them all, was a "man of worth" who lamented, as he perished under the arrows of his fellow countrymen, that "the wisdom which afforded me protection in Greece has been my downfall in Scythia."[23]

Such descriptions of virtuous Scythians actually go further back, and can all be found in abbé Rollin, who appeals to even older sources—the historian Justin and even Homer—while also introducing a discreet comparison with the lives of the Patriarchs. He nevertheless mentions out of honesty that a divergent and very ancient tradition also exists (dating back to Strabo and even further back to Ephorus, in the fourth century B.C.), according to which the Scythians were cruel and barbarous. But he hastily returns to Justin, who noted, as Jaucourt would later, that despite their ignorance the Scythians were wiser than the Greeks with all their statesmen and philosophers. Anacharsis is once again depicted as an entirely positive hero. In the light of all these elements, can we possibly, Rollin asks, "forbear to look upon them [i.e., the Scythians] with esteem and admiration?" Of course not. But, he continues, there came the time of corruption, brought about by "luxury." How, and by whose agency? "Strabo ... does not deny that this fatal change of manners was owing to the Romans and the Grecians."[24] Nothing could be clearer.

"The happy Scythians, whom the Greeks called Barbarians." This is the opening sentence of the *Historical Essay*'s Scythian chapters. Chateaubriand begins by adopting the traditional vision of the Scythians, following Rollin (or Jaucourt), but he adds a parallel between the three ages of the Swiss and the Scythians, on the basis that the Greeks were to the Scythians what the French are to the Swiss: agents of corruption! However, the parallel is not rigorous, he says, and there are some differences. Thus "the Scythians of the old, and the Swiss of the modern world, attracted the eyes of their contemporaries by the celebrity of their innocence. The different employment of their lives, however, introduced some difference as to their virtues. The first were shepherds, and cherished liberty for her own sake; the last were agriculturists and loved her for the sake of their property. The first approached towards primitive purity; the last had advanced a step nearer to civil vices."[25] In the wake of Rousseau, history could no longer be simple repetition.

Chateaubriand introduced two significant changes in relation to previous accounts. First, the Scythians are no longer assimilated to the Patriarchs, but quite simply to primitive man. The shift from Scythians to savages is thus not a problem or, more precisely, there is no difference between them since they are in equal measure men of nature. "Under the maples of the Erie I have seen this favourite of nature, who feels much and thinks little, who has no reasoning faculty beyond his wants, and who arrives at the results of philosophy like an infant, through his gambols and sleep."[26] Rollin before him had said nothing different, but Chateaubriand rewrites the comparison from the point of view of the savage. And as though further clarification were required, a note adds, "By depicting the mental savage of America, I supply a deficiency in Justinus, Herodotus, Strabo, Horace, etc. with regard to the history of the Scythians. People in a state of nature (some trifling differences excepted) resemble each other, and who has seen one, has seen all." As a result, Chateaubriand can exclaim: "Good Scythians, why did you not exist in our days? I would have sought among you shelter from the storm."[27] Scythia is thus depicted as a primitive America that no longer exists, that is, as a refuge. As such, quite unlike the young Anacharsis, the young Chateaubriand's one wish is to flee Greece and reach Scythia.

The other, more striking change concerns Anacharsis: not Anacharsis the Younger, but his ancestor, whom Chateaubriand is the only author to portray negatively. Introduced to illustrate Strabo's model of decadence, he is no longer represented as the wise man who traveled to Greece in order to drink in the wisdom of the Greeks, nor even as the "barbarian" who, in the tradition of the Cynics, came to poke fun at supposed Greek "wisdom." Rather, he is simply the man of progress, the bearer of corruption, that is, the philosopher. "He imagined that his fellow countrymen were barbarians, because they lived according to nature." So he undertook to enlighten them. Of course in no time at all he paid for his initiatives with his life, but the leaven "continued to ferment." The Scythians, "disgusted with their innocence ... drank the poison of civil life," thus illustrating this "philosophical and corrupted age."[28]

Historia magistra vitae

So this was the Scythian paradigm, or the "abridged, but complete history of man." Yet Chateaubriand dismisses it with a single stroke of the pen in a note from 1826: "These three chapters are no more part of the subject-matter of my *Essay* than is most of the work."[29] How come?! For Chateaubriand's procedure conforms perfectly to the principles of *historia magistra* that organize the *Historical Essay* as a whole, and have informed his relation to time up until then. In the form used by Chateaubriand, this famous doctrine of *historia magistra vitae* dates back to Cicero.[30] It expresses the classical conception of history as source of examples (*plena exemplorum*): "everything around us abounds with lessons and examples,"[31] Chateaubriand states in the *Historical Essay*. A summary of Koselleck's remarks on the disappearance of the model of *historia magistra* will be useful at this point to help elucidate both Chateaubriand's particular position and, more generally, the implications of a change in regime of historicity.

Koselleck's by-now classic analyses have shown how the development in Germany of the modern concept of history (*die Geschichte*) around 1760–1780 gradually devitalized its understanding in terms of exemplarity and repetition.[32] History in the singular (*die Geschichte*), understood as a process and conceived as history in itself, with its own proper temporality, abandoned the *exemplum* and redefined itself around the uniqueness of the event. A gap and a tension opened up between individuals' space of experience and their horizon of expectation.[33] The modern concept of history enabled the production of this gap to be understood and explained, and it could even illuminate historical progress in general. Although these theories from the German historical school were already in circulation earlier in the century, they were really put to the test by the French Revolution, which many experienced as a time of acceleration forcing apart, to breaking point, the space of experience from the horizon of expectation.

Chateaubriand's *Historical Essay* precisely faced this problem, and endeavored to reduce (as one reduces a fracture) this gap. He wanted not only to understand, but also to foresee events—with the intellectual tools available to him, namely the example and the parallel—by treating ancient and modern revolutions "in terms of their relations to the French Revolution."

Accordingly, Chateaubriand started with the past to explain the present, and even hoped to be able to reveal the future. A whole series of declarations throughout the *Historical Essay* suggest this aim: "With the torch of past revolutions in our hand, we shall boldly enter into the darkness of future ones. We shall scrutinize the man of former times, in spite of his assumed character, and compel the Proteus to give us an undisguised view of future man."[34] The Proteus mentioned is Proteus of Egypt, a figure from Homer and an immortal, who is capable of assuming all manner of different shapes. Menelaus can find out how to return home only by pinning him down to prevent him escaping, while he cross-examines him. Proteus is a seer, like Tiresias, whom Odysseus consulted, and as such he knows both past and future.[35] For Chateaubriand, however, Proteus is not a third party, but none other than the "man of former times" himself, whom the investigator must corner and interrogate, to make him reveal "future man." The past speaks to us, as long as we know how to question it. "Passing from the troubles of ancient times to those of modern nations I shall mount, by a series of calamities, from the first ages of the world to our own." The path climbed starts in the past.[36] "He who reads history, is like a man travelling in a desert through the fabled woods of antiquity, which predicted the future."[37] "If you wish to predict the future, consider the past. It is a sure datum which will never deceive you, if you proceed upon one principle—morality [*les moeurs*]."[38]

Chateaubriand calls upon an array of classical references, from Proteus to sacred groves, in his attempts to persuade himself that the past really can still shed light on the future. But this is clearly wishful thinking. Since "the enlightened ages have always been the ages of slavery," it follows that "judging from the data which history affords, I cannot but tremble for the future destiny of France."[39] Then, in conclusion to this demonstration, Chateaubriand affirms an "important truth": man is capable only of "incessant repetition"; he "moves in a circle, to pass beyond which all attempts are fruitless."[40] The conclusion to be drawn arrives abruptly, but it is no less desired for all that: the French Revolution has almost nothing new to tell us.

This relation to time and history encourages comparisons and parallels between the ancients and the moderns, and justifies imitation. Since history is basically repetition, the practice of comparison (understood as the search for and ordering of similarities) with antiquity is a first and essential step in the production of a well-constructed prognosis. And when it comes to parallels, Chateaubriand is fearless and certainly not beset by doubt: he compares Athens with Paris, London with Carthage, the Austrians with the Persians, Cook with Hannon, Critias with Marat—and more. "What chaos" he says several times in the 1826 preface. This is of course a conceit and an affectation, but also more than that.[41]

He also does not hesitate to use Tacitus to his own ends, citing "Experti invicem sumus, ego ac fortuna" ("Fortune and I now know each other";

Tacitus *Histories* 2.47) as the epigraph to the *Historical Essay* as a whole, and repeating it in the chapter concerning "the unfortunate."[42] These were the words Othon uttered when bidding farewell to his troops before withdrawing to take his own life. Chateaubriand wrote the passage while lying ill in London, adopting the pose of the dying man, half-Othon, half-Tacitus. The *Essay* is thus presented to the reader as the author's farewell to the world, his testament from beyond the grave, or at all events at death's door.

Yet despite the countless quotations, the classical mannerisms, and the numerous parallels, both familiar and surprising, Chateaubriand firmly condemns the harmfulness of imitation: "The danger of imitation is terrible. That, which is wholesome for one nation, is seldom the same for another."[43] This maxim is initially simply an acknowledgment of the variety and diversity of customs. But when it comes to the uses of antiquity, Chateaubriand does not doubt for an instant that the Jacobins are "fanatics in their admiration" of it and, because they are more "at home in Rome or Athens," have tried to reinstate ancient customs. Chateaubriand's stance here places him in the camp of the Thermidorian Reaction.[44] And he has just as little doubt that this imitation comes at the wrong time, due to a misrecognition of the "nature of things" (but he is not Thermidorian in his understanding of the "nature of things"). There follow some rather convoluted considerations which show that a maxim such as "other times, other customs" was not yet available.

This condemnation of imitation explains the terms in which Chateaubriand addresses the Revolutionaries: you seek to establish democracy just when "all nations are returning, from the nature of things, to monarchy, that is to say at the epoch of extreme corruption!"[45] Convinced that you are imitating Lycurgus, you "have inverted the motives of Lycurgus" (since Greece, at the time of Lycurgus, was in the process of abandoning monarchy). Furthermore,

> It was, nevertheless, at this moment that the body politic, stained all over as it was with the blotches of corruption, fell into general dissolution through a race of men, who at once arose, and in a sort of vertigo sounded the resurrection of Sparta and Athens. At the same moment the cry of liberty was heard. Old Jupiter, suddenly awaking from the slumber of fifteen centuries in the dust of Olympus, was astonished to find himself at St

Geneviève. The head of the Parisian Clown was covered with the cap of the Lacedaemonian citizen. All corrupted, all vicious as he was, the grand virtues of the Lacedaemonian were forced upon the little Frenchman, and he was constrained to play the character of Pantaloon in the eyes of Europe, attired in this masquerade dress of Harlequin.[46]

One can almost hear Marx's words on the French Revolutionaries dressed up in Roman costume.[47] Except that, for Chateaubriand, we have already left the domain of tragedy for that of farce and vulgar imitation, and at all events—Chateaubriand's parting shot—the Revolutionaries chose the wrong parallels at the wrong time. This tirade against imitation proves, however, to be wholly compatible with a certain nostalgia for antiquity, since on the very same page of the *Essay*, in an echo of Rousseau, we find: "I myself would wish to pass my days under such a democracy as I have fancied, as forming the sublimest of governments in theory; ... and I myself have lived as citizen of Italy and of Greece."[48] So antiquity can still function as a utopia—accessible in the form of a reverie—but it must under no circumstances be imitated. Explanations in terms of "different times" do surface here and there, but they are counteracted by the schema of history turning back on itself, a situation worsened by the progress of corruption: the Swiss have become the modern world's Scythians.

The well-trodden path of parallels between the ancients and the moderns, which is at once unavoidable and condemned (even if through other parallels), points toward the conclusion of the first part of the *Historical Essay*: "In vain do we claim to be politically free." Civil (or political) liberty "is nothing but a dream, a false feeling."[49] Adopting the point of view of the savage leads, in the last instance, to debasing the Classical model of political freedom as overvalued or even quite simply fraudulent. What, after all, does it mean to be a free man in Sparta? "A free man in Sparta, means a man, whose hours were regulated as completely as those of the school-boy under the rod." He is constantly under surveillance, checked, and constrained. Were things so very different in Athens? Yes, they were, but still "no one could be admitted into the administration of state affairs, unless he possessed a certain revenue; and when a citizen had involved himself in debt, he was sold as a slave." As for saying that citizens are slaves to the law, that is "pure verbal trickery. For what does it matter to me whether it is the Law or the King who drags me to the guillotine?"[50]

The traveler's only option, then, is to *return* to the life of the savage. And that is indeed the book's conclusion, somewhat surprisingly given its explicit claim to be a historical essay on revolutions ancient and modern. It is over there, finally, in America, that the only authentic liberty, namely "individual independence,"[51] can thrive. But the eventful course of the journey, with its twists and turns, indicates well enough its utopian nature: the crossing by boat, the shipwreck on the return journey, the "profound" sleep into which Chateaubriand sinks after his night of reverie in the forest are just some of the hallmarks of the utopian narrative. And, above all, the experience can be enjoyed only in the form of a memory.[52] As such, far from being simply an appendix to the *Historical Essay*, the "Night Among the Savages of America" can be read as something like its vanishing point, and at the same time as the vantage point from which to view the work in its entirety, that is, the position from which it could be written in the first place. It is a chapter which creates a narrative mechanism of "viewing from afar" by which all parties may be shown to be equivalent, and all the erroneous and criminal parallels used by the Revolutionaries may be denounced and exposed, at the very same time as the author produces other (supposedly legitimate) ones, capable of elucidating the present and the future. Above all, it represents a refuge preserved from the action of time: a place in memory [*mémoire d'un lieu*].

The American Trunk

In the *Historical Essay*, parallels are drawn predominantly between the ancients and the moderns. The savage is both central and yet outside the field of vision until just before the end (although he is prefigured by the Scythian, his double among the ancients). In the *Travels in America*, by contrast, the majority of the parallels concern the ancients and the savage; even the moderns (the Americans) are first apprehended as ancients, and judged by the yardstick of Roman Republicans.

When Chateaubriand himself arrived in Philadelphia, "full of enthusiasm for the ancients," like "a Cato," he imagined Washington as "of course Cincinnatus." But the glimpse he got of him passing in a carriage "somewhat deranged my republic of the year of Rome 296."[53] He expressed through self-irony and "political *disappointment*" [*désappointement*] his discomfort at the discrepancy between the unassimilable reality of modern America and the image he had had of it. Fortunately everything fell into place when he met Washington, who had "the simplicity of the old Roman."[54] Image and reality could coincide all the more easily on this occasion since, as a letter from Washington himself makes clear, the meeting never actually took place![55]

Still, he was impatient to leave this America, which "has no past," where nothing is really old, and where the tombs "are of yesterday." He wanted to push on to the Indian regions of an authentic, primeval America. On the way, a pilgrimage and a parallel nevertheless seemed called for: "I have seen the plains of Lexington; I have paused there in silence, like the traveler at Thermopylae, to contemplate the graves of those warriors of the two worlds who were the first to die in obedience to the laws of their country."[56] This is the point, or rather layer, in the *Travels* where a large number of comparisons (often taken from Lafitau) are made between the Indians and the ancients. Like Homer's heroes, the Iroquois Indians are at once physicians, cooks, and carpenters. Like them, they hurl abuse at each other in battle. Their war songs bring to mind the Spartans', and there are other similarities, such as the role of dance, the cruelty of their initiation ceremonies, and their respect for age. As for their custom of integrating vanquished nations into their own, there the comparison with Rome is more apt, bespeaking "the genius of a great people."[57] Chateaubriand also has no qualms in invoking the great names of Moses, Lucretius, and Ovid to characterize their fables.[58] All these classical, and above all Homeric, references must have seemed particularly appropriate or self-evident to Chateaubriand because they in fact matched his very first project on America, mentioned in the preface to *Atala*: that of composing an "epic on 'The Man of Nature.'" That was why, "in imitation of Homer's example," it was necessary to "visit the tribes I was desirous of describing."[59] The genre Chateaubriand chose thus encouraged Homerisms not only in content but also in form.

The "Journal without Date," from Chateaubriand's *Travels* (a title that adopts the *Historical Essay*'s viewpoint outside of time),[60] concerns a period of unanchored time, where only the hours are signaled, not the days or the weeks. It recalls the last pages of the *Historical Essay* ("Primitive liberty, at last I have found thee!"), to the extent of reproducing whole sentences: "I followed no trace, but went from tree to tree, and indifferently to the right or left, saying to myself 'Here there is not multiplicity of roads, not towns.'"[61] As in the *Historical Essay*, there are scenes of reverie and utopia. However, unlike in the earlier work, which ended on the perspective of the soul "los[ing] itself amidst boundless forests,"[62] the *Travels* stages a return. There is a "Conclusion" ("*Fin du Voyage*") to the travels in America: "Wandering from forest to forest, I had approached the American settlements. One evening, I descried ... a farmhouse.... I solicited hospitality and it was granted."[63] This sudden change of scene has transported the reader from the wilderness of virgin forest to settled land. So another America did exist, with its farmers—and even its English newspapers. Chateaubriand, at the fireside, glancing over "an English newspaper which I had picked up off the floor," sees the following words: "Flight of the King."[64] Suddenly, the call of the savage is replaced by the "call of honour," and Chateaubriand decides to return home. It is a turning point: he abandons the idea of being a "traveller in America," does not become a soldier either, and ends up a writer, exiled in London. The writings on America, partially destroyed, mislaid for fifteen years but never forgotten, were finally found again in a trunk. They inspired Chateaubriand's first writings, but also served as a resource and a reserve on which he would continue to draw. The *Historical Essay*—which could aptly bear the subtitle of *Journey from Greece to America*—was an integral part of these writings.

The Experience of Time

How do space and time interact here, or, more precisely, what effect does movement in space have upon Chateaubriand's relation to time when, having returned from America and left the Army of the Princes, he begins writing the *Historical Essay*? Time is above all the time of getting older: "When I left France I was young; four years of misfortune have put years on me."[65] Time's ravages are such that, as we have seen, this travel diary of a self in search of himself is presented, via Tacitus, as the writings of a dying man, or even as writings from beyond the grave. Already here time is figured as a river, a theme that, with all its variations, will come back and back, from the *Historical Essay* to the end of the *Memoirs*.

Each age is a river which carries us along according to the course taken by our destinies, if we abandon ourselves to it. But it seems to me that none of us are really in the current's path. Some (the Republicans) have thrown themselves in impetuously and crossed to the other bank. Others have stayed on this side and refused to take so much as the first step.[66]

That even defines our times, Chateaubriand suggests, times when some "are ahead of our age," while others "want to be men of the fourteenth century in 1796." But no one is squarely in the current, that is, *between* the two banks or two regimes of historicity. From the *Historical Essay* onward, however, Chateaubriand himself chose to be and to think in time, and to think about time, a thinking "shaped by the time which constitutes it, and incorporated into its order."[67] Or, to use an image from Hannah Arendt, he chose to dwell in the gap in time.

What takes center stage is the way time has speeded up:

I began writing the *Essay* in 1794 and it was published in 1797. I was often obliged to undo at night the picture I had sketched during the day: events moved faster than my pen; a revolution took place, which rendered all my comparisons useless; I was writing on a ship during a storm, trying to represent as though they were fixed objects the banks which flew past along the way and disappeared from view![68]

Time flies, swifter than the pen, and the craft caught in the storm is swept past an unrecognizable or unknown coastline, which races along. These remarks, from the 1826 preface, are crucial. They demonstrate what contemporaries were most struck by, namely, time's acceleration and their resultant loss of bearings (the boat is swept away and the coastline races past). The present is ungraspable, the future is unforeseeable, and the past itself has become incomprehensible.

In the foreword to his *Historical Studies*, published in March 1831, Chateaubriand returns to this theme, but from a different angle: time keeps accelerating, and ruins keep piling up:

I would not wish, in all the days remaining to me, to live again the last eighteen months. The violence I did myself defies description; for ten, twelve, fifteen hours a day I was forced to tear my mind away from what was going on around me, in order to accomplish the puerile task of composing a work of which no one will read a single word.... I was writing ancient history, while modern history was knocking at my door; in vain did I cry "Wait, I'll be with you in a moment," it thundered past to the sound of the canon, sweeping away with it three generations of Kings.[69]

Here Chateaubriand stages the gap between the daily grind of the historian and the speed at which history advances. Try as he may, by withdrawing daily for hours at a time, he simply tires himself out attempting—in vain—to catch up with contemporary events; his efforts are laughable and increasingly doomed to failure. Besides, who can take an interest in the "collapse of the old world" when one is living the "collapse of the new"?

Be that as it may, whether Chateaubriand was writing a history of France's present (as in the *Historical Essay*), or its past (as in the *Historical Studies*), he seemed always to miss the moment, to be out of step: always, ineluctably, too late. So what other option was there but to go on writing nonetheless, to exploit this gap as the mainspring or even the motive of his writing? When he began writing the *Historical Essay* he was not yet at that stage; he had simply experienced the impossibility of escaping the maelstrom of time. And, having crossed the Atlantic again, from West to East this time, the New World's island-in-the-storm and its untouched forests reverted to nothing more than utopias, which could be visited only in memory or in writing.

The Time of Traveling and Time in the *Travels*

Time occupies a prominent place in the *Travels in America*, published thirty-six years after the real journey. Far from being a straightforward piece of travel writing, the book in fact imaginatively revisits and reflects upon America. "The thirty-six years which have elapsed since my travels," Chateaubriand writes, "have made great additions to our stores of knowledge, and produced many changes both in the Old World and the New World."[70] Time is absolutely central to the work. Before the reader can even reach the beginning of the narrative "taken from the original manuscript of *The Natchez*" (that American trunk again), there is a foreword, a preface, and an "Advertisement" (an introductory "Address to the Reader"). One could easily be reading the last pages of the *Historical Essay*, except that there is yet another perspective superimposed on the text: the older Chateaubriand, in 1826, as though reading over the shoulder of the young traveler of 1791, makes statements such as "I shall now let the manuscript speak for itself," "the sequel of the manuscript contains . . ." or "the manuscript states that . . . ," or even "here is a main chasm in the manuscript." The repeated use of "at the time" and "today" introduces a further distancing effect.

This supplementary viewpoint is particularly evident in the preface, which contains a history of journeys from Homer to 1826, with the result that the young traveler in search of the Northwest Passage is utterly dwarfed. Whereas "formerly, when a man had quitted his home like Ulysses, he was an object of curiosity," nowadays, in a world where everything has been discovered, where everything is mapped out, and distance counts for nothing, Chateaubriand, as the "obscure traveler" he was at the time, has in fact seen "no more than every body has seen."[71] So what difference does it make that he hadn't seen, or hadn't seen in its entirety, what he nonetheless claims to have seen? Why nitpick! Chateaubriand here ruins his authority as a travel writer, but he regains it precisely through the passage of time. Time transforms him into "the last historian of the nations of the world of Columbus, of those nations whose race will ere long be extinct." It is "the register of their deaths" that he is about to open,[72] a phrase reminiscent of Michelet's definition of the historian as a go-between for the dead and the "administrator of the property of the deceased." The shift from traveler to historian also endorses the nineteenth century's self-representation as the century of the historian—understood as the memory of what is no longer and the harbinger of what is yet to come. Chateaubriand may well have seen what everyone else saw, but today there remain only traces of it, which will soon disappear completely. This distinction qualifies him as the "last historian." The "last" traveler is also the last historian, who is equally the first: he has seen what no one will ever see again.

The effect of the passage of time is above all that it brings to light another America, which is not a primeval territory and a utopian wilderness. This other America is not only caught up in time and grappling with it, but it is actually saturated with time. And this applies as much to the "America of the Savages" as to "Civilized America," which is consequently no longer viewed as an "Ancients' America," a limping Roman Republic forever out of step (with its Cincinnatus in a coach and four).

What clearly emerges is the older America of indigenous populations.[73] In the *Historical Essay*, the Indians appear abruptly, out of nowhere and within the space of a single sentence.[74] In the *Travels*, by contrast, the "introduction to the savage life" occurs in a comic scene, led by a Monsieur Violet, the "dancing-master to the Savages," who was "a little Frenchman, powdered and frizzed in the old fashion."[75] What is one to make—and, above all, what is a disciple of Rousseau to make—of these Iroquois dancing to the strains of a violin? However, what strikes Chateaubriand above all is an "Indian ruin" (which is almost a contradiction in terms).[76] So the deserted wilderness has its ruins too! It is as though the major organizational categories of the *Record of a Journey from Paris to Jerusalem* had momentarily crossed over into the *Travels*. Our traveler also dwells upon the monuments of Ohio (which had genuinely interested Chateaubriand). For indeed, what a remarkable archaeological ensemble, comprising bastions, entrenchments, and tumuli, which can only have been the work of a "much more civilized people than the present Savages of America." What?! *Grandeur et décadence* already then? So there were Indians before the Indians in this place? When can this have been? What nation was this? Where did it come from?[77] Suddenly America had a history, and a natural history too: Chateaubriand notes that a mammoth's skeleton had recently been unearthed in Ohio.[78]

Likewise for the political realm. People imagine, says Chateaubriand, that the native Americans had no form of government, but they are simply mistaking the savage state for the state of nature. There, too, the time factor was neglected. In actual fact, one can find in savage populations the "type," in the strict sense, of all governments known to "civilized nations"—from despotism to republicanism, via monarchy—but in their natural state. Chateaubriand proclaims, in passing, the grand principle that "[t]he extent of their wilds [*leur désert*] had done for the science of their governments what excessive population had produced for ours."[79] Besides, he adds, had one but cared to recall the history of the Greeks and the Romans, this error could or should have been avoided, since "at the origin of their empire, [they] had very complicated institutions." This remark is interesting for the double historicization it effects, of the native Americans and the ancients, and thus the double distancing it brings about. America, it evolves, is neither a pure state of nature, nor a utopia outside of time, but rather an "incipient civilization." And we shall never know what it might have become because European civilization came along and destroyed it.[80]

Without this attention to the changes occurring over a long period, Chateaubriand continues, one will inevitably end up with two "equally faithful and unfaithful" ways of depicting the savages. Either one describes only "their laws and manners," in which case one will see nothing but Greeks and Romans; or else one describes only their "habits" and "customs," in which case one "perceive[s] nothing but smoky and infectious cabins, the haunts of a sort of apes who possess the gift of speech."[81] The introduction of a time factor can alone enable one to move from "either ... or" to "both ... and." The savages are at once a sort of ape and they are Greeks and Romans—but was this principle not valid already for the Romans? Did Cato the Elder's modest dwelling appear much cleaner to Horace than the hut of an Iroquois does to us?

This America of native populations is not only old, it is dying out. The Indians, who in their Iroquois language called themselves "men of always," *Ongoue-onoue*, have "passed away."[82] Today, the savage is no longer a warrior, but an "obscure herdsman"; he no longer dwells in his forests, but has become a "beggar at the door of a trading-post."[83] He has swapped his grandeur for guile. All is decline and decay in this funereal portrait, which is reminiscent of Victor Segalen's *A Lapse of Memory* [*Les Immémoriaux*].[84] In it, people of mixed race, called "burnt wood," are accused of actively spreading corruption since, as interpreters and intermediaries, they have "the vices of both races," and are "bastards of civilized nature and of savage nature" selling themselves to the highest bidder.

As for "civilized" America, which had first seemed to be a land without a past (with its tombs dating from yesterday), it has paradoxically preserved the Old World's abandoned or ruined past because it is a land of exile. Athens, Marathon, Carthage, Sparta, Memphis, Versailles, and Florence are just some of the famous names carried over and transplanted. "The glory of all countries has placed a name in these same wilds where I met with Father Aubry and the obscure Atala."[85] And all the exiles who have found refuge there can, miming the gesture of Baudelaire's Andromache, revive the memory of their homeland from the banks of a false Simois. Furthermore, and as though to complete the transformation of the United States into a memorial to the Old World, Chateaubriand introduces a comparison with the famous Villa of Hadrian. The presence in America of all those famous European places is "like that garden in the Campagna of Rome, in which Adrian had models of the different monuments of his empire erected."[86] They are sites of memory, but simulated ones: the tombs are cenotaphs.

So the America of Chateaubriand's travels no longer exists, and the dreams of his youth have evaporated. He did not discover the Northwest Passage, French influence was eclipsed, and the savage is dying a slow death. Yet suddenly, at the end of this requiem for a dead America, the reader is presented with "a wonderful spectacle," painted in the glowing colors of modern freedom.[87] The *Historical Essay* ended on a hymn to the freedom (or independence) of the savage, as the only authentic freedom (in relation to which all others, including the freedom of the ancients, appear false). The *Travels* ends on the recognition and celebration of modern freedom: the United States' discovery of a representative republic is "one of the greatest political events that ever occurred." From this assertion Chateaubriand is led back to the familiar pair, ancient and modern freedom. The case of the United States has proved that there are

> two practicable types of liberty; the one belonging to the infancy of nations, the offspring of manners [*fille des moeurs*] and of virtue, the liberty of the first Greeks and the first Romans, and the liberty of the Savages of America; the other born in the old age of nations, the offspring of knowledge [*fille des lumières*] and reason, the liberty of the United States, which has superseded the liberty of the Savage. Happy country, which in less than three centuries has passed from one liberty to the other, almost without effort, and by means of a contest which lasted only eight years![88]

Unlike in the *Historical Essay*, Chateaubriand here historicizes the freedom of the savages, and also that of the ancients, which is thereby rehabilitated. The native Americans, the first Greeks, and the first Romans all belong to the same *moment* of freedom. That is the deeper meaning—and the miracle—of American history (which is the product of an acceleration of time).

Liberty as the "offspring of manners" "perishes when its principle deteriorates, and it is in the nature of manners to deteriorate with time," whereas liberty as the "offspring of knowledge" "advances with the principle which preserves and renews it," and knowledge increases with time.[89] Here again, time is an agent. But unlike Benjamin Constant, who theorized these two freedoms as ideal types,[90] Chateaubriand is giving a rough outline of a *history* of ancient and modern freedom. The principle of historicization he introduces (freedom as "offspring of manners" leading to freedom as "offspring of knowledge") situates the United States not only as the birthplace of a new sort of freedom, but also as the place where "almost without effort," and at great speed, the former gave way to the latter.[91] The Scythians had embodied an "abridged, but complete" history of the three ages of humanity. Here, the United States achieve a similar synthesis, but of their own past with their own present: they embody a *historical* development.

In the *Historical Essay*, the "Savages of America" represented both the vanishing point and the vantage point (outside of time) from which the work could be interpreted. In the *Travels*, the astonishing picture of freedom represented by America in its revisited version constitutes the vantage point (now anchored in time) from which to reconsider the real journey made. This is the place from which the *Travels* can be rewritten, or even written, and it is also the perspective from which the *Essay* can be reread and reviewed (but not rewritten, since that would effectively destroy it). The first and perhaps the most visible trace of this rereading, but by no means the most interesting or the most persuasive, is the distance Chateaubriand puts between himself and Rousseau, who is more or less excommunicated. The *Essay's* Rousseauist leanings had been the pretext for sometimes violent attacks on Chateaubriand. So the notes in the later edition, largely composed of Restoration commonplaces on Rousseau, should be read primarily as a reply and a defense.[92]

Above all, the American discovery of modern freedom ruins the whole system of parallels on which the *Historical Essay* has been constructed. In the 1826 preface, Chateaubriand writes: "I have always based my reasoning in the *Essay* on the Ancients' republican system of liberty, liberty the offspring of manners; I had not sufficiently reflected upon that other sort of liberty, liberty offspring of knowledge and a perfected civilization: my discovery of a representative republic has changed the whole matter."[93] This preface, which undermines the whole edifice of the *Historical Essay*, can be found almost word for word in the conclusion to the *Travels*. And every time this new principle is mentioned in the *Essay*'s 1826 notes, in which it occurs regularly, it unravels the book's arguments. The whole system of parallels comes out of it heavily compromised, and the very use of parallels as a heuristic device is effectively invalidated. When the gap between the ancients and the moderns is so great, we can no longer "with the torch of past revolutions in our hand, . . . boldly enter into the darkness of future ones." *Historia magistra* has had its day; it can teach us nothing about the present.

The "first" *Essay* conceives the development of humankind as an unendingly repeated cycle; the later edition describes the movement of history as, rather, "concentric circles—ever-widening, in an infinite space." According to this later model, the present can no longer be modeled on the past, nor measured against it: the movement no longer goes straightforwardly from past to present (but Chateaubriand, in his attempts to understand the past, is not yet ready to move in the opposite direction, from the present to the past).[94] Hence the *Historical Essay*, both through the relation to time constitutive of it, and through the relation it institutes, occupies a unique position, both reliant on the *topos* of *historia magistra* and challenging it. The principle of *historia magistra* continues to be applied while at the same time its inadequacy is demonstrated. The *Historical Essay* thus represents that fleeting moment when the Revolution has rendered this *topos* obsolete, while at the same time it cannot yet be discarded. It is a text between two centuries, between the ancients and the moderns, or between the two banks of the river of time, a book which to all intents and purposes is impossible—a monster. Yet Chateaubriand (who without this would not be who he is), far from abandoning the work, preserves it more or less intact, taking it up again and simply subjecting it to a slight displacement.

What he does is stage the work's impossibility and exploit this. The book's non-self-coincidence becomes its true meaning. Chateaubriand abandons neither the principle of *historia magistra*, nor the *exemplum*, nor the role of citation, but rather goes back over them, constantly introducing the dimension of time, displacing them, setting them in motion, undermining them, and putting them in perspective by putting himself in perspective. The *topos* of *historia magistra* is no longer possible, and yet it is equally impossible to relinquish it—at least for the time being. In its final form, the book displays a twofold impossibility: it belongs neither to the ancient nor to the modern regime of historicity, but lies between the two. In 1841, as he was completing his *Memoirs*, Chateaubriand returned for the last time to this experience, which he generalized as a hallmark of the times. The modern world, he claimed, is stretched between two impossibilities: that of the past and that of the future.[95] This was the first formulation of the gap in time.

Beyond the *Essay* itself, this double movement can be seen as typifying a rule of Chateaubriand's writing, with its wavelike movement constantly throwing out and taking back, preserving and reworking. It is fundamentally historical writing, obsessed by time and the discovery of history as a process. But whereas nineteenth-century academic historians separated the past from the present, Chateaubriand always sees the past *in* the present, the dead coming back to haunt the living. As such, his writing has a memorial rather than a historical character. His mania for dates also suggests this, for example in his feverish compilations of whole catalogues of dates and of the dead. Juxtaposing, or rather superimposing, two dates not only highlights their difference, their ineluctable noncoincidence, it also establishes relations between them, setting off echoes and producing effects of contamination.

Dates discriminate. That is why they are seen as the surest sign of history writing, given its attention to sequence and differentiation. However, juxtaposing and multiplying dates and deriving effects of meaning from the construction of seemingly arbitrary series amounts to methodically practicing anachronism, which was to be branded a cardinal sin by modern historians.[96] In Chateaubriand's practice, it is never one *or* the other, one *then* the other, but always one *and*, one *in* the other. As Chateaubriand states, "the varied events and changing forms of my life thereby involve one another."[97] Not in order to conflate them, but, on the contrary, in order to bring out their differences, the distance of "nevermore," of course, but first and foremost the distance between self and self.[98] Beyond Saint Augustine, Chateaubriand can thus be viewed as a close relative of Odysseus, but whereas the latter could only weep, wordless, on discovering this distance between self and self, this his radical historicity, Chateaubriand acknowledges it from the start and is forever reexamining it. In his writing and rewriting of the *Memoirs*, over a period of more than forty years, Chateaubriand makes of this fracture in time, this irremediable distance between the old and the new regime of historicity, the (reality and pleasure) principle of his writing.

In the case of autobiographical writing, ellipses and chronological parataxes convey an experience of the self as affected by a necessary and necessarily repeated lack of self-coincidence. Or, to put it another way, they are the realization and expression of the historicity of the world and of the self. Memory is the medium of this "writing of time, producing an infusion of the self into time by means of language."[99] Chateaubriand would in a certain sense be the first ego-historian! As he reminds the reader in a striking sentence from the *Life of Rancé*, "My first work was written in London, in 1797, my last in Paris, in 1844. Between these two dates there have elapsed no less than forty-seven years, that is, three times the span which Tacitus called a large part of a human life: '*Quindecim annos, grande mortalis aevi spatium.*'"[100] Tacitus is the author of the epigraph to the *Historical Essay*, Chateaubriand's first book, and he reappears in the preface to the work declared to be his last.

Above all, in the *Life of Rancé*, Chateaubriand talks of himself as though he were already no longer there. The work of time is what draws the self away from itself, until the final absence; it is alteration, the other insidiously taking the place of the same.[101] Chateaubriand notices some "marks of indecision" in Poussin's last painting, *The Flood*, and observes that "these imperfections of time embellish this masterpiece of a great painter."[102] One could suggest that Chateaubriand in his writing is likewise seeking to render something like these "marks of indecision." Hence the switching between time and place, in order to express time and its "imperfections": the recurrent patterns of returning to familiar places that have remained the same and yet not so, the theme of pilgrimage, the shifts from wilderness to ruins (and the wilderness itself revealing ruins), and so forth. Hence also the fact that Chateaubriand's writing is always on the move, but always also out of step or even *untimely*, with duration experienced as dissociation. The writer-traveler represents himself as always about to set sail again after a brief pause: "I always regard myself as a captain who will shortly board his ship again."[103]

Ruins

Finally, I shall play the game of dates a little myself. In April 1791, Chateaubriand had left behind an Old World in ruins, dreaming of a refuge in the forests of the New, from which he returned a few months later and wrote his *Historical Essay on Revolutions*, in exile. We have seen that this work, which fell between two regimes of historicity, was profoundly involved in questions of time. In September of the same year, 1791, Volney published his *Ruins; or, Meditation on the Revolutions of Empires*—still or already a question of ruins—but ruins in the ancient Near East this time.[104] Prior to this, on his return from his travels in Egypt and Syria between 1783 and 1785, he had published an account of his journey, which was particularly well received because of its wealth of observed detail and its denunciation of despotism. "Syria, especially, and Egypt, both with a view to what they once have been, and what they now are, appeared to me a field equally adapted to those political and moral observations with which I wished to occupy my mind." The question was thus the relation between their present and past state, yet the direction chosen was "to judge from their present state what was their situation in former times."[105] Volney's inquiry thus moved from the present to the past.

The *Ruins*, by contrast, which opens with a lengthy meditation among the silent tombs of Palmyra on why there are ruins in the first place, goes in the opposite direction. Why, asks Volney, are so many cities, which in former times displayed such opulence, now nothing but "desolation" and "solitude"? "Whence proceed such fatal revolutions?"[106] Volney then leaps from the ancient past to a distant future: who knows, he muses, if on the abandoned banks of the Seine, or the Thames, some traveler shall not sit and weep one day, just as he is doing now in what was once Palmyra? The traveler confronted with what seems to be the work of "blind fatality" cannot but feel a "profound melancholy." Humanity itself does no more than go from ruin to ruin.

At this point the Genius of ruins appears, to teach him how to "read the lessons" that ruins contain.[107] Man himself, it evolves, is at the root of such calamities, and not some vengeful God. It is his "self-love" (which is natural to man) which is to blame, a self-love perverted by "ignorance" and by "cupidity." The traveler's rejoinder is that if it is true that man is the source of his own ills, then the "lesson" is only the more dispiriting. To which the Genius replies with questions: are men "still in their forests" as in primitive times, and have societies "made no progress towards knowledge and a better state?"[108] "Embracing in one glance the history of the species, and judging the future by the past, hast thou shown that all improvement is impossible?"[109] Or else do you claim that "the human race is degenerating" and seek to prove a supposed "retrograde progress from perfection"?[110] But the course of history shows quite the opposite: "Especially in the last three centuries knowledge has increased and spread." And the Genius ends his paean to progress on a vision of a "prodigious movement" detected "at the extremity of the Mediterranean," ushering in a "legislative people" eagerly awaited by all humanity, and holding out the promise of a "new age."[111] However, Volney cautions, along this path one will first have to overcome the obstacle of religion, since each religion claims to have a monopoly on the truth.

Volney's *Ruins* are, in fact, a direct response to the Revolution—give or take a few years (or centuries). The opening meditation is presented as taking place in the course of Volney's journey, before 1789 therefore, but its contents are entirely dictated by the Revolution. The Genius of ruins is in fact a retrospective prophet, with Volney, now a deputy at the Constituent Assembly, in the role of prompt. The lessons to be drawn from ruins, in a movement from past to present which seems to follow the pattern of *historia magistra* and its cycle of repetition (chapter 12: "Lessons of Times Past repeated on the Present") are suddenly suspended. The "prodigious movement" heralded by the Genius and revealed to the traveler for encouragement—for "the past is, perhaps, too discouraging"—sheds new light on the ruins of the past. The book's conceit is evidently to present as yet to come something that has already occurred or is taking place. Volney does not get bogged down in trying to reconcile repetition and progress, nor in examining whether the Revolution is a culmination or a break, and he does not attempt to rewrite history in the light of it either. It is too early for that, and his goal is elsewhere. The future does not yet illuminate the past. One is left, therefore, with the model of *historia magistra*, while at the same time the latter is rendered inoperative by the advent of the new age. Volney would later criticize excessive and misguided uses of this model.

In 1795, while Chateaubriand was still piling up parallels with which to foretell what the Revolution would bring, Volney set off again on his travels, but headed west this time, to America, where he spent three years. In the interval, he had been imprisoned and released again in the wake of the 9th Thermidor, and appointed to teach at the École normale, where he gave a series of lectures called *Lectures on History,* in which he sought to characterize the type of certainty proper to history, while denouncing its perverted uses. He condemned with particular vigor the imitation of the ancients, seeking to "shake that respect for History which has become a dogma."[112] These *Lectures on History* are first and foremost an attack on the lessons of history as ordinarily understood: they are a critique of *historia magistra.*

By the time he sets off for America he harbors no more illusions. "Sorrowful at the past" and "anxious for the future," he sets out "with distrust to a free people, to try whether a sincere friend of that Liberty, whose name has been so profaned, could find for his declining years a peaceful asylum, of which Europe no longer afforded him any hope."[113] 1789 had lost its seductive brilliance, plunging past and future alike into darkness. No Genius will appear again. Volney returned from America with no new meditation or prophecy on the freedom and future of humanity, but, more prosaically, with a *View of the Climate and Soil of the United States of America.* After temporarily rallying to Napoleon, who made him a senator and a Count of the Empire, he retired to the country to devote himself to works of erudition on Oriental languages and ancient history. The Genius of ruins had forever fallen silent.

In March 1831, as we have seen, Chateaubriand was putting the finishing touches on his *Historical Studies.* While he was writing ancient history, modern history came knocking at his door, sweeping everything away. Charles X had been forced into exile by the July Revolution, and Chateaubriand felt like those historians who, as the Roman Empire collapsed around them, spent their time "rummaging in the archives of the past in the midst of the ruins of the present."[114] So it was ruins again, even more of them, and yet more revolutions, ancient and modern, unremittingly. Despite this, the foreword paradoxically presents the book, which is also the first major text on historical studies in France, as a farewell to history. In the end, he laments, he did not write the history of France he had so long planned on writing; the *Studies* are but the "building blocks" of an edifice he would never complete. He lacked time, or, rather, he did not have life enough for it.[115] Above all, this work, "the longest and the last," the one for which he had paid the highest price, was to be published at a time when "there were no more readers for it"! Here again we have that affected pose, reminiscent of the misfortunes of René, who is forever out of step and swimming against the historical tide. And now he is contractually obliged to finish and publish his *Complete Works*—nothing but money worries, as always! But there is worse to come. For who, today, could feel even remotely concerned by the fate of Constantine and Julian, the Vandals and the Franks? "It is a fine thing indeed to be interested in the collapse of the old world, when we are living the collapse of the new!"[116] This glaring untimeliness utterly invalidates the work: parallels are simply no longer operative.

Yet this final farewell to history cannot be explained solely by circumstances. Was Chateaubriand not aware, at heart, that the history-writing of his time was not for him? He acknowledged that France "must compose its Annals afresh, to make them conform to the progress of reason," and must reorganize them "according to a new plan."[117] He also had no difficulty recognizing that the nature of history "changes from age to age." And that, consequently, "nineteenth-century historians did not invent anything; they simply had a new world before their eyes, and they used it as a revised scale by which to measure the old."[118] But this was something Chateaubriand neither wished nor was able to do. His writing followed a logic of memory, zigzagging between the old and the new world. He was between the two banks of the river, swimming from one to the other, and as such he could write his *Memoirs* but not a history of France streamlined through the use of a "revised scale." Chateaubriand wrote *on* the gap in time and *as from* that point. Placed between two regimes of historicity, he continued using parallels, while conscious that they were unworkable, and he kept piling up and erasing dates, producing palimpsests.

1831: ruins once more. Tocqueville was a young man at the beginning of his career, when he set sail with his friend Beaumont for America, on the pretext of studying the penitentiary system there. He was from a long line of Norman nobility and, like Chateaubriand (to whom he was related) found himself on the side of the vanquished in the Revolution, in Koselleck's sense. He too was between the ancien régime and the Revolution, aristocracy and democracy. And it was precisely from the "archaism of his existential position" that he managed to derive the "modernity of his conceptual questioning."[119] As with Chateaubriand in 1791, it was the Revolution that brought him to America, but the circumstances were quite different. He was only there on an assignment, which he could additionally use to put some distance between himself and the Legitimists, and return "free of partisan engagement toward anyone at all," having acquired "among such a celebrated people" the acquaintances that "put the finishing touch on your being set apart from the crowd."[120] It was of course a full forty years since his young Breton precursor had set out to find the Northwest Passage with Rousseau under his arm. And Chateaubriand's uncharted forests, in which he sought to lose himself, were not those of Tocqueville: attempting to explain to a correspondent that everything in America derives from a single principle, Tocqueville compared America to "a big forest, cut through by a multitude of straight roads which end at the same point. One only needs to find that point of convergence, and everything becomes clear at one glance."[121] So it was a forest *à la française*! There is even a moment when Chateaubriand seems to pass the torch to the younger man: in a note written to Tocqueville to thank him for sending him *Democracy in America*, he says: "People were already talking about me a little when I saw you as a child in Verneuil. In your turn, you will see me in infancy: people will talk of you and I will be forgotten."[122]

If America is no longer a "refuge," then what is it? It is not so much a "New World" as a laboratory of a "World of the New," of what is yet to come. As observed by Tocqueville, America is like the Proteus "of former times" whom Chateaubriand had attempted to question, or like the Genius of ruins unveiling a revolutionary future to the marveling traveler. The interplay of regimes of historicity is absolutely central in Tocqueville. And, once again, everything starts with ruins, in the midst of which one can see "this irresistible revolution, which for centuries now has surmounted every obstacle."[123] These are not ancient ruins, but recent ruins produced by the Revolution, and "we seem ready to go on living complacently amid the rubble forever."[124] "The world that is on the rise remains half buried beneath the debris of the world that is in collapse, and in the vast confusion of human affairs no one can say what will remain of old institutions and ancient mores and what will ultimately disappear."[125]

Visiting America is the way to give voice to these ruins and dispel the confusion. Over there, the great social revolution—the long march toward equality of conditions—"seems almost to have attained its natural limits." America can thus provide the traveler with a vantage point from which to reconsider Europe: "Then I began to think again about our own hemisphere, and it seemed to me that I could make out there something quite similar to what I saw in the new world."[126] It is no utopia outside of time, as it was for Chateaubriand (at least in his first version). It is already caught up in the current of time and the future of Europe. At all events, it allows one to see further ahead, even beyond America itself: "I confess that in America I saw more than America. I sought there an image of democracy itself ... if only to find out what we had to hope from it, or to fear." Aspiring to bring back from his trip "lessons from which we might profit,"[127] Tocqueville scans the horizon, looking beyond the political factions who "busy themselves with tomorrow only." What he wants to do is to "think about the future."[128] It is again a question of viewing from afar, but practiced differently, in the form of viewing from the future.

In short, Tocqueville preserves the model of *historia magistra*, but inverts it; the lesson to be learned comes from the future, not the past. He himself explicitly recognizes this, toward the end of his work: "Although the ongoing revolution in man's social state, laws, ideas, and sentiments is still far from over, it is already clear that its works cannot be compared with anything the world has ever seen before. Looking back century by century to remotest Antiquity, I see nothing that resembles what I see before me. When the past is no longer capable of shedding light on the future, the mind can only proceed in darkness."[129] One can no longer, as Chateaubriand still thought possible in 1794, "with the torch of past revolutions in our hand, ... boldly enter into the darkness of future ones." The previous regime of historicity, in which the past precisely illuminated the future, was over for good. A world which is "totally new" requires a "new political science." This was precisely what Tocqueville set out to develop from his vanguard position, perched in his lookout to scrutinize the future.[130]

ORDERS
of
TIME 2

THE THREE MEDITATIONS ON RUINS AND THE THREE JOURNEYS TO America, described in the previous chapters, and which spanned more than half a century, gave form to three experiences of time. All three reflected a radical reappraisal of the order of time. Volney, Chateaubriand, and Tocqueville, each in his own way, expressed the realization that the old regime of historicity, which had so long been sustained by the model of *historia magistra*, could no longer work. In order for contemporary events to be intelligible, the categories of the past and the future had to be articulated differently, failing which "the mind could only proceed in darkness."

Unsurprisingly, it is Chateaubriand who undergoes the most fundamental change. In the space of a mere quarter-century he evolved from considering America to be a primeval land of refuge for those peoples still living in harmony with nature (as the Scythians had traditionally been represented) to seeing it as a country that in no time at all had invented modern freedom. No longer a museum or a utopia of the past, America was the place where the future was being forged. No longer a New World that had been discovered, but a world of the new, of an equality toward which the Old World was also proceeding, if more slowly and laboriously. The "Old"

World would henceforth be "old" in two senses: in the sixteenth-century sense, of course, but also in the (new) sense that it was less advanced than America. A gap had sprung up between the two shores of the Atlantic—between experience and expectation. Tocqueville's trip was, ultimately, a way of reducing that gap, by "seeking out" experience in order better to understand and even stabilize expectation by giving direction to action. In so doing he still maintained the schema of *historia magistra*, but inverted it and situated the source of intelligibility in the future rather than the past. Through this revised schema he could ground his "new political science."

Let us now leave the Atlantic and 1789 behind, to enter the waters of another major crisis of time, two centuries later, casting anchor around the now-symbolic date of 1989. The landscape is perhaps more familiar, because it is closer to us, but it is not necessarily easier to get one's bearings, because it is precisely too close. There is so much material, and so much has been said and written about it already, with new volumes appearing regularly in the bookshop window. That is why it is even more important than in the preceding chapters, which were exercises in viewing from afar, to find for the ensuing chapters, which are exercises in viewing a contemporary landscape close up, an angle of attack as precise and revealing as possible. At the same time, we should not lose sight of what viewing from afar has brought to the debate. Two contemporary watchwords, notions which organize our public space, seem to meet the criteria: "memory" and "heritage."

I shall not treat these two terms for themselves, nor explore them in all their many facets, but rather examine them for the light they throw on issues of time. The concept of memory will be introduced through Pierre Nora's *Lieux de mémoire*, and for heritage I shall give an overview of the key moments in the notion's development. What order of time do these concepts express or—perhaps an equally pertinent question—challenge? What crisis of time do they bring to light? Is the modern regime of historicity, which we have seen taking shape around 1789, still operative? That is, does the intelligibility of our world still and again come from the future, as the inventors of the idea of progress dared to imagine and later affirmed with increasing self-assurance? "New facts" could not but win out over "historical fact." Today, in the apparent self-evidence of the value of memory, and the centrality of heritage, just as in the polemics around memory and history, should we see a "return" of the category of the past, a nostalgia for the old model of *historia magistra*? Or, rather, a hitherto unknown dominance of the category of the present, the heyday of presentism? But is the notion of heritage necessarily backward-looking? Not, as we shall see, when the transformation of the natural environment into heritage brings back the idea of the future.

4

MEMORY, HISTORY, AND THE PRESENT

"France must compose its Annals afresh, to make them conform to the progress of reason." This maxim from Chateaubriand, which we referred to in the last chapter, comes from the preface to his *Historical Studies*, in which he was adopting the pose of the historian overtaken by history: "I was writing ancient history, while modern history was knocking at my door."[1] History, speeding ahead posthaste, was once again leaving him behind. As he observed in his *Memoirs*, ideally one would "write history in a calèche." Lorenz von Stein, a German theorist of history, noted similarly in 1843 that "it is as though historical writing is no longer in a position to keep up with history."[2] Of course for Chateaubriand this was partly posturing, since he had made his own anachronism into the driving force and ultimate source of his writing. As for composing the annals afresh to make them conform to the progress of reason—that is, to bring them into line with the modern regime of historicity—that task would ultimately not be for him; it would devolve upon the younger generation of liberal historians, above all Augustin Thierry.

And indeed, Chateaubriand's maxim could have served as an epigraph for any number of books written throughout the nineteenth and twentieth centuries, or at least for the most ambitious among them, certainly up to Ernest Lavisse, and maybe even up to Pierre Nora's *Lieux de mémoire*. French historians' great love affair with writing the history of the nation would last many a long year. Their contexts are obviously not comparable, but both Chateaubriand in 1830 and Nora in the early 1980s set out to take stock of the present and to draw conclusions from this. For Chateaubriand, this meant reconstructing history "according to a new plan," while for Nora the question was firstly what "compose afresh" could possibly mean: can one still, Nora asked, write a history of France? How? And why?[3]

The volumes of *Lieux de mémoire* (1984–1993) spanned the critical year of 1989: they were conceived and in part published before that date, but only completed afterward. In France at the time, the spotlight was on the bicentenary of the French Revolution, and people were busy rehearsing the spats between rival camps, with their predictable cast of characters.[4] But no one had foreseen the fall of the Berlin Wall. It took everyone by surprise. By contrast, the *Lieux de mémoire* were borne on the tide of interest in memory that had been sweeping over France since the mid-1970s. The work registered it, reflected it like a mirror, and also reflected upon it.

One could cite, among the many signs of this increasing preoccupation with memory, Marcel Ophuls's *The Sorrow and the Pity*, whose release was delayed until 1971, and the publication in the following year of Robert Paxton's meticulously researched indictment of the Pétain regime, *Vichy France: Old Guard and New Order, 1940–1944*, but also, in a different vein, the memoirs of "a Breton from the Bigouden" in Pierre-Jakez Hélias's *The Horse of Pride* (1975), which recreated the local Breton-speaking world of the author, born in 1914. The book had soon sold more than one million copies. Then came Claude Lanzmann's *Shoah* in 1985, Pierre Vidal-Naquet's *Assassins of Memory* in 1987, denouncing and exposing the logic of Holocaust denial, and, in the same year, Henry Rousso's *The Vichy Syndrome: History and Memory in France Since 1944*. Rousso's work on Vichy was prompted by the discovery that "what the case called for was a doctor qualified to treat the living, not the dead—perhaps even a psychoanalyst." Numerous other works could be cited, including Paul Ricoeur's last book, published for the millennium in 2000, *Memory, History, Forgetting*. Other, more visible and tangible markers included the energetic renovation, or museification, of historic city centers, the multiplication of ecomuseums and folk and crafts museums, and the extension of the idea of Heritage.[5]

Returning to the schematic parallel I made between Chateaubriand and Nora above, what is immediately striking are their different relations to time. The "new plan" required by the "progress" of reason implied a vision of time as a process of improvement and progress, which ushered in freedom "offspring of manners," as discovered in America. The *Historical Essay*'s many revisions show this clearly. Yet Chateaubriand could not ignore that the way liberal historians worked, taking this new world as "a revised scale by which to measure the old one," was poles apart from his own way of writing, constantly crisscrossing, and crossing out, from one world to the other.[6] By contrast, when Nora set out on what was to become the *Lieux de mémoire*, not only was there no question of a progressive time, but he remained entirely within the circle of the present. He aimed at a kind of inventory prior to a death foretold: "The rapid disappearance of our national memory seemed to me to call for an inventory of the sites where it had chosen to manifest itself."[7]

Further back, Fernand Braudel was still bold enough to embark upon a long solo voyage, a history of France similar in ambition to Michelet's. But whereas the latter devoted forty years of his life to it, Braudel started out on his *Identity of France* later in his career, and the book, in which singularity and permanence were brought together, remained unfinished.[8] Braudel was not interested in memory, but in the history that emerged from the very depths of the *longue durée*, that "immense surface of almost stagnant water" which imperceptibly but irresistibly "draws everything onto itself."[9] As for the *Lieux de mémoire*, the texts Nora contributed to each volume ensured that the whole enterprise, despite its exceptionally wide-ranging team of contributors, resonated with his own particular interpretation, almost in a musical sense, of the history of France: his own particular tone.

My guiding thread, as I have said, is the order of time. I shall examine the *Lieux de mémoire*, taken above all as an intellectual enterprise, in this respect. What does the privileged place of memory in the project tell us about how past, present, and future were articulated? They were obviously not organized in the same way as in the modern regime of historicity. And *Lieux de mémoire* will also help shed light on the temporalities mobilized in national history as a genre, in the course of its history. But first, let us take a step back again and practice another type of viewing from afar.

The Modern Regime's Crises

There are cogent arguments for situating the modern regime of historicity between the two symbolic dates of 1789 and 1989. I would suggest, at least provisionally, that the two dates mark the entrance and the exit of this regime on the stage of History. At the very least, one can suggest that they constitute two caesuras, or breaks, in the order of time.[10] 11 September 2001 poses no serious challenge to this outline, unless the American government has decided to make it into a new beginning of world history, a new present and one alone, that of the war on terror. That said, with 9/11 the contemporary event reached its logical limit. Under the glare of the TV cameras, the event exhibited itself in the making, undergoing a real-time transformation into history that was simultaneously, and already, a (self-) commemoration.[11] In this sense, the structure of the event had become absolutely presentist.

The French Revolution, for those actually involved in it, as for those who tried to explain it immediately afterward, was interpreted predominantly as a conflict between two regimes of historicity. The past, Rome, Plutarch, all were summoned to the cause, while at the same time the event was declared to be without precedent and imitation was to be proscribed. Napoleon's own trajectory takes on a different meaning in this light. He was inspired by the new order of time, which always drove him onward, ahead of himself—as Chateaubriand said, "he travelled so quickly he barely had time to take breath wherever he passed"—yet he remained fascinated by Plutarch's heroes, to the extent of entering his future backwards, as Paul Valéry put it, by fabricating for himself a pseudo-lineage.[12] He too was caught between two regimes of historicity, attempting to embody his destiny as a hero, and ultimately a tragic one.

Koselleck's by-now classic analyses, which we mentioned earlier, summarize the modern regime as the passage from the German plural *die Geschichten* to the singular *die Geschichte*, History. "Beyond histories," he says, "there is History," History in itself. In Droysen's words, as cited by Koselleck, History must become "knowledge of itself."[13] More importantly, it is conceived as a process, with the idea that events do not simply occur *in* time but also *through* time, with time itself as an agent, and even *the* agent. Since, today, the past no longer makes the future comprehensible, history's lessons have become obsolete, and what is required are, rather, predictions. Historians are no longer in search of the exemplary, but of the unique. The topics of *historia magistra* had allowed the past to connect with the future through the exemplary model to be imitated: in looking back at famous men, I could also find them in front or ahead of me.

The modern regime replaced the exemplary with the nonrepeatable. The past was, *a priori* or due to its position (which amounts to the same), outdated. Someday, later, when the time was ripe, historians would be able to formulate laws, as in the natural sciences, or, in the words of late nineteenth-century science-history, the glorious day of synthesis would eventually dawn. But in the meantime historians were like diligent craftsmen who must apply themselves to the daily grind of analysis. The time was not yet ripe. The future, or rather the view from the future, prevailed: "History has become an injunction addressed by the Future to the Contemporary."

One could add to this axiom of Julien Gracq's that it included the past in its scope, and was a powerful influence on those nineteenth-century historians who conceived and structured their discipline as a science of the past. The future illuminating the past and giving it meaning constituted a *telos* or vantage point called, by turns, "the Nation," "the People," "the Republic," "Society," or "the Proletariat," each time dressed in the garb of science. If history still dispensed a lesson, it came from the future, not the past. It resided in a future that was to be realized as a rupture with the past, or at least as a differentiation from it, unlike *historia magistra*, which was based on the idea that the future might not repeat the past exactly, but it would certainly never surpass it. And the reason for this was simply that everything took place within the same circle (notwithstanding Chateaubriand's daring image of concentric circles), was governed by the same Providence and the same laws, and, in any case, involved human beings who had the same nature.

Why do I suggest these two breaks, 1789 and 1989? Certainly not in order to discourage further thought, and go off ruminating on the end of everything and of history in particular, on the grounds that liberal democracy has won the day. On the contrary, the idea is to catalyze questions by unsettling the self-evidence of the present. If we read *Lieux de mémoire* in a broader perspective and within the *longue durée* of relations to time, we understand it as a way of responding to and working *with* that break (which cannot be reduced to the date of the fall of the Berlin Wall on 9 November 1989), and also working *on* it, suggesting how it may be broached, and what its history might be. Such caesuras can be called gaps in time, after Hannah Arendt, intervals which are entirely determined by things which are no longer and things which are yet to come.[14] Time seems to have come to a halt, to have lost its bearings. This recalls Chateaubriand's conclusion to his *Memoirs*, that the world of 1840 is lodged between two impossibilities: the impossible past, and an impossible future.[15] I shall come back to this in my conclusion.

However, I do not wish to suggest that the modern regime was uncontested before 1989, nor that the order of time experienced no other crises. On the contrary, that was precisely where I started out.[16] Besides, a regime of historicity has never been a universally applicable metaphysical entity sent from heaven. It expresses only a dominant order of time. Since it is woven together from different regimes of temporality, it is ultimately a way of expressing and organizing experiences of time—that is, ways of articulating the past, the present, and the future—and investing them with sense. In this respect, Augustine's phenomenological description of the three times still remains essential for apprehending and expressing these experiences. How many regimes are there? I do not know, but the example of the Polynesian heroic regime proves at the very least that the inventory is incomplete and that it is not simply derived from Europe's reflection on its own past. No sooner does a regime of historicity become dominant than it is challenged, and in fact it can never (except in an ideal world) be entirely secured. It establishes itself slowly and lasts a long time.

A case in point is the great classical archetype of *historia magistra* (whose uniformity or scope should not be overstated either).[17] It was adopted by the Church and by medieval scholars when their role became that of writing history. The Christian regime and the regime of *historia magistra* were compatible because both were turned toward the past, toward an *already*, even if the *already* of the ancients was nothing like that of Christianity (which opened onto a *not yet*). This regime of historicity was of course challenged over its long history. In the second half of the sixteenth century in

France, for example, there were Montaigne's *Essays* (1580), which destabilize the classical *exemplum*, in a world in perpetual flux; the *exemplum* was transformed into a "singularity."[18] Having set out to be a new Plutarch, Montaigne ended up writing the *Essays*, declaring "It is myself I paint" ("Address to the Reader"). In the following century, the *Querelle des Anciens et des Modernes* (1687) also marked a major crisis of time. Perrault argued that the moderns were superior to the ancients and that there had been progress and improvement in almost all fields. But the future was still not the source of illumination. Then, in the ensuing century, perfection was almost achieved: after all, how could one possibly venture to think beyond an absolute monarch?[19]

Lastly, the passage from one regime to another involves periods of overlap. Interferences occur, with often-tragic consequences. The French Revolution was one such moment. Chateaubriand, whom we situated between Volney and Tocqueville, guided us through one of these in-between times. He was forever observing and commenting on it, and also on himself enmeshed in and constituted by this in-between time. From a similar perspective, the course of Napoleon's life takes on new meaning.

The Rise of Presentism

The twentieth century, in retrospect, combined futurism and presentism. It started out more futurist than presentist, and ended up more presentist than futurist. It was passionately futurist, blindly so, and, as we know, embraced the worst. In futurism, the imperative dimension of the order of time decrees that the viewpoint of the future shall prevail. It is an order that presents itself as constantly accelerating. History is made in the name of the future, and it must be written in the same way. The futurist movement took this position to extremes. Like the *Communist Manifesto*, the *Futurist Manifesto*, published by Marinetti in 1909, was designed as a momentous break with the old order. Italy must be liberated from its "gangrene of professors, archaeologists, tourist guides and antiquarians" by celebrating "the splendor of the world ... enriched by a new beauty: the beauty of speed." It is symptomatic that Europe's altar to heritage, where the notion was forged, should be the very place from which it was radically challenged.[20] The most uncompromising expression of this defiance was the description of the "roaring" automobile as "more beautiful than the Victory of Samothrace." "We are on the extreme promontory of the centuries!," Marinetti went on, "What is the use of looking behind?" The *Manifesto of the Futurist Painters*, published the following year, was equally radical: "Comrades, we tell you now that the triumphant progress of science makes profound changes in humanity inevitable, changes which are hacking an abyss between those docile slaves of past tradition and us free moderns, who are confident in the radiant splendor of the future.... But Italy is being reborn. Its political resurgence will be followed by a cultural resurgence."[21] The artistic avant-gardes thrived on this momentum in their pursuit of the future's "radiant splendor."

But the *Futurist Manifesto* also showed how one could move from futurism to presentism, or how futurism was also (already) a presentism. When Marinetti declared: "Time and Space died yesterday. We are *already* living in a world of the absolute, since we have *already* created eternal, omnipresent speed," the present became "futurized," or, equally, there was already nothing but the present. Speed transformed the present into eternity and Marinetti, at the wheel of his racing car, could imagine himself to be God.

The catastrophe of the First World War, with the crises it provoked, followed by that of the Second World War, weakened and even discredited futurism. However, a whole series of factors—often taken up in slogans—gave fresh impetus to the paeans to progress. Not only was the modern regime of historicity kept alive, but it was even cast as the one and only temporal perspective. This new futurism, shedding its lyricism, was successful despite the nuclear threat and the need to find responses to it. In Europe, it took the form of the drive to reconstruct, to modernize, and to implement central economic planning, while on a global level economic competition became the rule, against the background of the Cold War and the accelerating arms race. The socialists' "Radiant Future," the German "Miracle," and the postwar boom years in France, the *trente glorieuses*, named after the book by Jean Fourastié,[22] were some of the watchwords of the time. Gradually, however, the present began replacing the future and encroaching further and further until, in recent years, it has seemed to take over entirely. The viewpoint of the present—the perspective of presentism—has established its dominion.

This present, which is apparently so self-assured and powerful, did not appear overnight (in the last third of the twentieth century), but it is not radically new either. In some sense, every group and society, today as in the past, can only build on its present. There may be strategies to privilege or minimize it, in varying and changing degrees, depending on the situation. One can entrench oneself in it or, at the other extreme, attempt to escape it at all speed. The linguist Émile Benveniste noted that the etymology of *praesens* is "what is ahead of me," hence something which is "imminent, urgent," and "will not permit delay," in the sense of the Latin preposition *prae*.[23] The present is imminent: it is the runner's body tensed forward at the very moment he or she leaves the starting blocks.

In Epicureanism and Stoicism the present was conceived as the only time on which it was possible to have purchase. In Horace's words, "Treat every new day as the last you're going to have, then welcome the next as unexpectedly granted."[24] And for Marcus Aurelius,

> If you separate from yourself, namely from your mind ... all that you yourself did or said, all that troubles you in the future, all that ... attaches to you without your will, if you separate [from yourself] what of time is hereafter or has gone by and practice only to live the life you are living, that is the present, then you will have it in your power at least to live out the time that is left until you die, untroubled and with kindness and reconciled with your own good Spirit.[25]

This was the presentism which inspired Goethe's Faust when, dazzled by his encounter with Helen, he says: "Now the spirit looks neither backwards nor forwards, the present alone is our happiness."[26]

In the revealed religions, by contrast, the present is at once devalued (nothing which happens has any real importance), extended (in some sense there is nothing but the present), and made more precious, since it is a present which anticipates the *eschaton*, a present in which the Messiah can come at any moment. Rosenzweig made a distinction between the "today which is only a footbridge to tomorrow" and "the other today which is a springboard to eternity."[27] In Christian dogma, the time inaugurated by the Incarnation is of the order of the present, and history has been, is, and will be the history of salvation, until the Second Coming (even if God the Father alone knows when the final hour will come). Hence Pascal's solemn reminder, returning to the sources of the New Testament and the eschatological dimension of the present: "The present is never our aim, and while it and the past are our means, the future alone is our end. Thus we never live, but are always hoping to live, and, constantly preparing ourselves to be happy, it is beyond doubt that we never shall be happy."[28] These, then, are the two major forms of presentism, the religious and the philosophical forms, with bridges between them, as in the case of Montaigne and Pascal.

Certain modern expressions of presentism, inspired by vitalist trends, have led to a denigration of the past. The past is challenged by the present in the name of life and art. Eric Michaud has drawn attention to the value of the present—what I would call presentist claims—in artistic avant-gardes between 1905 and 1925, right down to the titles of their manifestos: alongside Marinetti's presentist Futurism, which we described above, there were Simultaneism, Praesentism, Nunism (from *nun*, "now" in Greek), PREsentismus, and Instantaneism.[29] Literature was not standing on the sidelines either, if only because writers were also involved in a number of these manifestos—one need only think of Apollinaire. One could mention the inspirational role played by Nietzsche's *Untimely Meditations* (1874) and Gide's *The Immoralist* (1902), in which the hero Michel, after experiencing a near-fatal illness, finds that his scholarly study no longer interests him: "I discovered that something had, if not destroyed, at least altered, its savor for me; it was the sense of the present."[30] A similar vision can be found in Ibsen's *Hedda Gabler* and in Paul Valéry's meditations in the 1920s on, or rather *against*, history, which we cited earlier.[31]

This current was so strong that historians who wanted to challenge the accusations of the "bankruptcy of history" (which had become blatant with the First World War), had first to prove that the past was not synonymous with death and a desire to stifle life. Although the model of *historia magistra* had lapsed more than a century previously, a way of relating past and present had yet to be conceived in which the past did not presume to lay down the law for the present, but was not simply consigned to inexistence either. Marc Bloch's and Lucien Febvre's insistence in the first *Annales* on the need to be concerned with the present should be read in the light of this intellectual context.[32] Slightly later they would construe the historian's task as a double movement, from the past to the present and from the present to the past. This justified the practice of history, as well as being the source of its heuristic potential.

Sartre's *Nausea*, published in 1938, can also be read as a presentist tale. The narrator, Roquentin, is writing a history book, a biography of the marquis de Rollebon (who bears some resemblance to Talleyrand). But one day he suddenly finds himself unable to continue, since something has struck him as blindingly obvious: there has never been anything but "the present, nothing but the present." The present is "what exists and all that was not present did not exist. The past did not exist. Not at all. Not in things, not even in my thoughts." With the result that "M. de Rollebon had just died for the second time." He had been "my associate ... he needed me in order to exist, and I needed him so as not to feel my existence." But now "I exist." And "things are entirely what they appear to be—*behind* them ... there is nothing." So the past is nothing.[33]

But the future, or more precisely the perspective from the future, is nothing either. Sartre, this time in his "Editorial" in the first issue of the *Temps Modernes*, in 1945, was adamant: "We write for our contemporaries; we want to behold our world not with future eyes—which would be the surest means of killing it—but with our eyes of flesh, our real, perishable eyes. We don't want to win our case on appeal, and we will have nothing to do with any posthumous rehabilitation. Right here in our own lifetime is when and where our cases will be won or lost."[34] For existentialism, salvation lay only in a total commitment to action. "As a militant, I wanted to save myself by works."[35] Revolution thus took over "the role which once was played by eternal life"; it "saves those that make it," Malraux remarked.[36] Existentialism was a presentism.

Criticizing progress does not automatically imply advocating the present, but it does cast doubt on the supposedly positive character of striding toward the future. This was a *topos* that was certainly not new, but it was given a new slant when revived by Lévi-Strauss in the mid-1950s in his *Tristes tropiques*, which met with immediate success. In the context of decolonization, Lévi-Strauss was proposing a new version of the noble savage. Clearly Chateaubriand's night in the forests of the New World was not so far in the past! Lévi-Strauss's passionate defense of Rousseau and his critique of the narrow conception of progress in modern societies ended on a meditation on this world which "began without the human race and ... will end without it," and in which humankind has never done anything but "precipitate[s] a powerfully organized Matter towards a condition of inertia which grows ever greater and will one day prove definitive." Hence ultimately, he says, "Entropology, not anthropology, should be the word for the discipline that devotes itself to the study of this process of disintegration in its most highly evolved forms."[37] With this vision of the final cooling of hot societies, Lévi-Strauss was taking a really very distant view: something like a view from the heavenly spheres.

In a period when time itself was undergoing a severe crisis, when its old order was collapsing and the new had not yet found expression, Chateaubriand had had a brief taste of a utopian wilderness, outside of time. More than a century later, in the 1950s, Lévi-Strauss, as we saw earlier, challenged the modern regime founded on the apparent self-evidence of progress. He argued that history is only occasionally cumulative and, moreover, that we only recognize as cumulative what resembles our own development: forms of civilization and universal history had yet to discover their Einstein.[38] Then, in the 1960s, the "savage" became fashionable again. "Savage thought" was put to all sorts of untutored uses, and "mythic thought" became all the rage. The savage was held in higher esteem than civilization or the state, even if the direction was sometimes reversed,[39] before the great movements of "return to."

Perhaps the clearest sign of the radical exclusion of anything but the present in the Swinging Sixties was the slogan "forget the future." Revolutionary utopias were nothing if not progressivist and futurist, even if they were also backward-looking and retrospective (the revolutionary barricades and the Resistance). But henceforth they had to adapt to the narrow circle of the present. The slogans covering the walls of Paris in May 1968 were "Sous les pavés, la plage" ("Beneath the pavings, the beach") or "Tout, tout de suite" ("All, all at once, now"). But they were followed shortly by "No future," in other words, no revolutionary present. The 1970s brought with them disillusionment, or the end to an illusion. The revolutionary ideal disintegrated, the 1974 oil crisis struck, mass unemployment kept rising, and the Welfare State, which had been based on solidarity and on the idea that tomorrow would be better than today, began to run out of steam. All the remedies proposed, whether desperate or cynical, pinned their hopes on the present, and nothing but the present. There was nothing beyond. This was not an Epicurean or a Stoic present, and neither was it one of Messianic expectation.

Consumer society's rapid expansion undoubtedly led to this increasingly distended and bloated "now." It took over gradually, imposing its rule in ever more constraining ways, pitching both people and things into an obsolescence reached ever faster due to technological innovation and the search for increasingly rapid returns. Productivity, flexibility, mobility: these were the watchwords of the new managers.[40] There is nothing new about time being conceived as a commodity, but what characterizes contemporary modes of consumption is the value placed on the ephemeral. The media, which have expanded exponentially, try to keep pace with this movement (which quite literally justifies their existence), and they take their cue from it. They scramble for the live soundbite, and produce, consume, and recycle an increasing number of images and words in an ever shorter time. Time is reduced and compressed: one subject, one and a half minutes, thirty years of history.[41] Tourism is also a powerful agent of presentism: the world is on one's doorstep in a fraction of a second and in three dimensions.

This presentism also coincides with a period of mass unemployment in our European societies. An unemployed person takes one day at a time, without being able to plan ahead, inhabiting a time which has no future. If "time seems to be annihilated" for these "men without a future," as Pierre Bourdieu called them, this is because "employment is the support, if not the source, of most interests, expectations, demands, hopes and investments in the present, and also in the future or the past that it implies."[42] Unemployment is a key factor in this imprisonment within the present and within a presentism experienced henceforth as oppressive and without hope.

So futurism has sunk below the horizon and presentism has taken its place.[43] We cannot see beyond it. Since it has neither a past nor a future, this present daily fabricates the past and future it requires, while privileging the immediate. There are countless signs of this relation to time. For example, the present's expansionism increasingly eclipses death, as the poet T.S. Eliot noted already in the 1940s: "In our age ... there is coming into existence a new kind of provincialism which perhaps deserves a new name. It is a provincialism, not of space, but of time; one for which ... the world is the property solely of the living, a property in which the dead hold no shares."[44] The dead no longer have a place, or even, as Philippe Ariès declared in his historical study of the phenomenon, "In towns, everything goes on as if nobody died anymore."[45] The disavowal of aging (symbolized by the immediately popular figure of the Californian jogger) is another sign, alongside the premium placed on youth *as such* in Western societies, whose populations are aging. More recently, a wealth of technological innovations designed to abolish time have been developed, using the information superhighways, and "real time" seems to be universally endorsed, up to and including war in real time. Each of us could add to this list any number of daily gestures that betray our obsession with time, and our attempts to control it ever more finely, and more and more of it, or else to abolish it altogether. Would it not be true to say that any self-respecting person today owes it to him- or herself to have no time for anything?[46] After all, what is an overworked manager if not someone who basically suffers from a chronic lack of time?[47] These patterns of behavior characterize our present and express an experience of it which is widely shared. As such, they delineate one of its regimes of temporality.

The Fault Lines of the Present

In our media age, the present obeys an economy in which events are constantly produced and consumed, previously through radio and now through television and other media. But additionally the present, in the very moment of its occurrence, seeks to view itself as already history, already past. In a sense, it turns back on itself in order to anticipate how it will be regarded when it is completely past, as though it wanted to "foresee" the past, to turn itself into a past before it has even fully emerged as present. Yet this retrospective vision never steps outside the closed circle of its own domain, the present. The drive to make of every future a future anterior can be taken to caricatural extremes. Thus on 10 May 1994 journalists interviewed the man who was still president of France, François Mitterand, exactly one year before the end of his mandate (other times indeed, but not other customs!). The whole idea was to get him to behave as though it were already one year later, when he would already have left office, and would even—why do things by halves?—be dead and buried (he was asked to disclose his chosen epitaph). To ensure that one is the first to cover the news, what better solution than to announce that something has already taken place when it is yet to come! This is a mediated and media-centered response to Kant's provocative question, "How is history *a priori* possible? Answer: when the soothsayer himself shapes and forms the events that he had predicted in advance."[48] The *a priori* history practiced here is no more than a media product, but its embodiment politically in self-fulfilling prophecies is often criticized. In fact, the whole of Mitterand's presidency, from his visit to the Panthéon at the start, to his funeral, with its double ceremony, at the end, via the Bousquet affair, was marked by a crisis of time. It matters little, at the end of the day, whether Mitterand tried to avoid it or instrumentalize it; the fact remains that whereas the Left was still inspired by a certain futurism when it came to power, it was almost immediately swamped by the unfurling wave of memory and heritage, and the constraints of presentism.

In this economy of the present, we anxiously consume forecasts—treated as though they were predictions—and must constantly consult specialists. Historians have been appointed on several occasions as "memory experts," and have been enlisted to serve in the witness box.[49] Opinion polls supposedly hold the key to our world, although such projections into the future are used and abused without moving an inch from the present. The snapshot image taken today is simply transferred three weeks or six months hence, imperceptibly becoming the actual image of the situation three weeks or six months later. What you vote today is the true image of what you will vote tomorrow, so in some sense you have already voted. The only way time can be reintroduced into this structure is by a whole series of polls, to show a trend. But that is already a matter for the analyst, in other words for the expert. And obviously the polls can and do get it wrong. The future remains beyond our control, and so we go on yearning for an *a priori* form of history, in which time would precisely be abolished. In reaction to this situation, Mitterand's formula of the mid-1980s, "Give time to time," could precisely meet with immense success. He too was looking to the *longue durée* for France's identity, while he must in fact—but in secret—have been taking one day at a time, in the present dictated by his cancer.

Another fault line appeared in this present in the mid-1970s, as environmental protection, and preservation (of monuments, objects, ways of life, landscapes, and animal species), became major concerns. The unquestioned imperative to modernize began gradually—despite its brutal self-confidence—to be replaced by conservation and rehabilitation programs in town-planning policy, as though the idea were to preserve or actually reconstitute a past that had already disappeared, or was on the point of disappearing irrevocably.[50] The already palpable ill ease of this present was further compounded by the search for roots and identity, and the concern for memory and genealogy.

Coinciding with this movement of return to roots, a new public keen to consult archives developed. Regional funding was increased for county archives, and many medium-sized towns set up archival departments. Soon more than half the archives' visitors were amateur genealogists. French archives expanded enormously in this period: they were five times bigger than they had been in 1945 and measured 3,000 linear kilometers if laid out end to end.[51] In 1979 a law on archives was passed, the first since the Revolution, which stated the following: "Archives are the totality of the documents, whatever their date, form or medium, which have been produced or received by any physical or legal person, and by any public or private department or organisation, in the exercise of its activity." Ultimately, according to this broad definition, everything can be archived, and archives "constitute the memory of the nation and are an essential part of its historic heritage." The key terms are clearly "memory," "heritage," "history," and "nation," indicating that the heritage years had well and truly arrived. Archival institutions were certainly part of this trend, even if archivists in France had the feeling, which was not entirely unjustified, that they were less well endowed by the public authorities during this period than museums and libraries. This is one of the causes of the current crisis in archives.

Although archives were promoted as the memory, history, and heritage of the nation, they were also, foreseeably, overtaken by the present. This generated the other, more visible and more keenly contested, ingredient of the crisis in archives: the charge that documents were released too slowly and exemptions granted too rarely.[52] It was as though archives and the issues they raised could be reduced to contemporary archives alone (on collaboration during the Second World War, for example, or, more recently, on the Algerian War). Reports were commissioned, a new law (which was finally abandoned) was promised, support was rallied for a new "City of Archives," and the prime minister issued two notable circulars. The first one, dated 3 October 1997 (a few days before Maurice Papon's trial opened and shortly after the Church of France's Declaration of Repentance), relaxed the rules concerning consultation of documents from the period 1940–1945. It recalled "the duty of the Republic to perpetuate the memory of the events which took place in our country between 1940 and 1945," and encouraged further exemptions, for which "the personality or the motivation of the persons who are requesting an exemption" should be ignored. This was basically how the civil service interpreted the "duty to remember." The second circular, of 5 May 1999, stated that "in the name of transparency and out of respect for victims and their families, the government has decided to facilitate historical research into the demonstration organized by the FLN [Algerian National Liberation Front] on 17 October 1961."

Maurice Papon, who, in his capacity as former chief of police in Paris, had just lost his libel suit against Jean-Luc Einaudi concerning the victims during the October 1961 demonstration, once again brought the past into the present. The Papon case taken as a whole is a telling example of the changing attitudes to time. It was only in 1998 that Papon, the former secretary-general (administrative head) of the département of the Gironde, was sentenced in Bordeaux for complicity in crimes against humanity; that is, fifty-five years after the offenses had been committed, and after a ninety-five-day trial.[53] Before him, in 1994, there had been the case of the former chief of the Vichy Milice in Lyon, Paul Touvier. He had first been pardoned, in 1972, by the President Pompidou, who wanted to "draw a veil" over this period when the French "did not like each other." Then, twenty-two years later, he was convicted of crimes against humanity. Yet it was the very same man, Touvier. Time had worked backwards: far from ushering in forgetting, it had revived, reconstructed, and imposed memory. And with the new unique temporality of crimes against humanity, time really did not go by: the criminal would remain forever contemporary with his crimes.[54]

Urban development projects in Paris are another—glaringly visible—area through which the order of time, and challenges to it, can be apprehended. Let us recall a few scenes from these royal dramas, or *pas de deux*, of politics with redevelopment. The first phase still came under the sway of futurism, and was in tune with the modern regime of historicity. It featured Georges Pompidou, the modernizing president who wanted to "adapt Paris to the automobile," to make it expand faster, and also to make it internationally attractive again by creating a major contemporary art museum. The development of the area of the Halles, which took a full twenty years, shows clearly the transformations taking place. The government had decided to transfer the Halles to Rungis outside Paris in 1959, and for the following ten years, the local authorities examined different architectural projects, which all gave pride of place to skyscrapers: "high-rises, high-rises, nothing but high-rises."[55] Modernization and high profits seemed to be the only considerations.

Despite protests—May '68 had left its mark—Baltard's pavilions were finally destroyed in 1971, not dismantled and moved elsewhere, but actually smashed up. For an unbelievable length of time this central site was simply a hole, the "Halles hole," which was not filled in until 1980 and even then after many twists and turns of the plot in which Jacques Chirac, the mayor of Paris at the time, could give the full measure of his talents as a town planner. Had all this occurred a year or two later, the Halles would quite definitely have been preserved as exceptional nineteenth-century "heritage." Their destruction even marked the turning of the tide: the moment when the modern (and modernizing) regime ceased to be self-evidently persuasive. Shortly afterwards, Orsay station, which had also been earmarked for demolition, was saved, and Michel Guy, the secretary of state for culture under President Valéry Giscard d'Estaing, newly elected, began to promote contemporary heritage—from the nineteenth and twentieth centuries.

As for the museum project, finally called the Georges Pompidou Center, it was initially conceived, interestingly, as an "experimental" museum, in the sense of "a museum whose goal was not to preserve works of art but to allow all aspects of contemporary artistic creation to be freely expressed."[56] The glass-fronted building, with its multipurpose spaces and movable structures, was meant to unite a rigorously functionalist architecture with the idea of something playful and ephemeral. The Pompidou Center was to exhibit contemporary rather than modern art, and not only put it on show but show it in the making. Its mission thus combined a futurist element (inherent to any museum project) with a strongly presentist one: the museum would shun museification and instead display art of the present, as well as the process of its creation. However, in the course of various alterations and renovations, the art laboratory gradually gave way to the conservation center. Correspondingly, the space allotted to contemporary experimentation and production diminished, while the museum spaces increased,[57] as though the present had shifted from a playful and narcissistic presentist position to a much less self-assured one, and acknowledged its own self-doubt.

But it was François Mitterand who staged the total triumph of museums and heritage, when he inaugurated the Grand Louvre late in 1993, with its touch of postmodernism in the form of the glass pyramid surrounded by smaller ones with their little fountains. This was the new entrance to forty centuries of history down below. After the last trace of the Louvre's regal past had disappeared, with the Ministry of Finance's departure from the premises, the Grand Louvre became a vast museum space. It was the largest museum (no less befits a prince) and it ranked as France's top universal heritage site (not forgetting the basement vestibule connecting to a shopping mall).

Hence this "distended," self-contained, and self-assured present, which seemed to have unquestioned and exclusive dominance, revealed its fault lines. It discovered that it could not fulfill its desire to be both subject and object of its own vision—not even in the transparency of the great open-plan floors of the Pompidou Center. Having stretched to breaking point the gap between the space of experience and the horizon of expectation, this self-enclosed present suddenly found that the gap could not be sealed over again, and that the ground was receding beneath its feet. Magritte would have painted this admirably. Three keywords summarized and stabilized these shifting sands: *memory*, more precisely a voluntary, solicited memory (oral history), as well as a reconstructed memory (which amounted to a history, but with a view to narrating one's *own* history for *oneself*); *heritage*, with 1980 being declared Heritage Year, although the success of the word and the theme (the defense, enhancement, and promotion of heritage) coincided with a crisis in the notion of "national heritage"; and lastly, *commemoration*, given that the last twenty years could well be entitled "from one commemoration to the next." These three terms were all orientated toward a fourth one, positioned at a virtual point of convergence: *identity*.[58]

THE DATES AND RHYTHMS OF MAJOR COMMEMORATIONS increasingly shaped the political calendar and defined the political agenda. Politicians tried to make the best of this and to put across their political messages of the day in the context of edifying commemorative events. This was precisely Mitterrand's aim in visiting the Panthéon shortly after his election victory, on 21 May 1981. It was a highly symbolic inaugural gesture. With a rose in his hand—where Michelet's *History of France* required the magical golden bough—the new president descended into the kingdom of the Republic's illustrious dead in order to breathe fresh life into its deserted places, situate himself within an ennobling lineage, and reawaken a time that had started with the Revolution. The event's staging thus fused the dimension of heritage with a future-oriented message ... after which the problems started.

In the ensuing years, commemorations multiplied. But while France was busy adjusting to this new state of affairs, *the* major commemoration was fast approaching—the bicentenary of the French Revolution; this made it necessary to discuss and question the very fact of commemorating, that "strange activity which oscillates between presence and absence."[59] One polemical moment among many in these debates was a Capetian millennium celebrated in 1987 and finally ratified by a solemn mass in the presence of the president of the Republic: France's *longue durée* was alive and kicking. This first burst of commemorative fireworks was followed immediately afterward by a hail of quick-fire commemorations of the fifty years since the outbreak of the Second World War.

Far from being an exclusively French phenomenon, commemorations flourished more or less everywhere from the 1980s onward. Germany went about it with similar if not greater fervor, due to the rivalry between the two Germanys at the time. There was Luther in 1983 (the 500th anniversary of his birth), the foundation of Berlin in 1985 (its 750th anniversary), the transfer of Frederick the Great's ashes to Potsdam in 1991, and the inauguration of the "New Guard" (*Neue Wache*) in Berlin in 1993, which the chancellor, Helmut Kohl, had wanted as the Federal Republic of Germany's central memorial. At the same time, several histories of Germany were published by major publishing houses and a little later work began on the collective volume, *German Sites of Memory*.[60]

Memory and History

The three volumes of *Constructing the Past*, edited by Jacques le Goff and Pierre Nora, were published in 1974. The work sought "to illustrate and to promote a 'new type of history,'" one that could respond to the "provocations" of the other human sciences, in particular anthropology.⁶¹ Its contents, ranging from a history of mentalities to historical anthropology, reflected an awareness and an understanding of the gap that had opened up in our self-relation, understood as a distance in time and space. Neither memory nor heritage were yet included among the new objects or approaches. Although historians have always had to deal with memory, they have always regarded it with suspicion. Thucydides branded memory as unreliable due to its omissions and deformations, and the almost-irresistible temptation to please the listener. The power of the eye, the persuasiveness of the autopsy, must take precedence over the ear, without which history could not be a search for the truth.⁶² Nineteenth-century science-history was enthralled by Thucydides. Its first gesture was to draw a clean line between past and present, which is why Michelet, who crossed the river of the dead in both directions many a time, could only be regarded as a transgressive figure. History should begin where memory stopped, that is, with written archives.

Four years later, the dictionary *New History*, edited jointly by Jacques Le Goff, Roger Chartier, and Jacques Revel, reserved a place for memory, with the entry "Collective memory." This notion, coined by Maurice Halbwachs, was adopted by Pierre Nora and defended on the condition that historians used it correctly. He argued that the discontinuities characterizing modernity had led to a proliferation of collective memories, and these put pressure on how history itself was written. This was true even of the subjects and orientations of "scientific" history. Hence Nora wanted to "have collective memory play the same role for contemporary history as what is called the history of mentalities played for modern history." From this was born what would later become the *Lieux de mémoire*. It was a history of memorials, starting from the places—topographical, monumental, symbolic, or functional—to which a society knowingly consigns its memories. The aim was unambiguous: "Analyzing collective memory can and must be the spearhead of any history claiming to call itself contemporary."⁶³

Maurice Halbwachs had devoted more than twenty years of his life, from the 1920s to his death in the Buchenwald concentration camp in 1945, to developing a sociology of collective memory. This persistent focus can be read in part as an aftereffect of the First World War. Today his writings have themselves become a site of memory, particularly for work on memory. After a long period of neglect, they were taken up and quoted with increasing frequency, and were finally republished. They are thus both a tool for working on the subject of memory and a sign of our present. It should be added that Halbwachs, in opening up the field of memory to sociology, was writing both with and against Bergson: with him, because he adopted Bergson's analyses of duration; against him, because he was concerned to highlight the social (and above all familial) dimension of memory, its "social frameworks." He concluded that social thought is essentially a memory composed of collective memories, but only those memories survive which societies, working within their present-day frameworks, can reconstruct.[64] The stress was unambiguously on the present.

In *The Collective Memory*, an unfinished work, Halbwachs made a clear separation between history and memory, and came out in favor of the latter. He politely dismissed the historian, whom he sent back to his archives and his external viewpoint. History is unitary, he argued, whereas there are as many collective memories as there are groups, each of which has its own sense of duration.[65] In common with other figures I have mentioned, Halbwachs identified acceleration as a key factor: with the increasing speed at which society lives, there are more and more collective memories. Collective memory is "a current of continuous thought" (it retains from the past only what is still living), whereas the historian "can truly achieve his task only by deliberately placing himself outside the time lived by those groups that participated in the events concerned, which have more or less direct contact with these events and can recall them."[66] History, which "extracts changes from duration," forges "an artificial duration having no reality for the groups from which these events are borrowed."[67] The bird of history can thus spread its wings only when night has fallen entirely, that is, when the present is absolutely dead. A critical survey of historical scholarship in France, published in 1867, ended on the following forceful conclusions: "History is born for an epoch only once it has died away entirely. The field of history is thus the past. The present is the time of politics and the future belongs to God."[68] The author, J. Thiénot, described himself to the minister receiving this report as a "meticulous clerk."

However, if the historian who is thus excluded from the field of memory does not recognize himself in this portrait, then the rigid opposition between history and memory ceases to hold, whereupon the historian's "hunting ground" may include collective memory or, better still, collective memory may feed into contemporary history. Nora always rejected the idea of a break between the past and the present, which he considered artificial and illusory. Unlike the authors of the report to the minister, Nora argued that it is for "the historian of the present" to make "the past consciously emerge into the present (instead of making the present unconsciously emerge in the past)." Nora's reflections on the event additionally suggest a relation between the new status of the event in a consumer society and the perception of time: "Does our treatment of the event not transform time itself into something to be consumed, in which we invest analogous affects?"[69] This idea points to another aspect of presentism: time itself, Nora suggests, is trapped in the time of consumption, and itself becomes a consumer product.

The underlying premise of *Lieux de mémoire* is that the very mode of existence of the past is that it wells up into the present—under the watchful eye of the historian. The work's first volume was published in 1984, and the long opening text, entitled "Between Memory and History," was a kind of manifesto and overview of the problematics of the project as a whole.[70] What was important was the *between*: to be *between* history and memory, not to oppose or confuse them, but to use them both. Memory could revitalize and enlarge the field of contemporary history (and collective memory could thus play for contemporary history the same role the history of mentalities had played for modern history). It followed that a new field was being mapped, that of the history of memory. Moreover, Nora argued, when a history reached the stage of critical self-reflection, concerned to re-examine its methods and tradition, it was able to identify the course of the interactions between memory and history, particularly in the long tradition of national histories which, from Froissart to Seignobos, via Michelet and Lavisse, had taken the form of "memory-histories."

The whole of "Between Memory and History" is concerned with the idea of acceleration. It even opens with the words "*The acceleration of history.*" This phrase itself has a history, at least since Daniel Halévy's *Essay on the Acceleration of History*, published in 1948, and right up to Jean-Noël Jeanneney's *Does History Go Faster?* in 2001.[71] But already much earlier, Chateaubriand had viewed the phenomenon of acceleration as the irrefutable sign of the destruction of the old order of time, and Musil even invented the term "accelerism." Halévy's book opens with a quotation from Michelet and ends on the repercussions of Hiroshima. Michelet had observed that "one of the most serious, but least noticed facts is that the pace of time has completely changed. It has speeded up in a most strange manner. Two revolutions (territorial and industrial) in a single life-span." This increased pace is characteristic of the modern order of time[72] (although acknowledging this fact does not oblige one to take seriously all the modern world's declarations on acceleration).[73]

For Nora, acceleration had the effect not only of "multiplying" collective memories to such an extent that they become "impossible to unify," as in Halbwachs's version, but also bringing about a break with the past, with the field of experience. Globalization, democratization, massification, and the media boom all contributed to the demise of what Nora called "memory-based societies" and ultimately to that of memory itself. "Memory is constantly on our lips because it no longer exists," Nora stated. In other words, it is precisely because there are "no longer *milieux de mémoire*," environments of memory, that "sites" find themselves invested with residual feelings of continuity.

Are we living a paradox? Could it be that we are all the more obsessed with memory because it is disappearing? But first we need to agree on what we understand by the term. Nora noted that today's "memory" is not the same as the "memory" that regulated "memory-based societies." The same term covers widely different forms and practices. The older form of memory was in a sense "without a past," a memory that "eternally recycles a heritage." "Our" memory, by contrast, has been touched by history and transformed by it. Even if this vision of earlier, memory-based, societies is somewhat simplified or mythified, what counts above all is the contrast with today.

For "our form of memory" is "nothing but history, a matter of sifting and sorting." We have become obsessive archivists, transforming everything into memory, in furtherance of the present's immediate self-historicization, which we mentioned above. Memory has become a private affair, entirely psychologized, introducing a new economy of the "self's identity." "An order is given to remember, but the responsibility is mine and it is I who must remember." Hence "to be Jewish is to remember that one is such; but once this incontestable memory has been interiorized, it eventually demands full recognition. What is being remembered? In a sense, it is memory itself."

Lastly, "our" memory is based on a relation to the past in which discontinuity predominates. The past is no longer "solid and steady." Hence we have moved "from a history sought in the continuity of memory to a memory cast in the discontinuity of history." Today's form of memory "is no longer what must be retrieved from the past in order to prepare the future one wants; it is what makes the present present to itself."[74] It is an instrument of presentism.

This change in the regime of memory could not but have an impact on the *"milieu de mémoire,"* the long-standing framework in which collective memory had predominantly developed, namely the history of the nation. How to write such a history today? How should we regard the series of "memory-histories," up to and including Lavisse's, which were "at the intersection between critical history and Republican memory"? That was, for Nora, where historiography came into play. The *Lieux de mémoire* were predicated on a twofold awareness: our regime of memory is no longer the same, and, second, history has entered the era of historiography. What could link these two changes? The "site of memory."

"On 14 July 1790," Lavisse wrote, "monarchic unity was succeeded by national unity, which has proved indestructible." The Revolution could be identified with the Nation, the Nation with the Republic, and the Republic with a "regime one can consider definitive." This was Lavisse's historiographical move. As for the remaining twenty-seven volumes, they were simply a continuous narrative, including references to sources, divided into predictable chronological sections, which brought nothing new. Two important moments emerge from the whole, however. First, the opening, with its *Tableau de la géographie de la France* by Vidal de la Blache, and the *Louis XIV* episode, written by the head of operations himself. Here, Lavisse noted the singularity of French national history, namely that because the Revolution had cut France off from its past, reconstituting this past was a "question of erudition," of history therefore, not of memory. Such a position legitimated the role of history as a pedagogy of the nation: the *pietas erga patriam* (to borrow the motto of the *Monumenta Germaniae Historica*) presupposed knowl*edge of the nation, which could only be acquired through learning its history. The historian's function or, better, the historian's mission could not be clearer.*

Not only did Lavisse undoubtedly play a role in Nora's intellectual itinerary,[75] but more importantly, his *History* was a kind of testing ground for the

Lieux de mémoire. The volume of the *Lieux* devoted to *The Republic* came out of a critical reading of Lavisse, a Lavisse seen from the wings. Nora exposed as Republican *memory* what was precisely presented as national *history*, and showed how the latter was produced. It was effectively a trial run for the notion of site of memory. In order to gain purchase on what was happening in 1980 between memory and history, and the ideas feeding into the new demands for commemoration, Nora's first move was to go a century back, to Lavisse and a time when memory was not an issue. The year 1980 had a good look at 1880, and 1880, in turn, shed light on 1980. Bringing together these two moments was itself illuminating: it revealed that Lavisse's "history" was, essentially, (Republican) memory elevated to the rank of history.

As for the preliminary definition of a "site" (*un lieu*), understood as something at once material, functional, and symbolic (an object *en abyme*, through which the past is redeployed in the present), one could almost have taken the most obvious "commonplaces" (*lieux communs*) of the Republic—the Tricolor, the 14 Juillet, the Panthéon, and so forth—and analyzed them as such. Except that, as Nora points out, we have only very tenuous links with these symbolic sites today; they are "like shells left on the shore when the sea of living memory has receded." They are still there, but the only active relation we can have to them is a relation at one remove, created by reactivating the events of which they recount the history. This is precisely the relation sketched in the *Lieux de mémoire*. The first volume had a certain air to it of "the purple shroud within the folds of which slumber the Gods that are dead,"[76] in the sense that by the end of it the Republic was shown to be already a site of memory for itself, its own site of memory. The following two volumes fleshed out the notion of "site of memory," turning it into a more active principle, so that with it one could go still further toward the type of history—symbolic history, or history at one remove—that Nora advocated and practiced.[77]

The expression "site of memory" comes from the arts of memory, and before that from the Classical art of oratory,[78] long before Nora's use of it in his exploration of contemporary memory. Cicero's definition has become canonical: the site (*locus*) is the location—the rooms of a house, for example, or a colonnade—where the orator, in preparing his speech, may line up the *images* of the things he wants to remember. He is advised to choose active images (*imagines agentes*). One can see from this that the *Lieux de mémoire* used a rhetorical conception of place and memory. Just as the *site* of the orator is always an artifact, so the *site* (of memory), for Nora, is never simply a given: it is constructed and must even be constantly reconstructed. The historian of sites of memory must thus find Cicero's active sites, the *imagines agentes*, but unlike the orator, who memorizes his speech by means of the sites, the historian works in the opposite direction, starting from the sites in order to examine the "speeches" they underpin. Sites of memory are characterized by the fact that in them different paths of memory have crossed; the only sites to be still active (*agentes*) are those to which people have returned, which they have recast, reorganized, and reworked. An abandoned site of memory is at best a mere recollection of a site, like "the Gauls" or "the Franks" after 1914.

LES LIEUX DE MÉMOIRE WAS AN EXPLORATION OF NATIONAL history through the prism of memory. It showed the existence of periodic "flare-ups" of memory, with several peaks. There was 1830 (epitomized by Guizot's work), 1880 (when the Republic's rituals and history were finalized), and 1980 (when Nora's investigation started, and its endpoint also). Another date could be added, in my view a vital one: 1914 (or thereabouts). It remained less visible (including in Nora's work) because it did not leave behind any major institutions relating to history nor any great national histories, retrieved or recast. But it did lead to contestations of official history, a privileging of memory over against history—already then—and, in some cases, explorations of a different history, of other historical temporalities, which could produce new periodizations. Halbwachs's work on memory was part of this moment of crisis in the order of time and its associated challenges to the modern regime of historicity.

The architecture of Proust's *In Search of Lost Time* is a profoundly resonant sign of this crisis of time. Toward the end of the novel, in the prince de Guermantes's library, the idea of Time impresses itself forcefully upon the narrator, and he comes to the realization that his real artistic work is a book yet to be written, one which will deliver up time itself, "the form of Time." The idea of a site of memory is adumbrated here. Proust himself talks in terms of a "distant place" (*lieu lointain*) and a "present place" (*lieu actuel*), and of how memory, as the eruption of the past into the present, transfers the sensation of those former times from one "place" to the other, in a kind of resurrection. Madame de Saint-Loup appears to the narrator as a sort of site of memory: "Was she not ... like one of those star-shaped crossroads in a forest where roads converge that have come, in the forest as in our lives, from the most diverse quarters?" Those which ended in her were "the two great 'ways' themselves, where on my many walks I had dreamed so many dreams."[79] The book ends on the towering physical presence of time, in all its verticality. Man, who is endowed "with the length not of his body but of his years," is perched on the living stilts of time, which can "sometimes ... become taller than church steeples," as suggested by the elderly duc de Guermantes, wavering unsteadily on his legs. It is no coincidence that the last words of *In Search of Lost Time* should be "in Time."

Proust leads us to Bergson and his analyses of duration.[80] Charles Péguy should also be mentioned here. He was openly and fiercely opposed to the history practiced at the Sorbonne, as embodied in the great figures of Lavisse, Langlois, and Seignobos. He came down resolutely on the side of memory and, against history and the sacrosanct historical method, championed Hugo and Michelet. In *Clio*, he set "essentially longitudinal" history against "essentially vertical" memory. History "goes lengthwise," that is, it remains "on the side and on the sidelines," whereas "memory, since it is within the event, primarily involves not going outside of it, remaining within it and going back over it from the inside."[81] Péguy was of course constantly thinking of the Dreyfus Affair: "I kept talking about, discussing, evoking and transmitting a certain Dreyfus Affair, the real Dreyfus Affair, in which we were all steeped, we of that generation."[82] For Péguy, then, history was "inscription," whereas memory was "recollection." The modern regime of historicity was clearly under fire.

Bergson focused exclusively on individual duration, while Péguy ventured to explore the "time of the world":

> Look into your memory and therefore, and through it, into the memory of your people.... You will be led to ask yourself if there are not also *durations* of a people and a *duration* of the world, since it will seem obvious to you that life, the event of peoples and the event of the world, does not pass, expend or extend itself constantly at the same speed, with the same rhythm, according to the same movement.... Is it not evident that events

are not homogeneous, that they are perhaps organic in the sense that they have what are called in acoustics antinodes and nodes, peaks and troughs, a rhythm, perhaps some regulation, tension and release, periods and epochs, axes of vibration, moments of agitation, crisis points, monotonous plains and suddenly suspension marks.[83]

In other words, Péguy detected an order of time, or a series of waves of time, in which regimes of historicity can be identified, as though in cross-section.

A little later, Walter Benjamin made recollection (*Eingedenken*) into one of the central concepts of his collection of theses called *On the Concept of History*.[84] As an alternative to "historicism," an ideology that in his view embodied the bankruptcy of modern history and historical civilization, and in opposition to his "homogeneous and empty" epoch, he had been working, right up to his death by suicide on the Spanish frontier in 1940, on a new concept of history, which drew both on Marxism and on Jewish messianic thought. Through the notion of *Jetztzeit* ("the presence of the now"), which he coined, he sought to define historical time as that which was only really generated when "what has been comes together in a flash with the now to form a new constellation."[85] In Hannah Arendt's words, Benjamin knew that "the break in tradition and the loss of authority which occurred in his lifetime were irreparable, and he concluded that he had to discover new ways of dealing with the past." These involved "settl[ing] down, piecemeal, in the present" and "like a pearl diver ... delv[ing] into the depths of the past."[86] Recollection is not the sudden involuntary emergence of the past in the present, but an active orientation that, by aiming at a particular moment in the past, transforms it. Benjamin was a man of the gap in time, and undoubtedly a man of the present, but absolutely not of presentism. His *aura* has continued to grow ever since the challenges to the modern regime emerged. He developed a theory of revolution, while never advocating a *tabula rasa* of the past.

How did historians respond to these condemnations and questions at the time? The answer is "not at all," or at least "not directly." Lavisse was already ill, hurrying to publish the next part of his History, *The History of Contemporary France*. The last volume, published in 1922 and devoted to the 1914 war, ended on a "General Conclusion" written by Lavisse himself. In it he acknowledged that "the present is bleak," but he tried to summon reasons for having "confidence in the future." These reasons included an "indestructible" national unity, a mode of government "which can be considered definitive," and above all the conviction that progress would once again win out, after "feverishly marking time," and that "nations will set out again on a new stage. We have the right to hope and believe that in the vanguard will be France."[87]

The real, albeit indirect, response came from those historians who abandoned national historiography and began to examine economic and social phenomena whose temporalities were dictated by rhythms other than the simple linear succession of political events. Historical research, in its aspiration to the status of a social science such as the one vigorously advocated—and closely guarded—by the Durkheimians and, in France, particularly by François Simiand, sought to contribute, in its own field, to the production of society's knowledge about itself. This shift from Nation to Society went together with a new relation to time: "Once society had supplanted the nation, legitimation by the past, hence by history, gave way to legitimation by the future."[88] That was certainly the case, although one should add that the historiographical stance of the future illuminating the past had already emerged earlier, as from the moment when the Revolution became the point around which the whole past history of France came to be organized and the previous temporal perspective was reversed. We saw this already in Volney's *Ruins*.

One could object that the future in question was not a future yet to come but a future that had already taken place—except that the nineteenth century never stopped chasing after the true end of the Revolution, and, at least until the consolidation of the Third Republic, the century oscillated between the fear that the Revolution would be confiscated and the fear that it would remain unfinished. Thereafter, this issue was supplanted by the question, which came back and back, of the nature of the Republic. The founders of the Annales School advocated moving back and forth between the present and the past, so as to bring contemporary historians and historians of the past closer together, but without forgetting that "misunderstanding of the present is the inevitable consequence of ignorance of the past. But a man may wear himself out just as fruitlessly in seeking to understand the past, if he is totally ignorant of the present."[89] This was a way of encouraging historians to get involved in the intellectual discussions and social issues of the day.

National Histories

Throughout the nineteenth century, in which the idea of the Nation played such a pivotal role, the development of national histories in fact went hand in hand with discourses claiming to speak in the name of the future. In France, that future had already taken place, but it had somehow also been missed, had gone astray, or got lost—in any case, it was unfinished. 1789 was in the past, but the promise it held was still to come. Here again, we find a situation that is somewhere between the *already* and the *not yet*.

Let us start with the 1820s generation of liberals, who raised high the flag of historical reform precisely in the name of the Nation. These young thinkers ushered in a vibrantly inventive period, intellectually innovative, if naive, in which history as a science and no longer as one of the arts was first elaborated and advocated. For this generation, the Nation was at once a self-evident fact, a political weapon, a cognitive architecture, and a historical program. A self-evident fact, because the whole purpose of the Revolution was to replace the king—in whose person, as it was said, "the nation resided in its entirety"—with the nation as the "mystical receptacle of sovereignty."[90] The sudden substitution of one absolute for another created (enduring) problems of representation, with the question of how to understand this absolute, how to serve it, and how to embody it. Throughout the century, historians grappled with trying to understand this founding moment by putting it in perspective and making sense of it in the broader context of the history of France, in the light of what came before, but also afterward. This work was really where the modern concept of history and the definition of the historian's task (or even mission) originated. And this was also François Furet's starting point in his project of "thinking" (*penser*) the French Revolution, through rereading the nineteenth-century historians.[91]

The nation was also a weapon. It was vital to show that "the people of the nation in their entirety" were agents of history, and in particular that, although the 1814 Charter described an essentially if not exclusively monarchic history of France, the long march of the Third Estate had begun already in the twelfth century. Another continuity was at work, it was claimed, far more charged with history and above all harboring much greater potential for the future than dynastic succession alone. In Augustin Thierry's view, 1789 recalled the "revolutions of the Middle Ages," and 1830 was in the process of providing an "extreme" vantage point from which Thierry believed one could see "the providential termination of the labour of the centuries which had elapsed since the twelfth."[92] July 1830 fulfilled July 1789. History became intelligible in the passage from the present—which only yesterday was the future—to a very distant past, with 1830 figuring as roughly the end of history. On this particular point a political program (the establishment of a constitutional monarchy) and a new historical methodology were in harmony, and each could henceforth corroborate the other.

In order to write this new history "still buried within the dusty chronicles" of the time—the history of citizens and subjects, in a word, of the people—original documents had to be consulted, and this rapidly brought one to the door of the Archives. The pamphleteer became a historian. Thierry redeployed the old erudition of the Bollandists and the Maurists, but with a different agenda, and also read Walter Scott and the historical novel (hence the whole debate on "local color").[93] We might smile at the naivety of thinking that history writing and politics could so effortlessly join forces, on the strength of a superficial compatibility. Nevertheless, the national question really did catalyze this historiographical movement, which the July Monarchy institutionalized after 1830. Then came the events of 1848. Greeted with stupefaction, 1848 showed that history had not come to an end, was not even in the process of ending. How, then, could history be written? The Revolution was not over, and any elevated vantage point had been destroyed.

Michelet's starting point was also the "lightning bolt" of July 1830, which tore through the night, illuminating it as a moment of grace and total intelligibility in which, as in a mystical vision, history revealed itself in its entirety, came together, and took on meaning.[94] The break of 1789 could be both acknowledged and integrated, such as to mend the broken "thread of tradition." This relation to the nation as "soul" and "person" had several important consequences. First, what was expected of the historian changed: his role became that of bringing to light what was not immediately visible, less the secrets of the great than the murmurings of the anonymous masses, and even the silences of history. But, in order to uncover these and fully immerse himself in the task, the historian must do more than simply shake the dust off old chronicles: he must "plunge" resolutely into the archives. In Michelet's powerful words, the historian paying his visits to the dead as he passes along row upon row of archives must learn to hear "the murmurings of so many stifled souls," of all those no longer living, to whom the present is indebted. These funeral elegies, which (also) had an epistemological import, negated the break between the past and the present that had inaugurated modern history. As head of the Historical Department at the National Archives and an avid reader of Virgil, Michelet doubtlessly saw himself as a *vates*, but this posture and its accompanying style were also his way of developing his theoretical reflections on history.

Furthermore, the Nation as a "person" was, for Michelet, a living entity, at once already there and constantly evolving. It contained both failures and promises, the past and the future. Above all, in terms borrowed from Vico, it was constantly "working on itself." Hence there is no "fatality" in its history: neither "soil" nor "race," nor any other determinism. The Nation is freedom and so its history is open-ended. In opposition to the histories deemed either "insufficiently material" or "insufficiently spiritual," Michelet advocated a history that paid attention to "interweavings" (of powers, levels, and factors).[95] This vision and analysis of the nation as a complex organism had considerable heuristic potential. It encouraged ever finer and more complex analyses, leading to "France" itself becoming an experimental framework and a problematic. This was exactly what Fernand Braudel, taking his cue from Michelet (while also marking his distance from him), aimed at in his *Identity of France*. But that was a good century later, and three wars on: "I love France with the same demanding and complicated passion as did Jules Michelet.... But that passion will rarely intrude upon the pages of this book. I shall keep it carefully to one side."[96]

Prior to this, before and after 1870, the historian Fustel de Coulanges had been working on his unfinished oeuvre.[97] The "Three Glorious Days" of July were already distant, and the promises of 1789 were even further back. History had not come to a halt. 1830 had been followed by 1848, the Republic by the coup d'état, with in its wake the initially "authoritarian" and later "liberal" Empire. The Battle of Sedan and the Commune would soon be at hand. Throughout his career, Fustel reflected on the French

Revolution. His method involved subjecting it to a double displacement. There have always been revolutions, he argued, in antiquity just as in modern times, but revolutions are not what one thinks they are today. What is invisible in them is in reality more powerful than what is visible, and when a revolution "erupts," it is in fact already over. The time of the event itself is of little importance.

His *Ancient City* (published in 1864) was already a history of political institutions, but in antiquity. In it he examined the series of revolutions that had led to the establishment of the city-state. In order to understand the latter, he argued, it was necessary to trace it back to its origins. The first human institutions, he discovered, had a religious basis: the founding belief that death was not the end of everything was what gave rise to the social bond (since the cult of the dead presupposed the existence of the family, and ancestors' tombs represented the first form of private property). Fustel de Coulanges was still targeting the artificiality of Rousseau's social contract here.

This hypothesis had three implications. First, the historian should "extend his researches over a vast span of time," since without the long view, history was impossible. Second, the historian should focus above all on what Fustel called "institutions" (in the etymological sense of "that which institutes life in society"). Their establishment was "slow, gradual and regular," and anything but "the result of a chance accident or a sudden act of force." Hence institutions are never the handiwork "of the will of one man, and even the will of a whole nation is not sufficient to create them." Violence contributes "hardly at all" to their foundation.[98] All things told, man plays little part in his own history. Fustel's *History of the Political Institutions of Ancient France* (which he never finished and in fact abandoned) was to have been something like Braudel's *Identity of France*. One could even suggest that Fustel's *longue durée*, understood as a process of institutionalization, in fact found its way right into Braudel's thinking, admittedly with significant differences, since Braudel was exploring other depths.

> The history of the *longue durée* is thus a sort of reference by which every national destiny is not so much judged as situated and explained.... It helps us to take the measure of France in an unusual way, to enlarge its history, to arrive at what the identity of France *might be*. In the end, this

history coming from the depths of time and stretching on into the future its gently rolling course, poses all the old problems at once. Can we say that it limits—note that I do not say eliminates—both men's freedom and their responsibility?[99]

Lastly, as Ariès has noted, Fustel's approach highlighted the differences between periods, and sought to make sense of them, by showing the overall lines of coherence that found final expression in institutions. He stressed, for example, the "radical" differences between ancient peoples and modern societies, between Ancient France and Modern France. Although Fustel did not endorse the modern regime of historicity and its futurism, the premise of his entire work was that the old regime of *historia magistra* was no longer tenable: different epochs were too dissimilar. And he precisely worked on excavating the logics underpinning different periods. There certainly were discontinuities in history, he maintained, but these are not expressed in surface accidents. Yet despite his conviction that the past could no longer shed light on the future, Fustel never took the step of writing a history of France in which the future revealed the sense of the past. And as for the present, he declared after the events of 1870 that any historian worthy of the name must start by "forgetting it." By the time he published the first volume of his *History of the Political Institutions of Ancient France* in 1875, he was assigning no other finality to the work than to contribute to "the advance of historical science and the knowledge of human nature." The only progress to which he laid claim was that of knowledge. He too found himself between two impossibilities: that of the past and that of the future.

So, with Fustel, we hear no patriotic trumpet call and no mournful sounding of the bugle. Only knowledge and erudition are at stake. We are a far cry from Maurice Barrès's pronouncements a little later, and even from Gabriel Monod, who, in the following year, published the first issue of the *Revue Historique* (1876). In it he of course did not broach national history as such, but aimed to "contribute to the progress of historical study" by adopting "strictly scientific methods of exposition." It was a question of analysis, not of synthesis, since the latter, as mentioned above, was yet to come, and would be premature at this stage. But historians clearly had a social role, as we would say nowadays, and a responsibility. They were to be the pontiffs (in French *un pont* is a bridge), uniting France's past with its present. And they must understand and explain the "logical link between all the periods of development" of a country, from the past right up to the present. From this it ensued that history was of "national importance," since it gave the country "the unity and moral strength she needs."[100] We can see at a glance how far we have come from Fustel's (declared) withdrawal from the contemporary scene. The historian's position has changed yet again, as has the way the "progress" of historical study is understood. One can still detect some elements of Thierry's schema (in less triumphalist or naive form), but above all there reappears the motto of the German *Monumenta*, in which erudition and love of the fatherland are combined (*sanctus amor patriae dat animum*), even if Monod aimed to distance himself from this approach. Monod's historian was a Republican who sought to neglect neither the past nor the future nor the present, but without privileging any of the three.

Lavisse, Nora's sparring partner, came on the scene a few years later, between two wars (the one France had lost and the one for which it was preparing). Febvre mocked his refusal of a history "told by those who tasted defeat in 1870," its "wavering cautiousness," and "its almost exclusive penchant for diplomatic history."[101] Of course, France's history after the establishment of the Republic became that of "the nation fulfilled": 1889 replaced 1830 as the vantage point from which to contemplate, deploy, and teach this history. In terms, once again, of the overarching rhythm of the *already* and the *not yet*, the *already* (figured by the Revolution) and the *not yet* (the Republic's definitive consolidation) came together and were united in 1889. Even if much remained to be done, the torments of anticipation were over. National history understandably won out, a current that became synonymous with its foremost advocate, Lavisse (and with the *Lavisse* textbooks on the history of France).

The synthesis achieved by Lavisse played a major political and pedagogical role, but it was intellectually weak. Its triumph was also a swan song. Once the nation had been embodied, all that remained was to "write it up."[102] Basically, the idea was to abolish the historical frontier that split France's past in two (before and after the Revolution), so that France could rally united to the defense of another frontier—a geographical one this time—with a view to ultimately pushing it back (beyond the "blue line of the Vosges"). That was the general drift, and it already had the feel of mobilization orders about it. When war finally broke out, the youngest of that generation's historians were indeed mobilized, and most of the others considered themselves to be "mobilized in the rear services," as the historian Charles Petit-Dutaillis put it.

Then, as an aftereffect of the 1914-1918 war, a fault line appeared in the order of time, something like a rift. The bloody carnage of nations at war produced, in the 1920s, a historiography that either turned away from the nation toward social issues or precisely glorified it. These were two very different strategies for linking the past to the future. Valéry, who "despair[ed] of history" for its failure to foresee anything, denounced the dangerous substance that makes "nations bitter, proud, insufferable and vain."[103] It was as though there were no history other than national and empirical facts-based history [*l'histoire historisante*], on which Febvre would shortly pour scorn.

However, when Febvre took up his professorship at the University of Strasbourg in 1919, his inaugural lecture began by stating that "any history which is of service" is "a servile history. Professors of the French University of Strasbourg, we are not missionaries marching to the orders of some national bible."[104] It was due to this refusal to "serve" that he could ultimately reply in the affirmative to the key question he asked at the outset: "Do I have the right"—that is, *still* have the right—to do history "in a world in ruins"? And it was this refusal, again, that legitimated his continued practice as a historian, "picking up the thread again," and enabling a space of work and inquiry to be sketched for a (new) science-history in search of other rhythms, other depths, and other objects—in short, other temporalities. Some years later (after 1929) this history would give birth to the Annales d'Histoire Économique et Sociale. However, the retreat or even eclipse of national history did not mean that it was forgotten or abandoned. Later, both Bloch and Febvre planned to write a History of France, which finally neither of them completed.[105]

At the opposite extreme, Jacques Bainville, who was also affected by the 1914 war and its aftermath, took refuge in a national history. His *History of France*, published in 1924, was a real popular success, unlike academic history of the time. It was based on a simple idea, formulated in the foreword, that "the men of the past resembled those of today and their actions had the same motivation as ours." It was primarily an exercise in reactivating the model of *historia magistra*, using the standard devices of repetition and analogy. In 1916 he noted in his *Journal*, "Ignorance and lack of understanding of our past are killing us, and all due to the stupid democratic prejudice which says that time marches on." History still had lessons to dispense. And history must be "the memory of statesmen." The idea was to neutralize the feared future by expelling time from history. To counter stupid democratic prejudice, Bainville's *History* was obliged to prove that the modern regime of historicity was false, and that no, decidedly, time does not "march on."

Ariès, whom we have already mentioned for his work on death, was an avid reader and admirer of Bainville in his youth. However, he did not turn to national history after the "rupture" of the Second World War—what he called "the rifts of 1940"—but on the contrary, he carefully avoided it. He began with *The History of the French Population and Its Attitudes to Life Since the Eighteenth Century* (1948), was thrust into the limelight with *The Hour of Our Death* (1977), and later co-edited with Duby a multivolume *History of Private Life* (1985). In 1958, Georges Duby and Robert Mandrou published not a History of France but *A History of French Civilization*, whose foreword ended on the following words: "This book will have fulfilled its task if it arouses curiosity, if it inspires its readers to consult other, more scholarly and complete, books, and if it enables them better to grasp, oriented by ten centuries of history, the unique characteristics [*traits originaux*] of that 'person'—contemporary France."[106] This was a double reference, so discreet as to be almost for the happy few alone, to Michelet (the "person") and to Marc Bloch's *Caractères originaux de l'histoire rurale française* (translated as *French Rural History: An Essay on Its Basic Characteristics*).

SO FOR MORE THAN HALF A CENTURY, THE IDEA OF THE NATION ceased to be the driving force behind historical research; it provided neither the right scale nor the right depth of chronological perspective. It had done too much damage and seemed no longer to offer productive insights. New forms of science-history emerged, within the context of historical materialism, as well as quantitative and serial analyses whose tools were initially mechanized record cards and, later, computers. Yet by 1980 it had become clear that these scientific models, which were major consumers of futurity, and solidly anchored in the notion of progress (of society and of science alike), produced less and less fruitful results, and even began to lack substance altogether. There followed a period of stasis, a pause during which it became legitimate to cast a glance backward over the path taken, to try and make sense of where one was and why one was there. The move from a prospective to a retrospective viewpoint allowed some distance to intervene. The public turned to genealogy, and companies started worrying about their archives, and selling "business culture" as a loss leader. The modern regime of historicity was no longer convincing.

History, just like other disciplines, was affected by these changes. It was only an element in the total picture (which we sketched in our opening pages) and certainly not its instigator. However, the introduction of the historian into history, as practiced and professed by Febvre, and also advocated by Marrou and Aron in opposition to the positivist school, had paved the way for this movement. Henceforth, the historian seemed to want to "join the ranks of history," as Péguy put it: "They [the historians] do not want to write the history of historians. They want to exploit to the full the indefiniteness of historical detail. But they do not want to include themselves within the historical detail's lack of clearly defined limits. They do not want to join the ranks of history. They behave like a doctor who does not want to be ill and die."[107] The historian's claim to extraterritoriality and a commanding viewpoint was no longer tenable.

All these factors contributed to the emergence of a history of history, which was one of the sources, as we have seen, of Nora's reflections leading to *Les lieux de mémoire*. A reflexive and historiographical stance was obviously not the prerogative of just one type of history nor, of course, of history alone.[108] After all, to what was it responding if not, at least in part, to this new context, in which the hitherto paradigmatic temporality of the modern regime of historicity was being challenged? The light beaming in from the future was beginning to wane, what was ahead seemed increasingly unpredictable, the category of the present prevailed, and the recent past—which to everyone's surprise wouldn't move on or, on the contrary, passed with worrying speed—had to be constantly and compulsively revisited. As a result, history could no longer be written from the perspective or in the name of the future (or of any of its various hypostases). This directly affected the writing of contemporary history, but gradually affected other history as well.

Now it was precisely in these same years, the 1980s, and not only in France, that the question of the nation reemerged, generating intellectual and political interest, and a whole swathe of publications. There was arguably something highly paradoxical in the combination of a dominant presentism with the production of national histories. Given that "the Nation" and "Progress" had been so powerfully welded together in the nineteenth century, how could the idea of the Nation return when that of Progress was no longer sustainable? What was left of the Nation? It was often figured as a Nation without prospect(s), a retrospective and nostalgic entity, basically a refuge, linked to a form of history enthralled once again to the charms of *historia magistra*. Maybe, however, the return of the Nation was a relatively explicit and voluntaristic response to the issues of identity raised by the rising tide of memory. Yet could historians ever again become the instructors and institutors of the Nation (like Lavisse) or of a new Republic (like Claude Nicolet), even using the medium of television? Should they not simply remain its memorialists, better informed than others maybe, but one of many?

In his later years, Braudel was called upon to take a leading role in this debate between history and memory. He had just, to the delighted astonishment of historians, published the first part of his *Identity of France*. His France was of course not assimilated to a person but constructed as a historical object. And his goal was not to uncover an essence, whether located in the past or to be realized in the future. Identity was precisely given in the *longue durée*—in the *longue durée only* or only *as* the *longue durée*. "It is precisely that tide and the deep-flowing currents of France's past that I am seeking to detect, to trace, to better judge how they flow into the present, as rivers flow into the sea."[109] Thus toward the end of Braudel's career as a historian, marked by brilliant and acclaimed analyses ever since 1949, the history most antithetical to these, the short-winded and superficial genre of national history, was suddenly also admitted to the *longue durée*, through which it even revealed its truest and most expressive aspects. Although Braudel's *Identity of France* was published only in 1986, the seeds for it were sown by Braudel's experience as a prisoner of war in 1940:

> We the defeated, trudging the unjust road towards a suddenly-imposed captivity, represented the lost France, dust blown by the wind from a heap of sand. The real France, the France held in reserve, *la France profonde*, remained behind us. It would survive, it did survive.... Ever since

those days, already so long ago, I have never ceased to think of the France buried deep inside itself, within its own heart, a France flowing along the contours of its own age-long history, destined to continue, come what may. Out of this fascination grew the present book's ambiguous title, to which I have gradually become accustomed.[110]

It was a history penned by a man who had been forced to taste defeat, and who needed no less than forty years to approach the idea of the nation again, differently.

In another *History of France,* the editors André Burguière and Jacques Revel deliberately replaced the "classic narrative of the nation from its origins to the present" with a "thematic and logical approach." The book aimed not to "recount" France yet again, but to break with the official version and use the present as a prism through which to investigate the nation, "in order to discover the original characteristics of the national totality, through their emergence and transformations."[111] The approach was anything but teleological, retrospectively teleological, but instead it could be called regressive: the only perspective was that of the present, which was both the starting point and the endpoint of the inquiry.

More generally, the historiographical approach, in its concern to identify presuppositions and to examine the tools and categories mobilized, contributed significantly to how the theme of the nation was treated.[112] I mentioned above that the *Lieux de mémoire* went furthest in this direction in its integration of historiographical reflections on the work's methods as each new volume rolled off the press, such as to extend progressively the sense of the term "site." At all events, these different ways of approaching the nation as a problem broke with all the national memory-histories written from the viewpoint of the future. At the opposite extreme from the historical school called the *école méthodique,* which never talked of the present but always had it on its mind, the present had now explicitly become the dominant (and sufficient?) category.

Commemorations

The *Lieux de mémoire*'s strategy in trying to understand the unfurling wave of memorial concerns, and in anticipation of its size and force—like

Thucydides recognizing from the very start the importance of the Peloponnesian War—was to focus on how the major Histories of France had been written. How, at certain key moments, had the past been adopted into the present, and made into something meaningful? Which past exactly, and what in the past? Nora followed up on the ways in which the past was revived in and flowed through the present, enabled by a whole arsenal of rhetorical devices. But in this he never lost sight of the goal he had set himself at the outset, to return to the issues of the day, in order better to understand and explain them, informed by these long detours. Nora went from the present to the present, in order to question the present conjuncture.

Although Nora's starting point was his astonishment at the success of the topics of commemoration at the time, by the end of his inquiry he was formulating what he called the "inversion of the dynamics of commemoration." We continue commemorating in the name of the trilogy Memory, Identity, and Cultural Heritage, but the sense of the term "commemoration" has changed (as has that of "memory," and also of "heritage," as we shall see in the next chapter). Commemoration was initially religious: "Do this in remembrance of me" implies that the Last Supper presents itself from the outset as something to be commemorated, in the very moment it takes place. It thus necessarily incorporates absence into itself, or equally the invisible presence of he who henceforth must be constantly remembered and imitated. The rituals of monarchy involve a different logic, stressing continuity: "The King is dead, long live the King!" The Revolution and the Republic brought back the topics of commemoration, whose original sacred character was transferred to national, republican, and secular values.

So we commemorate "Bastille Day," in which 1880, 1789, and 1790 prefigure and echo each other.[113] Péguy, in his *Clio*, had striking terms for this: "The storming of the Bastille was a genuine feast-day, it was the first celebration, the first commemoration and in a sense the first anniversary of the storming of the Bastille.... The *Fête de la Fédération*, the first anniversary of the storming of the Bastille, was not its first commemoration. It was the storming of the Bastille itself which was the first *Fête de la Fédération*, a Federation *avant la lettre*."[114] Today, this phenomenon has become the norm, with every event already incorporating its own commemoration. This was the case in May 1968, and it was true again, in extreme form, for 11 September 2001, with all the television cameras trying to catch on film the moment when the second plane would crash into the World Trade Center's second tower.

The aspect of commemoration that Nora considered to be characteristic of his time was its "patrimonial" character. Commemorations had become wide-ranging and "denationalized," even when they sought recognition by the State (which in fact was overwhelmed by the flood of heritage-related demands).[115] Nora went even further: the nation itself has been transformed into cultural heritage, he argued, "as though France had ceased to be a history which divides us and had become a culture which unites us."[116] The question remained of who this *us* was, who defined it, how, and around what. Nora identified the emergence of a "nation without nationalism" in this movement from the political to the cultural. Could it be that late twentieth-century France was becoming a *Kultur Nation*, while Germany, which had adopted that path long before as a remedy for its lack of political unity, was becoming a Nation, even "despite itself," since it could not escape the question of nationhood? One can see in this the makings of an interesting historical chiasmus, against the background of European integration.

In summary, one could say that for France under the Third Republic and Lavisse's tutelage, a (Republican) memory that had been transformed into history gave way to history—or, as one more readily says today, *the past*—lived, read, and appropriated selectively as memory (in its new sense), sometimes spurred on by the "duty to remember."[117] The last twenty years would thus be the time of the transition from a "historical nation" (*la nation historique*) to a "memory-based nation" (*la nation mémorielle*). The *Lieux de mémoire*, like Proust's *À la recherche du temps perdu*, ends on a book that is yet to be written. It would be the "true" History of France written, as we can now see, in order to analyze and take stock of a crisis of time made manifest through the theme of the nation, and constituted by the sites we have just discovered. The aim of the *Lieux* was thus not so much to make the Annals "conform to the progress of reason" but rather to make them conform to the crisis of progress itself.

The Moment of the *Lieux de mémoire*

I have used the *Lieux de mémoire* as a way of situating the debates between history and memory, and in order to shed light on the relations between national history and the modern regime of historicity. But the work is also instructive in itself. It belongs to the moment that it sets out to map, and its very method teaches us something about our present. Its constant historiographical awareness, which I mentioned above, can be read as a further sign, at one remove, of the present's tendency to transform itself instantly into history.

Just as Lavisse considered the national unity created by the French Revolution to be final and indestructible, so he conceived his *History of Contemporary France* as the ultimate history of the fully realized Nation, addressed both to the present and to the future, a kind of timeless treasure. The Republic could always be improved, but nothing fundamental was to change henceforth. This was what he still wanted to be able to believe in 1921 when, an ill man, he was writing his *History*'s "General Conclusion," which went up to 1919. The *Lieux de mémoire,* by contrast, were conceived as a history of the present and in the present, taking into account the fact that the present had become "the category of our social self-understanding."

If one can say that the *Lieux* inhabits a specific moment, one should add that the work also constitutes a site (*lieu*) of this moment, or some possible sites. As well as being a History of France for today, it is also, quite explicitly, a history of our present. As a result, the historian can no longer be represented as the intermediary between past and future in the guise of a pontiff (Monod) or a prophet (Michelet), who can read in the past the future that has already taken place or is to be brought into being, and who then proclaims it. Even less can the historian "forget," or rather deny, the present, as Fustel did. And while the historian is indeed a go-between, this is only within the closed circle of the present, and "between the blind demand and the enlightened reply, between public pressure and the solitary patience of the laboratory, between what he senses and what he knows."[118] This is arguably a humble role, but at least the historian is henceforth fully and rightfully a historian of the present. And History, whether it is of the present or of other periods, must accept that it is history *in* the present.

But our contemporary present and its presentism have proved almost unsustainable. The demand for memory can be interpreted as an expression of this crisis in our relation to time as well as an attempt at providing a solution. And of course the memory claimed and proclaimed is not so much to do with transmission as with reconstruction of a forgotten and sometimes falsified past, a past that was never known. Despite this, the act of memory is conceived as *reappropriating* this past as totally legible. Epistemologically, the *Lieux* posits (and even champions) the centrality of the present, as both the origin and the destination of its exploration, but it simultaneously seeks to get round the present and escape its grasp. It does this by making the past's selective recycling, or the passage from the past into the present (which is how memory works) into the starting point of its historiographical operations: memory becomes, not so much in its content as in its form, a mode of historical inquiry and of history writing.

Traditionally, the historian's first move was rather to separate the two: history was to be the science of the past, a pure science, and the historian nothing but an eye deciphering documents in the silence of the Archives. The *Lieux*'s logic works quite differently, with the historian and the way he or she works being conceived, precisely, as a site of memory. Once again Michelet was the tutelary figure, but also Nora himself, who conceived and edited an *Essais d'ego-histoire*.[119] Just as Chateaubriand returned repeatedly to sites of memory of himself and for himself, so historians could take *themselves* as such sites,[120] leading logically to an ego-historical approach. They could write the histories of themselves as historical objects (but not all historians are great historians).

The *Lieux* can be regarded as a symptom of our times due to the immense success of the notion of "site of memory." It caught on rapidly, as an expression and in the real, including in law. Even places such as the Paris concert hall *L'Olympia* or the restaurant *Fouquet's* have been listed. The "site" came to the rescue of the "historic monument," which was oversubscribed and outdated. Although the Third Republic would have found the notion of "site" neither imaginable nor desirable, it was a quicker and simpler category to apply than the "historic monument."[121] But as a result, the "site of memory" found itself absorbed by the historical phenomenon that had led to its formulation in the first place, and which it had been invented to decipher. The cognitive instrument conceived in order better to define and understand the ubiquity of commemorative activity was itself co-opted into the latter's show and annexed to the arsenal of presentism, this time called to the rescue of Cultural Heritage and Commemoration. It was a clear sign that Nora's analysis was correct, but with the risk that the whole venture could be reduced to its immediate context, and would consequently be consumed by the very phenomenon it had helped to describe and understand.

The *Lieux* are a symptom of today's world also in their conception of memory. If we imagine for a moment the work being written in the mid-1960s, the unconscious would doubtless have played an important role (in the form of lapsus, memory blanks, amnesia, displacement, denegation, and so forth). Since, as mentioned above, the notion of "site" in the work is rhetorical, the memory referred to in the *Lieux* is a memory without an unconscious, except in the metaphorical sense, or only contingently and not essentially. The historian does not attempt to uncover the unthought of a "site" but rather to reconstitute what has made it thinkable. Whence perhaps a certain difficulty within the *Lieux*'s framework of conceiving what a "non-site" or a "bad" site of national history or memory would be.

Then came 1989. It was symbolized by the fall of the Berlin Wall on 9 November, marking the end of an ideology that had always regarded itself as the vanguard of modernity. History did not come to an end, not even in Francis Fukuyama's sense, but a break appeared in the order of time (first in Europe, then gradually in many other parts of the world). Understandably, after 1989, new relations to time were explored, as had occurred two centuries previously when the old order of time and its associated regime of historicity disintegrated. The future was still there, as unpredictable as ever, or even, we would be tempted to say, even more so than before.

The end of the tyranny of the future also had the effect of making the past inscrutable again, and at least partly unpredictable too. This was not simply linked to the issue of contingency, which Raymond Aron highlighted in his critique of causality in Simiand.[122] The past waiting to be rediscovered was neither linear nor unambiguous, and it was construed as a field crisscrossed by pasts that had for a time been possible futures, including those which had begun to exist and which had been prevented from doing so. Certain historians and philosophers, including Ricoeur, rightly dwelt on this.[123] Insofar as *Les lieux de mémoire* showed how certain sites crystallized, were remodeled and anamorphosed, but also how they were forgotten, it undeniably contained a whole critical inventory of France's memory-history. And since it was alert to the whole economy of the past in the present, the work also suggested a possible way of moving between the past and the present, starting deliberately, as I have said, from the present.

1989 also placed the nation once more in the spotlight. The nation was again something of a hit—or at least something of a problem. This came as a total surprise, even to those in Western Europe who had revived the idea of the nation in the preceding years. As mentioned above, although pre-Unification Germany readily defined itself as a "post-national" State, several histories of Germany were published in the 1980s, and an increasing number of conferences were organized around German identity and around commemoration. Yet at the same time, people on both sides of the Wall were convinced that Germany would remain lastingly divided. In France, the publication of the *Lieux* had the effect of foregrounding the question of the nation and its profound transformations. The nation was no longer a messianic but a heritage-based entity, or even a nation as shared culture, a nation without nationalism, alive but pacified. All that remained for France to do in its semi-retirement from history was to cultivate its memory, as one tends one's garden. This transformation of the French nation was precisely what the *Lieux* sought to make visible, to chart, and to describe. It was the *Lieux*'s critical context.

But can we be so sure? Can the shift from one model of the nation to another occur so neatly and irreversibly? What we have seen in whole areas of Europe since 1989, including in Western Europe, should prompt us at least to leave the question open.[124] How does Germany experience its status as a nation, with an East Germany rebuilt from scratch? And what can Europe be, with the enlargement of 2004, navigating like a heavy ship that is less and less responsive to the helm? Are we heading toward an all-heritage Europe, united by a common Heritage List? That would be a more presentist than futurist Europe, but for which "progress" would continue to play a major role.[125]

How are we to write Europe's history and even contribute to "The Making of Europe" (Faire l'Europe), to borrow the title of a series edited by Jacques le Goff, which was first published in 1989 as a collaboration between five publishers of different languages and nationalities?[126] It was certainly a voluntaristic project, and some even criticized it for reviving, this time for Europe, a teleological, nineteenth-century-style national history.[127] Le Goff stressed the "active title" of the series: writing history is also a way of making history. Did the project thus simply reactivate the modern regime of historicity, with the future once again used to explain the past? That was clearly not Le Goff's position, since "today comes from yesterday and tomorrow emerges out of the past." And he continued: "It is a past that should not paralyze the present but help it to be faithful to its inheritance yet different and innovative as it progresses."[128] Le Goff was not Lavisse, and both the futurism of the modern regime of historicity and the backward-looking vision of the old regime were rejected, in order to preserve the possibility of a present that would be at once new, different, and faithful to what it had inherited. As with Monod, it was a question of articulating the past, the present, and the future around the historical object called European (rather than National) History, and approaching it through the *longue durée*. Moreover, as the author of *Medieval Civilization, 400–1500*, who advocated a long Middle Ages stretching from the third century A.D. up to the modern industrial revolutions, Le Goff felt quite at home with the project: Europe came from a long way back. If there was such a thing as a European *identity*, it would be in and through this *longue durée* that one could best try to grasp it.

Whether one situates the nation in a mythical or distant past, or in the future, or both at once, people are yet again dying in its name or on the pretext of its name.[129] Ethnic nationalisms have killed many, and savagely. These more or less enflamed "returns to," or aspirations toward, the idea of the nation, which differ in form and intensity, can be attributed in part to a crisis of time. They are one of its components or expressions, although they cannot be reduced to or identified with it. As a *reaction* to this crisis, they have, alas, already proved their efficacy. But as a *response* to the contemporary situation, these nationalisms appear particularly out of place because the modern regime of historicity, flying its futurist or national-futurist flag, has in large part ceased to convince and mobilize.

5
HERITAGE AND THE PRESENT

LET US NOW TURN FROM MEMORY TO ITS ALTER EGO, HERITAGE, while asking the same question as before: how are we to understand, in terms of time and the order of time, the proliferation and universalization of heritage that we have witnessed over the last quarter of a century? More precisely, what regime of historicity is implied by the phenomenon that some have described as the "meteoric rise of the heritage industry" in the 1990s? Did this taste for the past, for everything old, emerge suddenly as a kind of nostalgia for an older regime of historicity that had in fact long been inoperative? And how could it be reconciled with the modern regime, which for two whole centuries had pinned all "hopeful expectation" on the future, as expressed in Marinetti's proclamations and prophecies? I shall suggest that our contemporary fascination with heritage can be understood as the expression of a crisis of time, and as a further sign of the emergence of presentism, which I have been exploring throughout this book. To broach these issues, I shall again move between different understandings of the notion of heritage in different epochs, with particular attention each time to the role assigned to the present.

In the period under consideration—and not forgetting that 1980 was decreed Heritage Year by the French government—heritage became a dominant and all-encompassing, if not all-consuming, category of cultural life and public policy. It was treated as though it were self-evident. Soon, all sorts of "new heritage objects" appeared, as well as "new heritage uses." In France, the Historic Monuments Division of the Ministry of Culture, which previously had had a whole department to itself, was cut back, uprooted, and transferred to a Department of Heritage that included, most strikingly, an ethnology unit.[1] Heritage Days were inaugurated in 1983, and by September 2002 they were attracting more than eleven million visitors to so-called heritage buildings. The results, duly recorded and publicized each year in the media, have become a kind of record to be broken the following year: the longer the queues, the healthier the figures! The only exception was 2001, when the Heritage Days had to be cancelled at the last moment due to the 9/11 attacks. Heritage days have now sprung up more or less everywhere. Thanks in large part to UNESCO's programmes and conventions, heritage has become a universal phenomenon, and every year the list of Universal Heritage Sites of Humanity, which can be consulted on the World Heritage Center's website, gets longer and longer: 730 in 2002. A National School of Heritage, set up to train future heritage curators, opened in Paris in 1991. And since 1996 one can even find a French Heritage Foundation, inspired, at least in its founding principles, by the United Kingdom's National Trust (but it remains to date remarkably inconspicuous). Lastly, the Ministry of Culture's Heritage Department has organized Heritage Debates (*Entretiens du patrimoine*) since 1984, where everything relating to heritage, including, recently, its "excesses," is discussed.[2]

In *Les lieux de mémoire*, Nora argued that the history of France—or even France itself—was becoming a "heritage object," insofar as the shift from one regime of memory to another had caused the regime of "memory-history" to give way to that of "heritage-history." In this respect the wording of the 1993 law on heritage was striking: "Our cultural heritage is the memory of our history and the symbol of our national identity." Heritage had gone over to the side of memory, incarnating the memory of history and, as such, becoming a symbol of identity. Memory, heritage, history, identity, and nation were seamlessly joined in the smooth language of law.

In this new configuration, heritage was linked to territory and to memory, which both operated as substrata of *identity*, that 1980s keyword. But there was nothing obvious about this identity. It was an identity aware of its own insecurity, teetering on the brink, or even already to a large extent forgotten, obliterated, and suppressed: an identity in search of itself, to be unearthed, pieced together, or even invented. In this sense, heritage came to define less what one possessed, what one *had*, than what one *was*, without being aware of it or without having been in a position to know it. Heritage could thus encourage collective anamnesis. To the "duty" to remember and, later, its public expression in the form of repentance was added something like the "zealous obligation" no longer toward the Plan, as in de Gaulle's time—other times, other customs—but toward heritage, with the attendant requirements of conservation, renovation, and commemoration. At about this time, ecomuseums and social museums (at least in France) became the testing ground in which a new hybrid heritage, at the crossroads between the cultural, the social, and the natural, was explored.

A History of the Concept of Heritage

How did this notion of heritage or patrimony, which had existed in private law since ancient times, come to dominate the field of collective cultural property? The term entered French dictionaries only recently.[3] The International Convention on Natural and Cultural Heritage of 1972 is a useful indicator: "heritage" had moved over to the natural world, to be taken up by economists and legal scholars, before swinging back to an overwhelmingly cultural definition. On the way, however, it became clear that applying the concept of heritage to nature was nothing short of a *coup de force*. For heritage had always been "the archetype of the appropriated good . . . , in opposition, semantically, to the natural, the wild and the inappropriable. Natural entities are the class of objects whose characteristics make them least likely to be able to be integrated into a logic of heritage."[4]

This remark is perfectly true, but it overlooks the fact that what defines heritage fundamentally is that it is something *transmitted*. The natural environment was qualified as "heritage" as soon as people realized that its deterioration, whether accidental or ordinary (pollution), temporary or irreversible, endangered its transmission. Hence the idea of making nature into a heritage object, so that it could benefit from legal protection and be preserved today for future generations. Taking the future into account involved acting in its name. So we appear to be on familiar ground again, within the modern regime of historicity. Yet is this future, and the approach to it, really the same as before?

The apparent self-evidence of the notion of heritage, which although recently established seems to have been overwhelmingly accepted, should not obscure the fact that it is a notion with a history: it did not exist in all places, nor at all times, nor in the same way. What was the situation outside of Europe, for example, and, more recently, in formerly colonized countries? A comparative analysis would identify how the notion emerged, how it circulated, and how it was received. In Europe, for example, heritage is a hybrid notion with a long history behind it. Scholarly studies tracing the concept back to its origins show that several conditions had to be fulfilled: a tradition of collecting, a concern for conservation and restoration, and the gradual elaboration of the category of the historic monument.[5] These were necessary, but not sufficient, conditions for the emergence of "heritage."

For something else was required, namely a certain way of life that links together and gives meaning to such practices; a certain mode of relation to the world and to time; and some awareness, more often than not uneasy, that something (an object, a monument, a site, or a landscape) had disappeared or was about to disappear. In short, what was needed was a crisis of time. Adopting Krzysztof Pomian's definitions, we can say that heritage objects are *semiophores*, or "visible objects endowed with meanings."[6] Clearly cultural heritage and social temporalities are inseparable, since heritage condenses the semiophores that a society produces at a particular time (and for a particular time). They are thus a sign of the type of relation to time that a society decides to establish. Heritage makes visible and expresses a certain order of time, in which the dimension of the past is the most important. More precisely, it is a past that the present cannot or does not want to relinquish entirely, whether the bond to it takes the form of celebration, imitation, banishment, reflected glory, or, simply, the possibility of visiting it. Is, then, the concern with heritage only or principally backward-looking? No, because we are dealing with a past—a certain past—whose visible embodiment is important for the present.[7]

So does that fulfill all the conditions? Yes, if one simply means to point out that all human beings or human groups become attached to certain objects that they have found, received, or cobbled together, however shabby they may be. No, if one is attempting to tease out the specificity of the notion of heritage in Europe, and the place it has come to occupy. In addition to the conditions enumerated above, and in addition to a certain relation to the world and to time, another factor was determinant: the high value placed on the trace, as such. And it leads us back to the life of Jesus, the passage of Christ on this earth, which became a foundational moment. The categories of presence and absence, of the visible and the invisible, were enduringly shaped by it. As we know, Constantine the Great had the Church of the Holy Sepulchre built around the empty tomb, that is, on the very spot that retained the trace of Jesus's passage, and that thereafter was treated as the epicenter of the Christian faith. I have already mentioned how radically Christianity transformed the order of time, stretching time between an *already* and a *not yet*; and how later the weight of the *already*—the accomplished, the past, tradition—grew ever heavier as the Church became institutionalized within the Roman Empire.[8]

Moreover, the relation to time rested on concrete objects that bore witness to the life and Passion of Christ. The empress Helena, mother of Constantine, discovered the True Cross on Golgotha. There were also the Crown of Thorns, the stone across the Tomb, the Holy Lance, and the sacred swaddling clothes, which ended up in Constantinople, the new capital of the empire. Old Testament relics, like "Moses's rod," also had a precise role in the rituals of the religious calendar's major festivals. The emperor was a new Moses, the heir to the kings of Israel, but he also acknowledged the authority of the "cross of Constantine." Gilbert Dagron's work on official ceremonials, minutely described with all their "sites of memory," has revealed the workings of this priestly monarchy.[9]

Saint Louis managed to appropriate some of these elements for the benefit of the French monarchy, in particular the Crown of Thorns in 1239, which he placed in the treasury of the Sainte-Chapelle.[10] Such emblems legitimating divine right had first been the signs by means of which the new "nation" of Christians could be recognized. Hence the rule that any altar used for worship had first to be consecrated, and often also authenticated by a relic. The cult of the relics of martyrs and saints prospered throughout the

Middle Ages. People came to see and touch them, and remain in silent prayer before them. As spiritual treasures but also sources of material wealth, these semiophores were stolen and traded, and gave rise to pilgrimages and donations. Bodily relics belonged both to this world and the next: on the day of the Last Judgment the saints would surely claim them back.[11] While relics were traces of the past, testifying to the sanctity of their owners, they were equally signs fully existing in the present. They were incorporated into the rituals of the Church, where they were constantly reactualized, and where their role of intercession made them into ever-contemporary "objects," functioning as particularly potent *imagines agentes* or sites of memory.

BEYOND THE CHRISTIAN WORLD, IT IS JAPAN THAT HAS MOST often attracted Western attention. The fact that almost immediately after the Meiji Restoration of 1868 legislation was passed protecting ancient artistic and architectural works makes it easier to establish comparisons with the European conception of heritage than in the case of other countries.[12] A first Heritage List was commissioned in 1871, followed in 1897 by a law on the preservation of ancient sanctuaries and temples, in which the notion of "national treasure" figured. The word "treasure" implied that the object's value derived from something intangible (its divine origin, for example).[13] At the time, religious (Shintoist) heritage was the primary focus. Then, in 1919, a law was passed on the preservation of historic and scenic sites, as well as natural monuments. Lastly, in 1950, a law on the protection of cultural goods included the category of "intangible cultural heritage" for the first time. We shall examine only two characteristics of this body of legislation and the heritage-related practices it codified.

The legislation provided for the periodic reconstruction of certain religious buildings. The fact that they were made of wood does not fully explain this provision, since the calendar for the works was fixed in advance, and involved exactly the same reconstruction every time. Such was the case in particular for the great Jingu Shrine in Ise: every twenty years the temple of the goddess Amaterasu, the mythic ancestor of the imperial dynasty, was to be rebuilt in Japanese cypress wood in exactly the same way. This ritual was established in the seventh century and has continued, naturally with some interruptions, until today (the next reconstruction was due in 2013). What counted most was that the form of the building should remain unchanged. Consequently, the Western dilemma of "preservation or restoration" was from the outset irrelevant.[14] A Japanese person visiting Paris will be struck (or more precisely would previously have been struck) by the effort expended on protecting objects and historic monuments from the marks of time.[15] The first concern of Japanese cultural policy was clearly neither how the objects looked, nor preserving the way they looked. There was another logic at work, a logic of actualization.

The label of "living national treasure," as defined in the law of 1950, can help us understand this logic. It is conferred on an artist or craftsperson not as an individual author but insofar as he "is the bearer of important intangible cultural heritage." Anyone, whether an individual or a group, who receives this title is obliged to transmit their knowledge, and receives an allowance for this. What this striking arrangement makes clear is that the object and its conservation count less than keeping alive a skill that is actualized in its transmission. Just like the wooden temples, the traditional arts are significant only insofar as they exist for and in the present. It follows that the notions that were pivotal in defining the concept of heritage in the West—the notions of original, of copy, of authenticity, and so forth—are not applicable in Japan, or at least are not invested with the same values. The past is not unimportant, but the order of time differs from that of Europe. Time is not essentially linear, and so a different representation of permanence and a different relation to the trace are operative. The above is simply a hasty sketch, the bare outline of a view from afar, but it is enough to defamiliarize the seemingly self-evident European conception of heritage. We can now return to a few moments in its long history, beginning when time was neither an actor nor a process, and when the model of *historia magistra* was unchallenged.

Antiquity

In order to situate the place of heritage in antiquity, or rather to repatriate it, could we not simply remind ourselves that "heritage" or "patrimony" derives from the Latin *patrimonium*, and that the Romans were great admirers of (above all, Greek) antiquities?[16] Monuments, statues, and paintings were restored in the Greek city-states, in Rome, and throughout Italy; collections and famous collectors existed, such as the Attalids of Pergamon, Atticus, or the notoriously corrupt Verres in Rome; and a whole imperial legislation existed for the protection of urban centers.[17] One could also mention the Library of Alexandria, even if its goals were less heritage-related than encyclopaedic, since it aspired to acquire all Greek and Barbarian books with a view to producing knowledge about knowledge, to knowing better and more.[18] But what was nonetheless lacking was the category of the *historic monument*, which presupposes that a certain gap has opened up: a moment comes when a monument can be regarded as something other than what it was or had been for a long time. It becomes visible again, but differently, as a semiophore bearing, precisely, "artistic and historical values."

We associate the Renaissance with this moment of renewed visibility: "The birth of the historic monument can be located in Rome around the year 1420."[19] A change in the order of time was required, namely a double movement in which the distance between present and past at once increased and was collapsed. The past is over, but it is still there as a resource or a model. This sort of relation to time was unknown in antiquity. It is perhaps what made Roland Mortier, the author of a pioneering study on the poetics of ruins, write that "the ruin—which was curiously non-existent for the Greeks—interested the Romans only as the material image of Destiny: it is not a presence but an *absence*, a *void*, the sign of a vanished greatness, the negative mark of greatness which has been destroyed."[20] This claim is no doubt true from the point of view of a historical psychology, but it is also true that ruins were present both in the landscapes and even in the minds of Greeks and Romans.

I shall take but one example, that of Pausanias, the author of the *Description of Greece*. Here we have a classical author who would seem to come extremely close to an awareness of something like cultural heritage, someone who, in the second century A.D., decided to visit Greek sites of memory. He was frequently portrayed in the modern period as an antiquarian busy writing the first Baedeker or Blue Guide to Greece. True, his book is a trip through the key sites of Greek history and memory. At one point he even chastises present-day Greeks for their instant admiration of the treasures of other nations, while they remain blind to the marvels of their own. People are always praising the Egyptian pyramids, he says, but no one makes even the briefest mention of the Treasury of Minyas or the ramparts of Tiryns, which are no less magnificent.[21] In selectively evoking certain sites, Pausanias behaves as though he were tracking down a long-lost and long-forgotten Greek identity. But he is, rather, constituting it in the very movement of his journey. As he states, "my narrative must not loiter, as my task is a general description of all Greece."[22] This was Pausanias's way of returning to Herodotus's original project, but at a time when there were no more *erga* (great feats) to be preserved from oblivion, and when all that remained were, precisely, ruins of former times. Rome had been in power for well over three centuries by then.

But one should not imagine Pausanias, a Greek from Asia Minor, as a distant precursor of Prosper Mérimée, a kind of Inspector of Historic Monuments on his rounds.[23] His ten books—starting in Athens and ending in Delphi—have nothing to do with compiling inventories, listing buildings, or, even less, recommending measures for conservation. The Treasury of Minyas and the city of Tiryns, for instance, had lain in ruins for many a long year, and had it not been for Pausanias's knowledge and his way with words, they would have been nothing other than what they were then, namely a few collapsed walls. He often chose to describe elements as still standing that no visitor could have seen intact even decades previously. Moreover, he felt under no obligation to describe everything a traveler would be able to see, since he deliberately ignored anything later than 150 B.C., treating the Hellenistic period as more or less nonexistent. All in all, his work contains more things *known* through written or oral sources than actually *seen*. As for restoring Greek temples, or recommending their restoration, the issue quite simply never arises.[24] All one needs is his book.

One of the key figures referred to for the theorization of monuments and cultural heritage, who was rediscovered in the early 1980s, could usefully be cited at this point. In 1903, as chair of Vienna's Commission on Historic Monuments, Alois Riegl had been asked to draft a new law on their conservation, and suggested that they be listed according to their "commemorative value." His starting point was therefore neither classical antiquity nor the Renaissance, but well and truly the present, and what he called the "modern cult of monuments." Riegl's analysis of this "cult" and his attempt to accommodate it led him to divide monuments into three categories, according to their different "commemorative values." First came "intentional" monuments, erected in antiquity and during the Middle Ages. Then with the

Renaissance came the "historic" monument, which we mentioned above: "People began to appreciate the monuments of antiquity anew... because of an increasing appreciation of their artistic and historical values." Lastly, whereas the nineteenth century focused exclusively on the monument's historical value, "the twentieth century appears to be [the century] of age-value." This last category, of monuments with age-value, "embraces every artefact without regard to its original significance and purpose, as long as it reveals the passage of a considerable period of time."[25] Ancient and modern are thus linked, with historical value accompanying modernity and even required by it.

Bearing in mind these points, which themselves have a history, I shall now return to the Greek and Roman worlds. Of course in antiquity practices such as preservation, restoration, and collecting were not unknown, but the question is what meaning could they have in the absence of the artistic and historical monument (in Riegl's sense). I shall go a little further with this question, using an example involving Augustus. In his *Res Gestae*, a short work written to his greater glory and destined for posterity, he wrote in the first person *feci*, "I completed," "I built" (followed by a list of temples and monuments) and, immediately afterward, *refeci*, "I rebuilt, restored, reconstructed" (followed by a list of 82 temples for Rome alone). The same *refeci* was also used to mean "repair," for example, the Via Flaminia and a number of bridges.[26] As for *feci*, although one might assume that it referred to new buildings, this was not necessarily the case. Thus the temple of Feretrian Jupiter, supposedly "built" by Augustus on the Capitol, is in fact one of the oldest buildings, traditionally dated as originating with Romulus. So Augustus must have been referring to a restoration.[27] As regards shows of power and the benefits anticipated, there seems to be little difference between the two activities, with *refeci* being as important as *feci*, and maybe even more so for an emperor who wished to be regarded as one who has re-founded Rome as its *restitutor*.

Similarly, Suetonius reports that Vespasian undertook the *restitutio* of the Capitol, which had been destroyed in a fire. In other words, he rebuilt it. At the same time he had three thousand bronze tablets, which had melted in the fire, "restituted" (they were in fact archives).[28] But how could they be restituted if they had been destroyed? Obviously, by using copies stored elsewhere. Hence *restitutio* did not mean restituting, but actually re-making, producing anew, based on a copy from somewhere else. Restoring, restituting, reconstructing, or making afresh—all these operations were covered by the term *restitutio*. In the Renaissance, the humanists saw themselves as agents of the *restitutio*, in all senses, of Rome's splendor.

Restoring a monument thus meant that an authoritative instance reestablished it as an "intentional" monument by adopting and reaffirming the monument's original intention. In so doing, the power in question also confirmed its own legitimacy, and made the return to law and order visible. In the case of Rome, restoration meant a solemn reaffirmation of the eternity of the *Urbs* and of the ongoing contract between it and its gods. Restoration, in this sense, is integral to any intentional monument. The logics of the *novus ordo saeclorum* and of refoundation were championed during Augustus's reign, since he styled himself as the *restitutor* (restorer) of tradition in all fields, including the urban environment.[29]

Since antiquity was a time of "inertia and not creative development," as Paul Veyne put it (with a nod to Bergson),[30] building meant building for today, but also and equally, for eternity. Nowadays, by contrast, one tends to build for today, and today alone, with the result that buildings are anything but durable, even if we pretend to be surprised by this. In thirty years, according to a historian of architecture, "they will no longer exist.... We will not even be able to afford to maintain them in their original state, because they will have to be constantly rebuilt."[31] Will they be rebuilt as they were originally, or given a supplementary "facelift," as one sometimes says? One way of introducing something new is to play, precisely, on the paradox of the durable and the ephemeral, by transforming a monument into an event. This is Christo's strategy in wrapping up buildings. When "wrapped," the monument's everyday invisibility and its drab patina of historical time fall away, showing it to be strikingly contemporary and endowing it, temporarily, with a new visibility.

As for preserving the external aspect of buildings and cities, let us attempt to define or date the moment when it became important. A first-century imperial *senatus consultum* aiming to preserve urban centers has come down to us, but according to specialists, its goal was above all to prevent and control speculation.[32] Yan Thomas has devoted a remarkable study to the legal dimension of urban ornamentation, in which he shows that the *ornatus* (marble decorative elements, columns, etc.) in their totality were considered to be attached not to particular monuments but to the Town, and that as such they were under the jurisdiction of the ruler.[33] One can find, from the first to the fourth century, a whole panoply of legislation concerning the aspect, form, and appearance of buildings, and reading between the lines, the spectacle of towns threatened with being dismembered, demolished, and reduced to ruins. However, what seems to me most important here is that "such damage was criticized not so much because of its ugliness but because it betrayed the indifference of the powers that be, the disasters brought about by civil war and the incapacity to ensure an eternity of time: neglecting buildings or allowing them to get defaced signalled the triumph of a dilapidation (*vetustas*) which was directly contrary to the supposed eternity of Rome, Italy and the Empire."[34] As a general rule "re-using *spolia*, breathing new life into the marble ornaments, was an attribute of the ruler's majesty."

Thus "the Eastern Emperors continued to exercise their jurisdiction over Roman marble ornaments for a time, even though Rome was governed by its bishop." Then the movement reversed, from centrifugal to centripetal, and it was no longer a case of spoils pouring into Rome to constitute "a bodily universality," but quite the contrary, everything "wrested from Rome would end up constituting the Roman substance of the Christian world."[35] For instance, Charlemagne had the mosaics and ornaments of the imperial palaces of Ravenna and Rome transported to Aachen, with the pope's consent.

In fifth-century Italy under the Ostrogoths, Cassiodorus, a Roman senator, describes how Theodoric, the king of the Ostrogoths, was worried about the upkeep of his palace, whose beauty was threatened by "the approach of old age." So he decreed that the "ancient monuments" be returned to their "originary splendor," while having "new ones built on the model of the old."[36] But apart from that, his administration continued to oversee the reuse of blocks of marble, columns, and other precious materials.[37] In 608, Pope Boniface IV authorized the reuse of the materials from pagan temples (having himself been authorized to do so by the Byzantine emperor Phocas), and in particular the Pantheon, which was converted into a church dedicated to the Virgin Mary. The logic of spoils was thus still largely operative. Reuse of materials was above all the sign of the spectacular triumph of the new religion.

Returning to Rome once more, Trajan's Column is a striking example of the changes taking place. How was the column regarded by the Romans? An edict of 1162 provides for its protection on the grounds that "We wish for it to remain intact as long as the world endures." Even if Rome was no longer assured of eternity, it would still like to last as long as the world! Since the column could no longer figure as the intentional monument of a triumphant Rome, it came to be identified with something else: Rome's emblem and a patriotic symbol. It thus came to represent Rome in the present, but the requisite detachment was still lacking for it to be considered a historic monument. The above examples suggest the composite and transitional role of the monument, on which different systems of understanding temporarily converged. The intentional monument no longer quite fitted, but the historic monument was not yet an available category either.

In France, the first conservation order has always been attributed to Francis I, who, on a visit to Nîmes in 1533, decreed that the buildings adjoining, and masking, the Maison Carrée should be knocked down. However, the order was never carried out.[38] Besides, the very same Francis I did not hesitate to have "the great tower of the Louvre," that is, the fortified keep erected by Philip Augustus (its foundations have now been laid bare within the Grand Louvre complex), razed to the ground. As late as 1788, Louis XVI, without batting an eyelid, signed an edict decreeing the demolition or sale of a whole series of châteaux: the château of la Muette and of Madrid in the Bois de Boulogne, and those at Vincennes and Blois. Crown assets might well be inalienable in theory, but economic necessity had reasons of its own. The first two were demolished, and the Revolution saved the two others.[39]

It was in 1790 that the expression "historic monument" [*monument historique*], coined by Louis Aubin Millin, was used to refer to a building for the first time.[40] "Only in 1790?!," you might reasonably exclaim. Are we to infer that prior to this date France had no historic monuments, or at least none perceived as such? Maybe that would be a slight exaggeration, but let us add a significant detail here: the very first historic monument described by Millin was the Bastille, which was being dismantled at the time—so, at once a historic monument and earmarked for demolition. The purpose of Millin's inventory was precisely to record those buildings and objects that had suddenly become "property of the nation," and whose status and visibility had been radically transformed by this. Through his work, these objects were changed into semiophores of a completely new sort.

Rome

I shall now return once more to Rome and move, via Cicero's praise of the scholar Varro, from the *Urbs* of the end of the Roman Republic to Quattrocento Rome, before paying a rapid visit on the Rome Winckelmann so yearned to see.

Cicero painted an unforgettable picture of Varro, the patron saint of antiquaries, whose vast body of work, most of which has not survived, included forty-three volumes of *Antiquities*:

> When we were sojourning and wandering like foreigners in our own city, your books, I may say, escorted us home, and enabled us at length to perceive who we were and where we lived. You have revealed to us [*aperuisti*] the age of our fatherland, its chronology, the laws of its religion and priesthoods, the plan of our home and foreign administration, the position of our territories and districts, the titles and descriptions of all things divine and human, with the duties and principles attaching to them, and you have shed a vast amount of light on our poets and on Latin literature in general and on the Latin vocabulary.[41]

The scholar of antiquities is one who opens people's eyes to what they could not see before, and helps them understand the meaning of gestures made and words spoken without understanding why. Although he probes the past and reminds people of it (*commemorat*), he also contributes knowledge that is useful for living in Rome today. With the Republic in crisis and its *aeternitas* under threat, there is no question of proposing a nostalgic itinerary through the forgotten or destroyed Rome of yesteryear. The crisis of the present makes the present forgetful, and that is what must urgently be remedied.

Moving on to Renaissance Rome, my question will be how the relation between past and present was envisioned at a time when monuments and sites were acquiring a new commemorative value (on which Riegl was to base his classification). What would be the status of all those monuments in ruins, and all those texts so passionately pored over and edited?[42] Was this *historia magistra*'s triumphal moment, in the form of the reactivation of classical models? And if so, was this vision and use of *historia magistra* simply backward-looking?

I shall begin with a letter from Petrarch written in the spring of 1337. He had already recounted the emotion he had felt on first entering Rome (which was larger than he had imagined). Then, in this long letter to his correspondent, the Dominican friar Giovanni Colonna, he undertook a lengthy description of classical Rome on the pretext of recalling their walks in the city together, and inserted it into a meditation comparing pagan and Christian wisdom. The itinerary started with Evander's palace and went all the way through the history of Rome, including the grotto in which Constantine the Great was supposedly cured of leprosy, and the place where Peter was crucified and Paul decapitated. It would have been fitting material for a *De viris illustribus* or a dramatized tale from the Early Church.[43]

Like Varro, Petrarch wanted to show the Romans their own city, since they had become blind to it. But in actual fact the letter was written not *in situ*, but later, in his study (despite the words "on my journey" that figured in it). His descriptions were inspired by other works, "principally ... Livy, Florus, Suetonius, the *Scriptores Historiae Augustae* and Pliny the Ancient."[44] The stroll through history is above all a stroll through texts. As regards the experience of time, Petrarch makes a distinction, which has since become famous, between two times: "Our conversation was concerned largely with history [*historiis*], I being more expert, it seemed, in the ancient [*in antiquis*], by which we meant the time before the Roman rulers celebrated and venerated the name of Christ, and you in recent times [*in novis*], by which we meant the time from then to the present."[45] So the "new" history, which had started with Constantine, was still in force.

Moreover, Petrarch's list of famous names, proper names, and place-names does not lead to some meditation on ruins, but rather to a direct moral condemnation of the present. Petrarch insists on the dire ignorance of the Romans of his time: "I do not deplore only the ignorance involved (although what is worse than ignorance?) but the disappearance and exile of many virtues. For who can doubt that Rome would rise again instantly if she began to know herself?"[46] This marks the first appearance of what would become a major theme for the humanists, namely the *renovatio* (renewal) of Rome. *Knowing* Rome would already be *reinstating* it, renewing its *imperium*, and confounding the false doctrine of transfer of political and cultural power (*translatio imperii et studii*) to outside of Italy. This theme also precipitates the first exchanges between philology and reality, words and things: recovering the purity of Latin would be (like) restoring Rome.

A century later, Lorenzo Valla would champion through his textual scholarship the identification of Latin with Rome. For him, language was the real: "Rome as empire has disappeared but Rome as Latin lives on."[47] Hence restoring Latin to its former excellence was the same thing as *refounding* Rome. That is the ultimate meaning of *renovatio* for Valla. Livy in particular embodies the splendor of the empire: he *is* Rome. Restituting Livy's text is therefore, Valla states, an act of *restitutio in patriam*, "a restitution of (in view of) the fatherland" and a refusal of the doctrine of the transfer of political and cultural power.[48] Valla's struggle was for Rome to exist again in Rome. More specifically, he called for a new Camillus, who would come and save the nation and drive out the Gallic—French—oppressors. Philology, polemics, politics, and concern for the present were all tightly interwoven.

In 1448, and still in Rome, Poggio Bracciolini published *On the Inconstancy of Fortune*, which contained a long description of the ruins of Rome. A colorful and many-sided figure, who occupied important positions in the Roman Curia, serving several popes, Poggio became an epigraphist, in Rome, a manuscript-hunter, and a translator. He also produced meticulous critical editions. At around the same time, Flavio Biondo, Cyriacus of Ancona, Leon Battista Alberti, and Lorenzo Valla also spent time in Rome, which had attracted a whole scholarly community. Petrarch's words deploring Romans' ignorance of Rome were no longer applicable, nor was a predominantly text-based description of the Eternal City. Poggio's portrayal is still today qualified by modern archaeologists as "decisive for the birth of scientific archaeology."[49] Yet what is the real status of the ruins detailed by Poggio? What relation to time do they imply?

Poggio's treatise is in the form of a dialogue in two parts. The description of ruins is followed by a meditation on fortune, which is based on several classical authors. Poggio and his friend Antonio Loschi first view the city from the top of the Capitoline Hill, from which it resembles an "immense cadaver laid out rotting and eaten away all over." The corpse's remains are then identified. After reminding the reader of all his work salvaging inscriptions and identifying buildings, Poggio inserts a long list of monuments into the text. His descriptions are quite different from Petrarch's abstract and historical digest; we are genuinely accompanying Poggio as he walks through the city and punctuates his progress with an "I saw," "I read [on an inscription]," "I noted."

But the treatise does not stop there. It is more than a simple description, since the visit only takes on meaning in relation to the central theme, that of the inconstancy of fortune. The grandeur and decay of ruins precisely testify to fortune's injustice. But there is no place for pure lamentation: ruins figure both in their own right (monuments to be identified as precisely as possible) and as an imposing illustration of a theme whose relevance is not confined to the past.

In further illustration of this, the dialogue ends on a carefully prepared inversion. Contemporary vicissitudes of fortune are no less significant and influential than they were in the past, Poggio maintains. Now as then, what is lacking are the writers capable of rendering these. However, the situation could change: "I am not one to forget the present for the sake of remembering the past," Poggio announces forcefully. "I am not so attached to antiquity, so wholly attentive to her and her alone that I would despise men of our time and consider that nothing comparable with what was achieved in former times is achieved today, or would allow the historian's talent to shine."[50] We have seen therefore that from one description of Rome to another, and from one century to the next, there are clear differences. But what comes across equally strongly is the constant focus on the present.

Flavio Biondo, who was in Rome at the same time as Poggio, wrote his lengthy descriptions of Rome's monuments there, for which Varro's *Antiquities* were the core reference and model. He conceived his three-volume *Roma instaurata* [*Rome Restored*], published in 1447, as a contribution to Eugene IV's great project of *renovatio*. He also defended the Rome of his day, considering its fame and majesty to be linked to the papacy. His focus on the topography of ancient Rome and the names of its monuments, and his detailed presentation of Rome as a great *model*, were designed to complement the concrete restoration work undertaken by the pope. So in presenting this "mirror" of ancient Rome, he was also working for the benefit of the present.[51] Likewise Leon Battista Alberti, who perfected a new method of mapping monuments, using polar coordinates and a set scale, for the restoration work planned by Pope Nicholas V. Alberti's *Descriptio urbis Romae* also contained a message for contemporary architects. In it he declared that he treated Rome's monuments first as "a lesson in construction, then as an introduction to the question of beauty ... where the architects of the Quattrocento may come and learn from the example set by these remains."[52]

In summary, can one infer from the above that the "artistic and historical" value of monuments only really emerged when principles of conservation were introduced by papal brief? That is, when Paul III took the first preventive measures, in 1534? But we have already seen, through Yan Thomas, that Roman emperors were far from indifferent to the *ornatus*; and here the papacy, as in other matters, simply followed suit. Of course the declared concern for conservation was not enough to prevent pillage, nor even the reuse of materials; the sheer number of papal briefs is an indication of this. Antiquities were resources for Rome, in all senses of the term: it lived off them and on them. Even Pope Nicholas V, who saw himself as the restorer of the Eternal City, did not hesitate to treat the Forum, the Coliseum, and the Circus Maximus as travertine quarries. Similarly, Pius II published a bull against these practices while at the same time cannibalizing the Villa Hadriana for the construction of his own palaces. It is not insignificant in this light that the director of antiquities at the Vatican bore the title, granted by papal bull in 1573, of "Commissioner of Treasures and other Antiquities, and of Mines." By putting treasures, antiquities, and quarrying on the same level, "the papal administration revealed ... that the control of antiquities was an instrument of power."[53]

The interest in preservation coincided with the establishment of the first museums. In around 1470, Pope Sixtus IV offered "the Roman people" a collection of antique bronzes, to be exhibited on the Capitol. Shortly afterward, his nephew Pope Julius II created a rival museum, in the Vatican, the Villa Belvedere collection.[54] A century later, it would be the turn of the Uffizi Gallery in Florence, housing both ancient and modern works.[55] The juxtaposition of the two is clearly significant. Although the past and the present were not yet separated, a new regime of visibility for such objects had been introduced.

In 1515, Raphael was commissioned by Pope Leon X to make a comprehensive map of Rome. Adopting Poggio's image of Rome as a corpse, he described how he "sees with immense sorrow as it were the corpse of this noble fatherland thus horribly lacerated, when once it had reigned in majesty over the entire world." Despite this vision, he made a clear distinction, as director of Roman antiquities, between buildings that were "old and very old, until the Sack of Rome," and those built subsequently by "Goths and other Barbarians": the former were to be preserved, the latter not. So there was some awareness of a break, a before (of value), and an after (valueless). But preserving the old did not mean one should not tamper with it. One could preserve the memory of something by noting down the inscriptions on it, but one could equally remove the travertine facing from the Coliseum and the Baths of Diocletian in order to use it for the newly designed St. Peter's Basilica, itself built over the ruins of the Old Saint Peter's Basilica erected by Constantine the Great.[56]

I shall now turn to our last Renaissance visitor to Rome, Michel de Montaigne. He was in Rome for a few months between November 1580 and April 1581, departing with the title of "Roman citizen." The *Essays* leave the reader in no doubt as to the strength of his attachment to the city and his long-standing familiarity with the Romans of former times, as he himself states: "I knew the Capitol and its plan before I knew the Louvre, and the Tiber before I knew the Seine."[57] Also, seeing the very places "which we know to have been frequented and inhabited by persons whose memories are recommended in story, moves us in some sort more than to hear a recital of their acts or to read their writings."[58] Montaigne was sensitive to the commemorative value of sites, but he also immediately made the link to the present: it would be ungrateful, he remarked, to despise "the relics and images of so many worthy and valiant men as I have seen live and die, and who, by their example, give us so many good instructions, knew we how to follow them." Through the mediation of the example to be imitated, the "relic" could become meaningful in and for the present. Montaigne thus reactivated and adopted the Ciceronian model of *historia magistra*.

The image we have of Montaigne through his *Travel Diary* is that of an insatiable tourist, rapidly becoming more knowledgeable than his guide, as his secretary admiringly noted: "in a few days he could easily have reguided his guide." However, from isolated remarks, one might get the impression that Montaigne was not at all interested in ruins: "one saw nothing of Rome but the sky under which it had been grounded and the outline of its form; . . . those who said that one saw at least the ruins of Rome affirmed too much, for the ruins of so awe-inspiring a machine would bring more honour and reverence for its memory: it was no more than a sepulchre."[59] In fact quite the opposite is true. Montaigne refers to the *tomb* and not even the *ruins* of Rome, since the world, "hostile to her long domination," had fallen upon this body and, after breaking it to pieces, "buried her very ruins." What was still visible was thus nothing compared to what was buried. To consider Rome as a tomb was in fact a way of paying homage to its past grandeur, and presenting a variation on the theme of the injustice of fortune that Poggio had expounded earlier.

Thus from Petrarch to Montaigne the ruins of Rome took on increasing significance. However, although their grandeur endured, they were increasingly ruins. They were still legible for Petrarch through Virgil and Livy, but by Montaigne's time they were nothing but a tomb. On the one hand, these ruins appeared more distant and less enchanting; erudite procedures such as epigraphy were needed to bring them back to life. On the other hand, like the past of antiquity in general, they remained closely bound up with the present. That is where the *exemplum* played a powerful role, since humanism was constellated around the paradox of a "hopeful expectation turned toward the past," in Alphonse Dupront's striking formulation, or equally "the vision of a new world rebuilt upon an ancient word," in Francisco Rico's terms.[60] The Renaissance broke new ground, but it "needed an example, and it could be none other ... than the entire reality known through texts of the ancient world in all its radiant splendor and self-sufficiency, prior to the birth of Christianity."[61] The Renaissance's audacity consisted in choosing this particular past. Hence the "order of reverence," which was also an order of time. Antiquity was no more, *and yet* its example was authoritative.

So the movement went once again from the past to the present, in accordance with the logic of *historia magistra*. But at the same time, the declared break in continuity that gave rise to the Middle Ages made the classical past into an "available" present, immediately accessible. Or, to put it differently, it was "a kind of eternal within easy reach." This was the real meaning of *renovatio*, the watchword and rallying cry of the humanists: at once to recall and to begin afresh. The philosophy of "returning" of course implied a philosophy of time, but one should add, with Dupront again, that it expressed "a certainty about time, a plenitude of the present." The Renaissance humanists "did not get as far as a modern philosophy of progress, which requires time to be ongoing; time stopped with them.... This feeling of a time which they alone occupied expressed their positive dependence, since it was through this very plenitude that the succession could be achieved."[62] Christian time, in which the present inaugurated by Christ would open onto eternity on the day of the Last Judgment, defined the limits of their world.

WHEN JOHANN JOACHIM WINCKELMANN LEFT DRESDEN and set foot in Rome for the first time, in 1755, both his approach and what he perceived were totally different from Montaigne's experiences. No ruins, no corpse, but rather statues. For Winckelmann, who was going to blaze the trail to the Greeks for the Germans, Rome meant antiquity itself, that is, the place in which Beauty resided. In order to come closer to it, he had decided to forsake Lutheranism and convert to Catholicism. For him, the journey to Rome represented the promise of a new birth: a rebirth. Thirty years later, Goethe would be equally moved on seeing Rome for the first time, and would likewise experience a kind of rebirth. On his arrival on 29 October 1786 he lodged at the Bear Inn, as had Montaigne before him, and on 3 December he obtained the new Italian edition of Winckelmann's *History of Art*, noting that "the history of the whole world attaches itself to this spot, and I reckon a new birthday—a true new birth from the day that I entered Rome."[63]

There is a paradox here, however. Rome is the place of Art and yet art is not Roman but Greek. The Romans simply copied the Greeks.[64] So why Rome and not Athens, which Winckelmann in the end never visited, despite often planning to do so? It was to Rome that Winckelmann was again heading, unable to tear himself away, when he was assassinated in Trieste. The reason was that Athens was an ideal, and not, or no longer, a *place* one could really reach. By contrast, John the Evangelist's injunction "Come and see" could be applied to Rome, and Winckelmann used the expression on several occasions to encourage his correspondents to come and look for themselves.[65] But at the same time the experience of Rome fell short of total plenitude. It was also shot through with absence, since what the person who had learned to look saw was the trace of what was no longer visible. In such circumstances, learning to see meant choosing to develop a historical eye, in order to accommodate the loss. This was Winckelmann's startling conclusion to his *History of Art in Antiquity*: "we ... have as it were only a shadowy outline of the subject of our desires remaining; but this arouses so much the greater longing for what is lost, and we examine the copies we have with greater attention than we would if we were in full possession of the originals."[66] Hence every birth, even a new birth, is also a separation and an awareness of a distance that thereafter remains unbridgeable. This break is at once recognized and denied, or rather, it can produce aesthetic enjoyment, and also a history of art. It signaled that times had changed: Winckelmann is much closer here to Chateaubriand than to Poggio.

The French Revolution

After this brief excursion to Rome, as at once the real and the symbolic place in which Europe's notion of cultural heritage was largely fashioned, I shall examine the notion of heritage as it emerged during that profound crisis in the order of time constituted by the French Revolution.

The Letters to Miranda and Canova on the Abduction of Antiquities from Rome and Athens, or *Letters to Miranda* (called after their addressee, General Miranda) were published in 1796. Their author was a certain Antoine-Chrysostome Quatremère de Quincy, who was already quite well known at the time. He was born into the Parisian bourgeoisie, and spent many years in Italy.[67] On returning to France he compiled a *Dictionary of Architecture*. In 1791, he was commissioned by the National Assembly to oversee the transformation of the St. Genevieve Church into a temple devoted to the memory of great men. In his treatise *Considerations on the Arts of Design*, also published in 1791, he drew on Winckelmann in lauding the "just proportion" of the Greeks, who had taken "nature as a model."[68] He sat in the Legislative Assembly, on the right, and was arrested and then liberated in the wake of 9 Thermidor. Found guilty of "inciting armed insurrection" against the Convention during the 13 Vendémiaire, Year 4, he went into hiding in Paris between October 1795 and July 1796.

In his letters, Quatremère de Quincy criticized the seizure of works of art by the "Great Nation," in the form of the French Army of Italy acting on the instructions of the Directoire. "The arts and sciences have long formed a Republic in Europe," he wrote, and so it was as a "member of this Republic," whose ideals the Enlightenment had promulgated, that he was taking the floor. Anyone seeking to appropriate these "common goods," he claimed, would be committing a crime against learning and reason, and against the betterment of humanity.[69] So Quatremère de Quincy was protesting in the name of the Republic of Letters and the Enlightenment. He also summoned Cicero to his cause, citing the latter's criticism of moving Greek works of art, since "these things [statutes] lose their value in Rome," because in order to appreciate them one requires "the peace and philosophical serenity of Greece";[70] he appealed to the authority of Winckelmann, whom he read and admired, as the first to "bring the genuine spirit of observation to the study of antiquity. He was the first who thought to analyze antiquity and specify the periods, ... and discover[ed] a method."[71] It was as an art historian who had found a "method" for "analyzing times" that Winckelmann impressed Quatremère. Without Rome, Quatremère argued, Winckelmann's project would have been inconceivable, and now no one would be able to pursue it. Unsurprisingly, Quatremère praised Pope Nicholas V for being the first power to have had "the idea of reestablishing ancient Rome down to the very last edifice." This was an interpretation of *restitutio* or *renovatio* as the restoration of ancient monuments for their own sake alone.

Quatremère's *Letters* are not just one more lamentation on the dismemberment of the corpse of Rome. On the contrary, he is concerned with the future of art, and takes the future into account in his arguments. He is convinced that the arts in Europe will soon take on a "new aspect,"[72] due to the way in which the ancient world is currently coming to light through the enthusiastic efforts that he himself is following closely. That is precisely why Rome must remain what it has always been, namely the only "home" of antiquity. The doctrine of imitation again takes pride of place: what, after all, are the antiquities of Rome if not a "great book" whose pages have been destroyed and dispersed by time? Or, in another image, the Eternal City is a "museum" which is "immovable ... in its entirety." Moreover, the country itself, with its light and landscapes, is also part of this museum. A certain Pirro Logorio, an antiquarian and architect in the service of the cardinal of Este in the mid-fifteenth century, declared, as self-appointed historian of Italy's "population of statues," that were they to be uprooted from their original scenery and context they would "as it were die a second death."[73]

So artists would always have to undertake the journey to Rome if they wanted to "learn to see." Consequently, the institution of the museum, as conceived by the Revolution in the name of reason and with a view to instruction, could not but be roundly condemned, in the name of the role of place in preserving memory, and in the name of a certain idea of heritage. The Museum of French Monuments would soon be the target of this essential hostility toward the museum and the gesture of museification. But for the time being, the issue was Rome and Italy. We must, says Quatremère, maintain the unity of this scholarly collection, this museum which is Rome and indeed the whole of Italy, in the face of those who seek to dismantle it and bring it to Paris: "Rome has become for us what Greece once was for Rome."[74] While the doctrine of the "final home" for humanity's artistic masterpieces was being elaborated in Paris, Quatremère was defending a localized and rooted conception of heritage, according to which transplanting meant mutilating. Any attempt to dismantle artifacts was "an attack on science and a crime against public instruction [*un crime de lèse-instruction publique*]."[75] Genuine instruction involved and must involve making a detour via Rome. The stakes were nothing less than artistic progress itself. Two centuries later, Marinetti would want nothing more than to "get rid of the innumerable museums which cover it [Italy] with innumerable cemeteries."

QUATREMÈRE WAS ACTUALLY IN HIDING IN PARIS WHEN HE WROTE his *Letters*, although he took up the cause of Rome as though from Rome itself. After 1789, Paris styled itself as a "new Athens," in the name of and by virtue of the freedom it represented, and as an effect of the regeneration—that great revolutionary rallying cry—that would give rise to the new man. Jansen, Winckelmann's translator, declared that "under freedom's dominion the arts have flourished. The august assembly of our representatives need only express the wish and the self-same marvels which illustrated the most magnificent times of Ancient Greece will be produced amongst us."[76] Without discussing the whole topic of the arts in Paris between 1789 and 1796, as Edouard Pommier has done, I shall simply highlight the way in which the slogan of the early period of the Revolution, to the effect that "the marks of despotism must be effaced," gave way in only a few years to its polar opposite, "a legacy to be preserved and transmitted." This move went together with another shift, which led from Greece and Rome to the "National

Antiquities," from the ancient world to the Middle Ages and "from iconoclasm to cultural heritage."[77]

In terms of the major categories of thought and action mobilized, this shift corresponds to a move from intense politicization to growing concerns with time. A good example of this transition can be found in the decree of 14 August 1792. Its preamble insists that "monuments raised to ostentation, prejudice and tyranny should no longer continue to offend the eyes of the French people." Here again we have the theme of a people "offended by the sight" of the emblems of despotism. But not all the articles of the decree stipulate the removal or destruction of these emblems, and some paradoxically recommend preservation and conservation. In the following months, and particularly in the policies of the interior minister, Roland, a conservationist discourse began to emerge, to the greater glory of France, and with educational ends. The obvious instrument for the implementation of this policy was the museum. For Roland, the Louvre was to become a "National Monument" whence, as in Greece, the arts could shine forth.

A new argument emerged during these months of lively and conflictual debate. It tended to associate the Revolution with cultural heritage or even to treat national heritage as an emanation of the Revolution. The arts, the sciences, and philosophy were the Revolution's creditors; the Revolution should now make good and repay them for preparing the ground for its emergence. There is a debt to be repaid, and the new present acknowledges this. A cardinal text of 15 March 1794, which established doctrine and allowed the two contradictory discourses to be articulated, was the Instruction of Year II, on the manner of inventorying and conserving, throughout the Republic, all the objects that could be useful to the arts, the sciences, and teaching (*Instruction de l'an II sur la manière d'inventorier et de conserver, dans toute l'étendue de la République, tous les objets qui peuvent servir aux arts, aux sciences et à l'enseignement*). There was no cause to be "offended by the sight" of these monuments of the past, because henceforth they belonged to the nation. On the contrary, such testimonies could be instructive for all. "The lessons of the past can be assembled by our century, to be transmitted, with new pages, to posterity." The Instruction stressed that free peoples can find "models" in the arts of antiquity, and hence that one of the most important tasks was to "cultivate a taste for and encourage the teaching of" this area of study, "which links Greece and Republican Italy to a regenerated France."[78]

At almost the same time (13 février 1794), François-Étienne Boissy d'Anglas brought to the attention of the Convention a treatise entitled *Some Ideas on the Arts, on the Need to Support Them, on the Institutions Which Can Ensure Their Progress, and on Various Institutions Necessary for Their Teaching* (*Quelques idées sur les arts, sur la nécessité de les encourager, sur les institutions qui peuvent en assurer le perfectionnement et sur divers établissements nécessaires à l'enseignement*).[79] In this text on the arts, time (both the future and the past) and history play an important role. Time, he wrote "can *complete* the great work of regeneration of the human spirit." Regeneration is not immediate, like the holy sacrament of baptism or the Holy Spirit descending at the feast of Pentecost; it involves a question of time, a "horizon."[80] And one should not make a *tabula rasa* of the past, because from it comes a legacy to be transmitted: "Preserve the monuments of the arts, of the sciences and of reason . . . , for they are the prerogative of the centuries and are not your private property. You may only have them in your possession with a view to ensuring their conservation."[81] We should note this expression "prerogative of the centuries."

Henceforth, time would have supreme authority over these accumulated masterpieces. It became history's great protagonist, bearing a legacy that on this occasion was well and truly "preceded by a testament," and a binding one at that. And Greece, despite the fact that its greatness was so far in the past (as France's would be one day), was nevertheless exemplary. How so? Precisely because what saved Greece was the "reciprocity" established between culture and freedom, by which it escaped the ravages of time. "Even after their [the Greeks'] demise, they still appear, thousands of years later, to be a model of a civilized and free nation."[82]

So there had been a phase of intense politicization in which time was short-circuited, condensed into the searing apprehension of the present alone, or else introduced only as an absolute beginning. This gave way gradually to an awareness of time stretching back to the past and opening onto the future. In its demise, to cite Boissy d'Anglas once more, despotism had bequeathed a vast legacy to a regenerated France, and "it *restituted* to it [France] for the centuries to come and for the whole of the universe the immense storehouse of all human knowledge."[83] Regeneration legitimated restitution, understood as the return of an object to its rightful owner. But one should add immediately that this restitution was a far cry from the active *restitutio* of the humanists, in which the past was recuperated for the sake of the plenitude of the present, since after the Revolution the works were only held in safekeeping in the name of the centuries to come and the universe as a whole. Time restitutes and one must restitute to it; that is how we gain a perspective onto the future. But what can such a legacy mean for whoever receives it? The idea of restitution generates the novel and acute problem of the conservation and restoration of semiophores.

The doctrine of freedom that the new France incarnated, and the theory of safeguarding works for the future, and being accountable for them to posterity, were combined in the most striking way in the idea of a "final home," which I mentioned above. The notion drew on a mystique of the nation and of freedom, combined with some pure sophistry to justify what was simply pillage. The masterpieces of the past, the argument went, were waiting for France to "liberate" them by at last hosting them on its soil. Only then could the message they had been bearing since their creation be fully communicated. "Are the masterpieces of the Greek republics," abbé Grégoire asked, "to adorn a nation of slaves?."[84] Of course not, and the Louvre, where they would "leave the tyrants behind," was ready to receive them. This extreme understanding of the role of the museum and of cultural heritage was what sparked Quatremère de Quincy's condemnatory pamphlet, even if he was anyway essentially hostile to the museum in principle.

The festivities of 9 Thermidor 1798 brought these subtle reasonings to a close. On that occasion, François de Neufchâteau, the minister of the interior, made an extraordinary speech in celebration of the triumphal entry of works of art seized by Napoleon in Italy: "With religious fervor preserve this estate bequeathed to the Republic by the great men of every century, this repository entrusted to you as a mark of the esteem in which the whole universe holds you ... their sublime paintings are the testament by means of which they bequeath to the genius of freedom the task of providing them with a true apotheosis and the honor of awarding them the true laurels they have deserved."[85] Repository, testament, laurels—the picture is complete. France both is a repository and is called upon to pronounce a last judgment. The works of art are an inheritance based on a testament, but one which has waited a long time to find its true beneficiary, who now becomes aware of her election. The link with the past is not only reestablished, bracketing out the centuries of despotism, but it is reactualized, and a relation to the future is introduced, founded on the new obligations acknowledged by the testament's beneficiary. This is how the model of *historia magistra* comes to be revived. Or, more precisely, through the intermediary of national-universal cultural heritage, a renewed form of *historia magistra* takes shape in an attempt to articulate at once an appeal to the past and an openness onto the future. It is a way of sealing over the rift in time—or at least getting by with it.

There was another Revolutionary museum, the Museum of French Monuments (*Musée des Monuments français*), against which Quatremère de Quincy mounted dogged and, at the end of the day, successful attacks. This museum gradually materialized on the basis of the national treasures held in the Couvent des Petits-Augustins, under the aegis of Alexandre Lenoir. Quatremère, whom Napoleon had marginalized due to his *Letters*, was showered with honors by the Restoration and named permanent secretary to the Academy of Fine Arts in 1816. Thereafter he had every means at his disposal to act. Several texts prepared his offensive, including his *Moral Considerations on the Destination of Works of Art*, published in 1815, in which he condemned these deposits made supposedly in the name of "conservation," where the works transferred "lost their effect in losing their cause": "Who can enlighten us," he asked, "as to what these statues signify, since their poses no longer have a purpose, their expressions are just grimaces, and their details have become enigmas? . . . What do they convey, these mausolea without tombs, these doubly empty cenotaphs, these graves which death no longer quickens?"[86]

And if that were not clear enough—since every word already targeted Lenoir—Quatremère added, "Moving all these monuments, gathering together all their decaying fragments, classifying their debris methodically, and claiming that this recomposition is a practical lesson in modern chronology is to make oneself into a dead nation for a living cause; to attend one's funeral during one's lifetime; and to kill Art in order to write its history; yet this is not its history, it is its epitaph."[87] Clearly Lenoir's own epitaph and that of his museum were writ large.

A pupil of David, Lenoir identified totally with his museum-in-the-making at the Couvent des Petits-Augustins. In 1791, he was appointed as

"Guardian" to the "Parisian deposit of artistic monuments" (*Dépôt parisien des monuments des arts*), which had become national assets. Then, in 1794, he was named curator of what he managed to get recognized a year later, after many trials and tribulations, as the Museum of French Monuments.[88] Lenoir had devoted the intervening years to intensive lobbying, while also compiling inventories, purchasing, salvaging, restoring, reconstituting, and even making from scratch all sorts of objects, statues, portraits, and cenotaphs, with increasing interest in the Middle Ages.[89] Like Quatremère de Quincy, Lenoir looked to Winckelmann, whose bust presided over the entrance to the museum. The only foreigner on the premises, Winckelmann was present on two accounts, first—or still—as prophet of Athens and of freedom, but also and perhaps above all as the inventor of the history of art. As the author of *Reflections on Imitation* and of a *History of Art*, he was a figure attentive both to the politicization of the arts and to their relations to time.

Thus, under the watchful eye of Winckelmann, Lenoir succeeded in transforming his repository into a museum, that is, with works arranged historically. Not, however, according to the canons of a history of art, but such as to reveal progressively, in Lenoir's words, "a genuine history of the French monarchy in monuments."[90] This is what Quatremère contemptuously referred to as a "practical lesson in modern chronology." And yet it was a visit to this museum—"there, and there only"—that gave Michelet the most "vivid impressions of history." As he wrote in *The People*, "In fancy I filled those tombs—I felt the dead, as it were, through the marble; and it was not without some terror that I visited the vaults, where slept Dagobert, Chilperic, and Fredegonda."[91] Thus, setting out from Winckelmann, and in the latter's company, Lenoir marked out a path which led the visitor through the national antiquities "successively from century to century," as he stated in his *Notice*. The order of time began to leap forward by century, and at the same pace the visitor advanced toward the light. *Our* cultural heritage, the antiquity that belonged to us *historically* and was properly *ours*, was finally neither Greek nor Roman but medieval. In the bric-a-brac of his repository, the mostly self-taught Lenoir could thus dream on, cobbling fragments together, restoring works, and building up contexts such as to produce, ultimately, the first visual representation of a post-Revolutionary "national history."[92]

Quatremère, however, put all his energies into getting this first historical museum closed down, even if it was in fact a quite different venture from Vivant Denon's Louvre and had nothing to do with the doctrine of a "final home." He finally succeeded in 1816: he dispersed the collections, restituted monuments to churches and families, and made over the premises to the School of Fine Arts. What was unpardonable in Quatremère's view was that the museum should be the product of vandalism. That was his final word, even if the rift of the Revolution had also generated a theory of inheritance and a philosophy of time, and even if the Museum of French Monuments was far from being the only national institution founded between 1793 and 1795 to be devoted to or involved in conservation: the National Archives were established, the *Muséum central des arts*, the former King's Library, and the *Conservatoire des arts et métiers*. Although these had been created in response to particular needs, they became the matrix in which new relations to time, linking past and present, began to be expressed.

The Revolution was a moment of collective appropriation. Its protagonists "felt proud to see a family inheritance become a collective legacy" (*l'orgueil de voir un patrimoine de famille devenir un patrimoine collectif*).[93] Just as there was a transfer of sovereignty, so there was a transfer of property, in the name of the Nation and into the Nation's name. That was the first episode, which was genuinely political and presentist, soon to be followed by a second act, in which time was recognized as a protagonist in its own right, in two forms. First, the "long" time which restituted and to which one must restitute; and second, the time of immediacy, embodied in the novel experience of acceleration. The old order of time had shattered, and after an initial period of *tabula rasa*, the emergent modern order was still uncertain of its direction.

Indeed, how to pass from *destroying* to *preserving*? Destruction had been carried out with excitement, frenzy even, and tenacity, whereas preservation had to be rationally justified at least. The solution found was to mobilize the idea of heritage and especially to make time into an agent. Time gives, and to time we must entrust. This was a way of linking the past to the present, and on to the future. A thoroughly reworked form of *historia magistra* could thus be (re)introduced, opening onto a future and in no way denying the rupture with the present (on the contrary, France's regeneration precisely qualified it to host this consignment of masterpieces from the past). It was a *historia magistra* compatible with the modern regime, in phase with it, and able to formulate it by linking the categories of time differently. Quatremère remained premodern, at least concerning the arts, because there was no change in his relation to the past. There was no gap in time, no transitional period, and there neither could nor should be. It became clear on his appointment as the permanent secretary to the Academy of Fine Arts in 1816 that for him all roads emanated from the French Academy in Rome and that the history of art ought to tread an unbroken path from an instructive past right up to the present.

By contrast, all those writers who experienced discontinuity, rupture, and acceleration—for example Chateaubriand, again, for whom these were the inexhaustible source of his writing—felt their relation to time to be profoundly altered. For some, the past became an object of nostalgia, burdened by regret for what had disappeared, by the *nevermore* of real or mostly fantasized loss. Soon the young Romantics would explore this theme with all its variations. On its publication in 1802, Chateaubriand's *Genius of Christianity* met with instant public, and even political, success.[94] Despite describing as "something of a distraction" his "walk[ing] among the ruins" of what had only recently been churches and monasteries, he encouraged his readers to "look back with regret on the days that are past"—and all the past. He wanted to convert his "distraction" (which was simply a watered-down version of the "offence to the eyes") into regret.

With Gothic churches, the past was indeed distant, and even very distant, since "the forests of Gaul" themselves "were introduced" into their architecture. It was the recent past, however, which re-emerged as he wandered through Versailles, that place where "all the splendors of the religious age of France had been brought together. Scarcely a century has elapsed since these groves rang with the sounds of festivity, and now they are animated only by the music of the grasshopper and the nightingale." The immediate past appeared with the evocation of a deserted Saint-Denis: "the bird has made it her resting-place; the grass grows on in shattered altars; and, instead of the eternal hymn of death which resounded beneath its domes, naught is now to be heard save the pattering of the rain that enters at the roofless top, the fall of some stone dislodged from the ruined walls, or the sound of the clock which still runs its wonted course among empty tombs and plundered sepulchers."[95] In short, the entire past of pre-Revolutionary

France, which was a religious past, could be "converted" in this way. One set of ruins followed another, linked by the steps of the visitor. The path even took in the empty tombs, which spoke of the death of the monarchy and of the "religious age" itself. Yet Chateaubriand trusts, despite everything, that if only we would let ourselves be touched by this past, we would understand that it points to a future, which should again be religious.

Toward Universalization

The nineteenth century was a crucial period for the development of a politics of cultural heritage, its future orientations, and its instruments. But for that very reason, this period has tended to monopolize scholars' attention ever since memory and heritage came to occupy such an important place in public debate and academic research. So I shall move on swiftly here, on my path back to the issue of our contemporary preoccupation with heritage and the relations to time subtending this. *Les lieux de mémoire* has mapped the nineteenth-century field, giving due prominence especially to the July monarchy, with its new institutions devoted to history, its inventories, and its policies on national memory. The figures of Arcisse de Caumont, Mérimée, and Viollet-le-Duc are given a fitting place in the work alongside François Guizot, the driving force behind these innovations.

A department of historic monuments was created after 1830, within the Ministry of the Interior. Through its activities restoring and listing buildings, the past of pre-Revolutionary France became the business of central government. Louis-Philippe decided to transform Versailles into a history museum (ending in 1830), to recall the glory of the national past, with painting after military painting hung in the Galerie des Batailles. Viollet-le-Duc started on his large-scale restorations in 1840, from Vézelay to Carcassonne via Notre-Dame de Paris and many others. Proust and Rodin meanwhile deplored the way he "ruined France."[96] National history was consolidated, a process that continued under the Third Republic.[97] The legislation of 1887 and 1913 encapsulated what would for a long time be the official doctrine on historic monuments.

The 1887 law was very restrictive, applying only to historic monuments "of national interest." It was extended slightly in 1913 to take into account "the public interest from the point of view of history or art." However, within this extended definition, only monuments of national interest were protected by being listed. After the separation of Church and State, Barrès's campaign around the "the pitiful plight of the churches of France" (1911) came up with a different definition of cultural heritage: *all*, and not simply the finest or the most representative, of France's churches should be protected, because "through the church which sinks its foundations deep into the accumulated dust of generation upon generation of our ancestors, the latter still reach up to life, and what the church proclaims is what similar monuments standing in every village across France have proclaimed throughout the centuries."[98] But this decentralized and locally rooted conception of cultural heritage was not acceptable to the lawmakers, and postwar reconstruction further reinforced the centrality of the Department of Historic Monuments.

Even later, in 1959, one of the tasks awaiting André Malraux as the very first minister for cultural affairs was to "make the major works of humanity...accessible." The logic was still that of the historic monument and the masterpiece. In 1982, twenty-three years later, Jack Lang in the same role had the task of "preserving the national and regional cultural heritage, and that of different social groups, for the benefit of society as a whole."[99] In the wake of France's 1980 Heritage Year, heritage had thus diversified and become more decentralized. Meanwhile, Germany was examining the extension of the notion of the monument, while England was pondering the phenomenon of the "Heritage Industry."[100]

During that period, the rising tide of heritage, in tandem with that of memory, began to submerge more and more areas. Just as people declared or demanded commemoration of just about anything, so everything was, or could be ordained to be, heritage. A similar inflation was at work in both fields. The transformation of objects into museum pieces or heritage eventually won the day, encroaching ever further on the present.[101] The need, for example, to stipulate that "no living architect's work can lawfully be a historic monument"[102] clearly points to the tendency of our present to transform itself instantly into history, as mentioned above.

One particular sign of the impact of the theme of heritage and of the associated changes in relations to time can be found in policies concerning urban rehabilitation, renovation, and renewal. These seek to create museum pieces while at the same time keeping places alive, or better still, to revitalize through rehabilitation. Does this mean a new museum, without the limits of the museum—a kind of museum coextensive with the community? A museum genuinely *of* society rather than *about* society? Such a vision naturally implied moving beyond the category of the historic monument and conceiving urban heritage protection in a holistic way. The shift from the Athens Charter of 1931 to the Venice Charter of 1964 embodied this move.[103] Paradoxically, the result has been that the most authentically modern urban developments today take the form of the historic past spruced up to modern standards. Taken to its logical conclusion, all we preserve are façades.

When this past happens to be lacking—adding to the malaise of deprived urban neighborhoods or dormitory towns—it is simply invented. Urban heritage sites are produced in order to bolster identity. A history is chosen, which then becomes *the* history of the town or district, one's own; a history discovered, rediscovered or unearthed, and then displayed. Everything revolves around it, even literally. For example, at Port-de-Bouc in France, the shipyards, which closed in 1966, were chosen as the location of the central square. At Épinay-sur-Seine, the Eclair Film Studios similarly became the focal point of the town's identity. Heritage introduced an element "of temporality and singularity." But, an anthropologist asked, can one both consume cultural heritage and live in it?[104] Senart, a new urban cluster of one hundred thousand inhabitants, treated the problem differently. It built a city center (or "a space of centrality," in the words of its developers) a full thirty years after its inauguration in 2002. Called the "Carré Sénart," it provides this town-in-the-country with a central green space that currently accommodates a vast shopping mall, understood as the first link in the town's future "life-hub."[105] The development's sole ambition seems to be to connect the natural environment (or rather, the natural environment signposted as heritage) with consumption.

"Heritage" has also become extremely diverse. One example among many would be the French Heritage Foundation Law which, in its concern to be inclusive, itemized "protected cultural heritage," "local cultural heritage" (the "connective tissue" of national territory), "natural heritage" (including the "notion of landscape"), "living heritage" (animal and plant species), and intangible heritage (including traditional know-how, folk traditions, and folklore).[106] The "gene pool" as heritage is already a familiar expression in the media, and "ethical heritage" has come on the scene. No one can ignore the increasing pace at which heritage is constituted—one could even say produced—more or less everywhere. A series of international charters coordinated, shaped, and enshrined this movement (even if ratifying, and respecting, such charters can be two very different things).

The Athens Charter for the Restoration of Historic Monuments, the first of the series, was concerned only with major monuments and ignored the others. The Venice Charter, thirty years later, had a much wider range of objectives, including "the Conservation and Restoration of Monuments and Sites." The first article also gave a much broader definition of the historic monument: "The concept of a historic monument embraces not only the single architectural work but also the urban or rural setting in which is found the evidence of a particular civilization, a significant development or a historic event. This applies not only to great works of art but also to more modest works of the past which have acquired cultural significance with the passing of time." The preamble emphasized heritage protection in particular, and introduced the notion of a common heritage of humanity: "People are becoming more and more conscious of the unity of human values and regard ancient monuments as a common heritage. The common responsibility to safeguard them for future generations is recognized. It is our duty to hand them on in all their manifold authenticity." Heritage was conceived as a set of testimonies, however minor they might be. As with any act of witnessing, our responsibility was to acknowledge them in all their authenticity, and to assume additionally a responsibility toward future generations.

Instrumental in this growing awareness around heritage was the campaign to save the Abu Simbel temples during the building of the Aswan Dam in 1959. The case received extensive media coverage and alerted public opinion to the issues on a grand scale. Miraculously enough, the distant past and modern technology seemed to work together on this occasion, and the future did not erect itself on the ruins of the past. On the contrary, the operation gave them the chance to remain visible in the future, as a sort of duplicated semiophore. Malraux's speech during this campaign expressed this aspect admirably: "Your appeal is historic, not because it proposes to save the temples of Nubia, but because through it the first world civilization publicly proclaims the world's art as its indivisible heritage." And the parting shot: "In days when the West believed its cultural heritage had its source in Athens, it could nonetheless look on with equanimity while the Acropolis crumbled away."

The more "heritage" (or at least its concept) was fleshed out, the more the "historic monument" (or its category) withered away. As we have seen, the 1913 law replaced "of national interest," as the only criterion for listing a monument, with "of public interest from the point of view of history or art," thus extending the notion's field of application. But today the sovereign privilege of defining the nation's memory-history finds itself challenged by partial, particularist memories (of specific groups, associations, businesses, local communities, and so forth), all of which wish to be deemed equally legitimate or even more legitimate than the others. The nation should no longer be imposing its own values but rather safeguarding with all speed what in the present moment, immediately and even urgently is considered to be "heritage" by the various social players.[107] The monument itself tends to be replaced by the *memorial*. It is less a monument than a site of memory, through which one seeks to keep a memory alive, to maintain it as a living memory and to pass it down. History, as Daniel Fabre observes, tends to merge into *the past*, perceived as "a relatively undifferentiated entity, more to do with sensation than with narrative, giving rise to emotional participation rather than analysis." The producer of local history, Fabre rightly points out again, is less concerned with history than with an "emotional past" to be made present and palpable using all available technology.[108] It is a classic case of a presentist use of the past.

The number of associations whose declared focus was cultural heritage or the environment ("minor heritage") came to 2,241 between 1980 and 2000. The vast majority were established after 1980. Since they sometimes gave wider definitions of "heritage" than the official categories of the ministry involved with "major heritage," they tended to upset the administrative classification machine. Moreover, the associations' battles to have such heritage recognized at least partly accounted for the value they ascribed to it.[109] The initiatives were mostly to do with local heritage, in which memory and social space could be combined to produce a sense of territory and of continuity for those living there: "Heritage associations show that since memory is not a given, it cannot be lost—but it can be constructed. They devote themselves to the creation of a symbolic universe. Hence heritage should not be viewed in relation to the past but in relation to the present, as a category of action of the present on the present."[110] And, as a key branch of the leisure industry, heritage is the site of important economic stakes. When the recommendations of guidebooks are taken up by travel agents, heritage enters the globalized world. "Adding value" to heritage thus brings it ever closer to the market economy, exposing it to the market's rapid rhythms and temporalities.

NO CENTURY CAN RIVAL THE TWENTIETH FOR ITS FASCINATION with the future, for building and butchering in its name; and it certainly went the furthest, in line with the modern regime of historicity, in producing history written from the vantage point of the future. But, especially in its last third, it was also the century in which the category of the present expanded most sharply. The present became something immense, invasive, and omnipresent, blocking out any other viewpoint, fabricating on a daily basis the past and the future it needed. The present was already past before it had completely taken place. But from the end of the 1960s, this present showed signs of disquiet in its search for roots and its obsession with memory. In the contemporary attempts to mend the thread of tradition, in Michelet's terms, one could say that neither thread nor tradition is self-evident. Confidence in progress has given way to a desire to preserve and save—but preserve what and whom? This world, our world, future generations, ourselves.

Hence the world appears to us already as a set of museum pieces. Torn between amnesia and the desire to leave nothing out, we try to foresee today the museum of tomorrow and to assemble today's archives as though it were already yesterday. And for whom if not for us? A good example of this process is the demolition of the Berlin Wall: it instantly became a museum object and just as immediately, a commodity, with pieces of the Wall going on sale duly stamped with *"Original Berlin Mauer."* It is heritage that defines what we are today. The movement whereby everything must be transformed into heritage, a movement itself caught up in the spell cast by the aura of the duty to remember, remains a distinctive feature of our present and recent experience. It signals a certain relation to the present and a certain form of presentism.

The Time of the Environment

In my overview of how the notion of heritage developed, there is one aspect I have already noted, but whose importance should be explored further: the transformation of the natural environment into heritage. UNESCO provides a good way in, since it is both a powerful echo chamber and a vast, worldwide laboratory, in which theories are developed and principles laid down.[111] In 1972, the General Conference adopted the "Convention Concerning the Protection of the World Cultural and Natural Heritage." The text seemed to include everything in its scope: heritage is global, cultural, *and* natural. And why an international convention? The preamble gave an unequivocal answer: because universal heritage is increasingly threatened with destruction "not only by the traditional causes of decay, but also by changing social and economic conditions which aggravate the situation with even more formidable phenomena of damage or destruction." This led to the introduction of a new notion, that of "protection." "Protection," which is the responsibility of the international community as a whole, should be mobilized for "cultural and natural heritage of outstanding universal value."

But what is heritage of "outstanding universal value"? How can the "universal" and the "outstanding" be associated? According to what criteria? Relatedly, how to draw up a list of world heritage? These were some of the questions addressed by the numerous expert meetings. They all concluded that the selection criteria should be enlarged. No longer should the emphasis be on the historic monument (and thus on Europe), but rather on the notion of "cultural landscape." The formal definition of authenticity should not exclude other definitions (one need only think of Japan) and an anthropological understanding of culture should be adopted.[112] In 2002, the World Heritage List numbered 730 items; 175 countries had ratified the convention, which was thereafter redescribed as an instrument of sustainable development.

Moreover, some fifty years after Lévi-Strauss's enjoinder in *Race and History* to take the "fact" of diversity seriously, UNESCO's director general announced that a new international convention was in the pipeline, on intangible cultural heritage this time, understood as a "mirror of cultural diversity." This further expansion of the notion of heritage was preceded, in 2001, by a "Universal Declaration on Cultural Diversity." Today, UNESCO wants to bring together its commitments to cultural diversity, biodiversity, and sustainable development by linking them through a common focus on protection or, better, through the imperative to preserve.[113] But what is really at stake? Protecting the present or preserving the future? Both, of course—and yet it is not necessarily a pointless question. For does the reasoning work back from the future to the present or out from the present toward the future? We shall come back to this. At all events, according to the director of the Center for World Heritage, preservation should be envisioned not in terms of a year or two, but "for ever."

Thus, at least since 1972, culture and nature have been united under the single notion of "heritage," defined as both cultural and natural. In France, the first stage in the recognition of nature as heritage began as late as the 1960s, with the creation of nature reserves, that is, circumscribed protected areas. The reserves, which were open to walkers, aimed to preserve the local flora and fauna. For the first time an official text talked of "natural and cultural heritage."[114] The following stage was that of ecomuseums. The fact that they multiplied so rapidly was the most visible—and also, some argued, the most significant—expression of the new heritage policies, in which associations played a major role.[115]

"Preservation" was the key term again, but of skills, ways of doing things, and landscapes, rather than of objects. The heritage in question was intangible and actualized. The ecomuseum was inseparable from a particular territory, but it was always an inhabited territory, part of the natural environment, to be sure, but as the matrix of a social group. Max Querrien, one of the key architects of the concept of "ecomuseum," wrote, "The ecomuseum's heritage is really collective memory, from which an identity emerges which, in its singularity, sees itself as grappling with present history and giving birth to the future." That is why it is, essentially, "more concerned with saving skills than with preserving objects in museums." It aims to "draw attention to the things which generally pass unnoticed."[116] The ecomuseum's aim and mission were to make visible what is commonly overlooked, what soon no one will be able to see, or what already one can only glimpse.

So was the ecomuseum a "degree zero" museum or a museum coextensive with the community at large? It must not, we are told, merely see its role as

> fostering nostalgic regret for the natural, material and human heritage which is disappearing, or has already disappeared—and which should most certainly be consigned to memory since it constitutes the roots without which nothing new can grow.... Its role is rather, by explaining the lessons which can be drawn from the past, to help build the future; its role is to be one of the instruments (as at once agent and place) of both technological and social transformation. It must be able to explain the adaptable and ingenious spirit of our ancestors, as an example for those faced with difficult changes today.... The ecomuseum must teach this knowledge to ward off despair and help life rise from the ashes.[117]

This set of guidelines was as prescriptive (it *should*, it *must*) as it was ambitious, since the ecomuseum's theoreticians wanted at once to avoid attachment to the past, nostalgia, and tourism, and for the ecomuseum to constitute an interactive and transitional space between the past and the future. The ecomuseum should be a pedagogical project, with lessons to teach, in a visitor-friendly and even playful environment. It should not encourage imitation of the past, since its very identity stemmed from a break in time, involving a particular awareness of the end of (industrial, artisanal, or agricultural) activities and ways of life. The ecomuseum was a museum in the present, seeking to produce a living site of memory.

The ecomuseum's function was thus construed as eliciting memories and raising awareness. Through it, society (a community) was urged to become aware of its heritage. Its advocates would say that this sort of museum had no visitors, only "inhabitants," and that it aimed to "mobilize cultural heritage to creative and not solely museum-focused ends."[118] Clearly the hopes vested in it were immense. In the way it appealed to memory, it both manifested the crisis affecting the modern regime of historicity, and constituted a response to it, a response of the present and directed at the present, yet anxious to avoid the trap of presentism. Was it successful, or could it be, as "inhabitants" transformed into "visitors" and even into tourists among other tourists? At all events, nature reserves and ecomuseums helped highlight the transition from an aesthetic view of nature to a heritage-oriented one, in which memory and territory were interwoven. With this last stage in the rapid transformation of everything into heritage, "heritage" had become universal and the concept had reached its limit. It brought with it a concern, or even a duty, to preserve not only what had long since disappeared, but also what had recently disappeared, and even what was just about to disappear, in a sort of anticipatory speculation on the transformation of use-value into age-value.

WHAT DID (AND STILL DOES) THIS PROLIFERATION OF HERITAGE imply in terms of changing relations to time? It was undoubtedly the sign of a break between past and present, experienced, for example, as a feeling of accelerating time. Or—and this was Pierre Nora's starting point—as a sign that one regime of memory had tipped over into another.[119] Our overview of the development of the notion of heritage has shown that it certainly never thrived on continuity, but rather on breaks in and challenges to the order of time, combined with all the fluctuations between absence and presence, visibility and invisibility by which the constant and constantly changing ways of producing semiophores were shaped and oriented. And it all started a long time ago with the intrusion of that inaugural absence, Jesus, into what became—and would long remain—the Western tradition. This set in motion a new order of time. The trace left by the event was indestructible and unforgettable: *the* trace itself.

Cultural heritage is a way of overcoming, that is, at once acknowledging and reducing these breaks by identifying, selecting, and producing semiophores. In the *longue durée* of Western history, the notion has gone through several states, each of which has corresponded to periods of heightened questioning of the order of time. One resorts to heritage in times of crisis. Given these "moments" of heritage, it is impossible to settle on a single meaning of the term. Across the centuries, heritage-type practices have shaped different times of heritage. These correspond to different ways of articulating the present and the past, in the first instance, but with the Revolution, the future too; the times of heritage thus reflect different ways of articulating past, present and future.

I have identified some of these temporal configurations. When Varro took on the task of exhaustively describing Rome's antiquities, he did so because he was convinced that the crisis of the Republic would endanger the eternity of the *Urbs*. When the Renaissance humanists aspired to achieve Rome's *renovatio*, their "hopeful expectation" turned toward the past was addressed first and foremost to their own present; while not abandoning a Christian order of time, they could fully deploy the principle of *historia magistra*, through use of the example and imitation. In response to the breaks brought about by the French Revolution and the traumatic experience of an acceleration of time, the revolutionaries managed to develop, in the space of a few years, a new interpretation of *historia magistra*, in which time itself became an agent. Past and future were reconnected, but only via the transitional space of the regenerated present (the France of freedom). The nineteenth century would have the task of taking on cultural heritage in its modern form, classifying and restoring it, and also feeding it into the grand narrative of the nation's history: from the Restoration to the Third Republic. The historic monument, characterized in the law of 1887 as "of national interest," marked the entry into the era of the "the nation fulfilled." But despite being awe-inspiring—since it was, after all, the incarnation of history—the historic monument did not invite identification.

After the catastrophes of the twentieth century, the numerous breaks in continuity, and the momentous acceleration of time we have experienced—so palpable in our everyday lives—the fact that memory and heritage have come to the fore is hardly surprising. One could even ask why it took so long. The answer would surely be that they could not appear in an instant, and also that earlier the time was simply not right. The order of the world and of time had made it well nigh impossible for them to take shape, since a whole series of conditions had first to be fulfilled, including generational ones, as we mentioned at the outset of this journey through time(s). However, what distinguishes the contemporary burst in heritage activity from the preceding phases is the variety of its forms and its strongly presentist character, while the present itself has extended immeasurably (it is at least sixty). We saw several signs of this: the memorial is more popular than the monument, or the latter is resuscitated as a memorial, and the past is more popular than history; conjuring up the past in the present in an emotionally engrossing way is preferred to the values of distance and mediation; the current primacy of the local goes hand in hand with the quest for a "history all one's own";[120] and, lastly, heritage is itself affected by acceleration, through the imperative to act quickly, before it is too late, before evening falls and the light fades to a darkness that may be total.

Remembrance and commemoration, whether construed as objects of a demand, a duty, or a right, are the other phenomena which have, like heritage, emerged both in response to presentism and as a symptom of it. Heritage, however, has an additional dimension as regards experience and, ultimately, the order of time. The redefinition of the natural environment as heritage, which is probably the most momentous and novel extension of the concept, unquestionably points toward a future, or to new interactions between present and future. This might suggest that we have moved out of the closed circle of the present, since concern for the future is integral to this redefinition of heritage. Except that this future is perceived not as a promise or a "principle of hope," but as a threat. That is the reversal we have witnessed. And since we are also the cause of this threat, it is accepted that we must take responsibility for it, as from today, since we failed to do so in the past. Hence our exploration of heritage and its regimes of temporality has led us unexpectedly from the past to the future, but to a future which is no longer to be conquered or brought into being, if need be by brutalizing the present. This future is not a radiant horizon guiding our advancing steps, but rather a line of shadow drawing closer, which we ourselves have set in motion. At the same time we seem to be caught on the treadmill of the present and ruminating upon a past which simply won't go down.

OUR DOUBLY INDEBTED PRESENT

THE REIGN OF PRESENTISM

OUR RELATIONS TO TIME MAY BE DISSECTED BUT NOT DECREED. For how could we ever pronounce upon our own present? Perched on what stilts or standing on the shoulders of what giants? We have seen that the present's immediate self-historicization is a defining trend of our time. And we credit ourselves with the power to extend and intensify this trend? To push presentism to its very limits?

If there was a time when Chateaubriand's stance could be ours, it is certainly long gone. I shall mention it one last time, as a way of bidding farewell to the self-styled swimmer between the banks of time, between the old and the new regime of historicity. Having described the July Days of the 1830 Revolution as they unfolded, Chateaubriand notes that "a certain contemporary colouring" sheds a cast over his portrayal, which is "true at the moment when it occurs" but "false when the moment has gone." In order to "judge the reality that remains impartially, one must adopt the point of view from which posterity will consider the completed event." Chateaubriand does not for an instant doubt his success in this: he entitles this chapter of his *Memoirs* "How the July Revolution will be viewed," or, a variant, "The July Revolution in the Future."[1] We may well be as eager as Chateaubriand, or even more so, to historicize the present, but we cannot be even half as certain that we will succeed. What of 1989 in the future? What of 11 September 2001?

Ten years later, as Chateaubriand was preparing to lay down his pen and step into his grave, he observed, "The world now, the world without consecrated authority, seems lodged between two impossibilities: the impossible past [because "the old society is breaking up"] and an impossible future."[2] Yet he can almost immediately move on from this aporia, from what we have called a pause or a gap in time. First, he still has the example of Rome to refer to, even if in the same breath he declares *historia magistra* to be officially dead. Although the excesses of freedom may well lead to despotism, he states, excessive tyranny has never led to anything but greater tyranny: "Tiberius did not return Rome to a Republic; he simply left Caligula as his successor."[3] Second, as regards the future, he appeals to the virtue of Christian hope as "more permanent than time." It alone can help the future come into being, through a combination of eschatological belief and faith in progress. Hence the last sentence of the *Memoirs*, "I behold the light of a dawn whose sunrise I shall never see."[4] But leaving aside the particular (and well-tried) remedies Chateaubriand proposes, could such an analysis, namely the assertion of this twofold impossibility, still shed even a modicum of light on our own contemporary situation? Can our present conjuncture be addressed in these terms? Is the image of the swimmer between the banks, or equally of the gap, still adequate today?

"Tell me how you interpret the present and I will tell you what philosophy you are," said Péguy.[5] What, then, are the salient features of our present? How do we conceive it? What order of time does it point to, and—a related question, which has accompanied us from the very start—are we to believe that a new regime of historicity has emerged? Or is emerging? A regime which might be visible only in sector-based, local, or even disciplinary areas, but which would as yet have no general or unified expression. Then again, it might be useless to look for unity, if a certain dispersion or simply a multiplicity of different regimes of temporality happened to characterize (and distinguish) our present. And it might also be simply premature, given how long it takes to bring to light and delineate a regime of historicity, as we have seen, and given also that a regime of historicity never exists in pure form.

Let us nevertheless add some finishing touches to the depiction of our present, which this book has, explicitly or implicitly, never lost from view. In moving back and forth between presents and pasts, while consistently focusing on the category of the present in its relations to the past and the future, I have attempted from one chapter to the next to shed light on how the present has been construed—long ago, more recently, and today. Each chapter could doubtless have stood alone, which is a sign that it covered the ground of its journey too swiftly. Our Polynesian trip, with which I began, showed up the misunderstandings arising down there between Maoris and Europeans, while over here we glimpsed the debate between anthropology and history on the issue of types of history. We crossed the seas with Odysseus, and encountered the question of the past. It led us from the shores of Phaeacia to the Christian order of time, with Augustine. Then came the French Revolution, and the rapids of a crisis of time through which we accompanied Chateaubriand as he navigated between the Old and the New World, moving from the ancien régime's *historia magistra* to the modern regime of historicity.

Then came the journey across the recently unearthed continent of memory and history, prompted by the crisis of the future that unsettled the modern regime. The powerful spotlight of *Les lieux de mémoire* sweeping over the landscape of the 1980s caught in its beam the old and familiar theme of national historiography. Thereafter, on our last journey, which was already a recapitulation, we traversed the *longue durée* of European culture on the traces of heritage, noting its key moments, which were also crises of time. I even went so far as to say, at the end of the last chapter, that heritage was a notion fashioned by and for crises of time, in which the issue of the present or the dimension of the present had always played a pivotal role.

These five chapters can be read as just so many reconnaissance trips. The range of knowledge areas covered and the different periods spanned made the journeys challenging, but they have already yielded a rich crop of insights, even if each of these crises of time could still be mapped more precisely. However, in relation to the overall movement underlying this book, the shifts between yesterday and today, down there and over here, can only have the status and value of brief halts. They have enabled the reader to experience some of the forms taken by the order of time, and to assess the position of the present within each.

To characterize our present, I have used the term "presentism" throughout, and primarily in opposition to futurism, which had long dominated the European scene. When it disappeared, there emerged a disoriented time, marked by greater uncertainty, although uncertainty also became a category of thought and the object of scientific research. But I used the term also because I wanted to compare today's present with those of the past, some of them at least, the most notable ones, those which have left the most indelible marks on European culture: the Homeric present, the present of the classical philosophers, the Renaissance humanists' present, the eschatological or messianic present, and the modern present, produced by the modern regime of historicity.

Let us call on Péguy again: "And suddenly one turns away, and nothing looks the same again."[6] For us too, everything looks different. The crisis of the future unsettled our idea of progress and produced a sense of foreboding that cast a shadow over our present. The future did not disappear, but it seemed opaque and threatening. The atomic bomb on Hiroshima, initially hailed as a "scientific revolution," inaugurated the era of nuclear threat, while in the same period Europe conclusively lost its "spatial and temporal centrality."[7] The development of the notion of heritage, as I traced it from the ruins of Rome—ruins which certainly came from the past but with a view to Rome's *renovatio* in the present—up to the inclusion of the natural environment and the human gene pool within the category of heritage helped us grasp this reversal. But whereas a logic of heritage was previously summoned to seal over a perceived break, today it must additionally avert a perceived threat. In this configuration, intangible heritage has become increasingly important, and the issue of transmission is perceived as particularly critical.

These shifts in our experience of time have given rise to two compelling new areas of thought, the first organized around the "imperative of responsibility," conceived and advocated by the philosopher Hans Jonas, and the second, a later development, organized around the "precautionary principle."[8] Although the two principles certainly differ—having neither the same origins, nor the same scope, nor the same applications—one can nevertheless consider the former to be the "philosophical bedrock" of the latter.[9] I mention them in conclusion because they are particularly meaningful in the light of Péguy's remark. Both principles seem to turn their back on presentism, understood as a confinement to the present alone and to the present's vision of itself. And both are essentially concerned with taking the future seriously and even taking it in hand, with all its uncertainties. For the imperative of responsibility, this future has no visible end, while for the precautionary principle it is characterized first and foremost by uncertainty. But, as the philosopher Jean-Pierre Dupuy has argued recently, it is perhaps not a question of uncertainty but of belief, since in fact we know well enough what catastrophes await us, but we refuse to believe them. This argument forms the basis of Dupuy's theorization of what he calls a "rational catastrophism."[10]

The Imperative of Responsibility: In Search of an Ethics for the Technological Age was published in 1979, but according to Jonas its conception dated back to the early 1960s. Its starting point was that Prometheus was "finally unbound." Having mastered nature, man now took himself as the object of technological manipulation. Jonas was (still) targeting the Marxist futurist utopia, but his criticism was also (and already) valid for technology "in the anticipation of its extreme possibilities."[11] The book's success was probably due in part to the fact that it arrived at a crucial moment for relations to time, when a radiant future was fast transforming into a future of threat. The book targeted the illusions produced by the "principle of hope,"[12] which in Jonas's view endangered the future while blithely sacrificing the present. Its publication also coincided with a time of particular vitality in ecological thinking. But by the time the French translation came out in 1990, one year after the fall of the Berlin Wall and the final collapse of the Marxist utopia, concerns had shifted over to the other side, onto the crisis of the future.

Hans Jonas countered a "politics of utopia" for which it seemed legitimate to "use those living now as a mere means to a goal,"[13] with the need to construct an ethics for the future, since unquestionably "action takes place for the sake of a future which neither the agent nor the victim nor their contemporaries will live to enjoy." In other words, "the obligations upon the now issue from that future."[14] Also, "the ethic of revolutionary eschatology," as Jonas calls it, is "an ethic of transition," whereas the ethics he seeks to found should be noneschatological and anti-utopian: concerned both with the future and with the present, both with our contemporaries and with the generations to come, in the name of humankind. Against the temptation to "sacrifice [of] the present for the future," Jonas posits that "every feeling and striving being is not only an end of nature but also an end-in-itself, namely, its own end," while immediately adding to this first maxim an imperative: "Act so that the effects of your action are compatible with the permanence of genuine human life."[15] Unlike Kant's categorical imperative, which does not extend beyond my present act, this imperative demands attention to the long-term effects of my actions. It can be formulated in Ricoeur's terms: "Responsibility extends as far as our powers do in space and time."[16]

The present is in some sense responsible for the whole of the future, since "a degraded legacy simultaneously degrades its heirs." When we come to understand this "futurology of warning" and can recognize the "fate staring at us out of the future," we feel "a mixture of fear and guilt: fear because what we see ahead is something terrible; guilt because we are conscious of our own causal role in bringing it about."[17] Jonas even readily uses a "heuristics of fear" in order to give full weight to the dangers ahead. His ethics is unreservedly critical of (utopian) futurism and its dangers, and he looks unflinchingly at the future staring out at us, which we endanger through our actions. In terms of relations to time, Jonas's ethics wants a future without futurism and a present without presentism, associated or even linked one to the other by a legacy which must not be "degraded," since in so doing both those who bequeath and those who receive are themselves "degraded." Since we are already indebted to future generations, our responsibility begins today and starts afresh each day—in order that the humanity of humankind may endure.[18]

The second area of thought I mentioned above concerns the "precautionary principle." It represents another figure of indebtedness in response to the same crisis of progress and new technological risks. In addition to the already-present risks of irreversible environmental changes, there are now the dangers associated with the biotechnologies. The precautionary principle caught on very rapidly, and on an international scale, to become a key 1990s term, partly due to ecological thinking, and to certain contemporary disasters and scandals. A report to the French prime minister of the time mentioned in its conclusions that precaution "responds to an evident social demand."[19] What had once been the nightmare of politicians could now become their mascot or, more trivially, a convenient way of passing the buck. And indeed, their tendency or temptation to make the precautionary principle into a principle of abstention was soon apparent, in a new version of "If in doubt, don't," countered by the adage "Nothing ventured nothing gained!"

This principle was first adopted at the International Conference on the Protection of the North Sea in 1987, concerning the protection of the environment. The Rio Declaration on Environment and Development in 1992 gave rise to a French law in 1995 providing that "the absence of certainty at a given stage of scientific and technical knowledge should not delay the adoption of effective and proportionate measures, at an economically acceptable cost, designed to avert a risk of serious and irreversible damage to the environment."[20] The principle was thereafter applied also to the food industry and to health, and was extended further to become the central point of reference for advocates of sustainable development. It was the nodal point of debates around the debt to future generations and our corresponding duties.[21]

The precautionary principle was conceived precisely for situations of radical uncertainty, when science itself is unable to decide. The principle applies to risks that are not, and might never be, ascertained, but which are presumed to exist. It differs from the more familiar, even if not always implemented, principle of prevention, since the precautionary principle counts in terms of long or very long temporalities. But, as an economist asked, how are we to identify and interpret these "unclear signals coming from the future"?[22] This is where Hans Jonas's ethical meditation on the "fate staring at us out of the future" came into play, as well as Jean-Pierre Dupuy's critique of precaution.

According to François Ewald, responses to uncertainty have taken three forms: foresight, prevention, and, today, precaution.[23] The paradigm of responsibility (linked to the advent of liberalism) can be associated with foresight, that of solidarity (represented by the Welfare State) can be associated with prevention, and perhaps a new paradigm, for which a name has yet to be found, will come to be associated with precaution. Ewald proposes the paradigm of "security" and the concomitant emergence of a "Precautionary State."[24] "Foresight" implies not overlooking the ups and downs of life, "prevention" means evaluating risks on the basis of scientific knowledge, and "precaution" acknowledges that even science is not infallible. With it, a new relation to harm and to time is introduced: "there exist the irreparable, the irremediable, the unpardonable, the harm which is beyond compensation and the crime whose prosecution is beyond time restrictions [*imprescriptible*]."[25] Irreversibility and sustainable development are concepts whose temporalities carry with them the idea of time as continuous and seamless, from us to future generations or from future generations back to us. Of course we look toward the future, but on the basis of an extended present, without interruption or revolution.

Critics of the precautionary principle have highlighted its negative effects, namely encouraging passivity and inaction, or at least excessively obstructing innovation. The principle could, paradoxically, generate a sort of defensive withdrawal into the present and hence bolster presentism even further. Along the same lines, Ewald has drawn our attention to an "extreme form of the figure of precaution," according to which development itself would constitute a risk. Let us imagine a product with "an undetectable and unforeseeable defect, which only becomes apparent after a certain length of time. Moreover, the responsibility for the defect can be imputed to the product or producer only due to a scientific context different from the one existing when the product was first put into circulation, used and consumed."[26] How determine civil or criminal liability in such a case? How can someone be held responsible after the fact for something he or she could not possibly have known at the time? In France, the law's nonretroactivity was established already in 1789: "Legislation provides only for the future; it has no retrospective operation" (French Civil Code). Yet with development risk, when a danger is discovered at some future date, the past (in which the danger was unknown) is still considered to be part of the present of the risk's discovery. This means that we never leave the present (or at least a legal present). The as yet unsuspected risk is (already) present, and once it has been proven, after the fact, it will continue to belong to that present; it will not be considered as past.

Thus a whole new configuration took shape, in which the direction of debt was reversed and reoriented toward the future through the pivotal concept of "responsibility." Ricoeur proposed that responsibility have "an orientation that is more deliberately prospective as a function of which the idea of prevention of future harm will be added to that of reparation for harm already done"[27] (responsibility toward the past, particularly in the form of an acknowledgment of the duty to remember, had already been reinforced). And the Nuremberg Charter lifted statutory time limitations on the prosecution of crimes against humanity, an innovation which was incorporated into the French Penal Code in 1994, and is now recognized by a majority of countries (since the decision, ratified by France in 2000, to create an International Criminal Court).

The nonapplicability of statutory time limitations to certain crimes means that ordinary justice, which is precisely governed by these, is annulled, as is the principle of the nonretroactivity of the law. The jurist Yan Thomas commented that, "the opposite of lifting statutory time limitations [*l'imprescriptible*] is not time passing but time having a term [*le temps prescrit*]." Both are equally constructions.[28] The lifting of statutory limitations here means that the criminal in crimes against humanity remains contemporary with his crime until his death, but by the same token we too are contemporary with the facts to be judged. Maurice Papon, for example, despite his ninety-two years, was not a day older: till the day of his death, vehement in his denial, he remained the administrative head of the Préfecture of the Gironde. If the "very nature" of crimes against humanity makes statutory time limitations fall away, then they ground a "legal atemporality" which can be understood as a sort of past in the present, a present past or rather an extension of the present, as from the present of the trial. The only place for historians in this temporality is, logically enough, as witnesses, called upon to express orally what they remember. The notion of responsibility generates here a certain elision or certain transfers between the time of law, with its own regimes of temporality, and the time of society. The extent to which the temporal regime associated with crimes against humanity has permeated public space is probably linked to the increasing litigiousness of our societies, which is another characteristic of our contemporary world.

The present has thus *extended* both into the future and into the past. Into the future, through the notions of precaution and responsibility, through the acknowledgment of the irreparable and the irreversible, and through the notions of heritage and debt, the latter being the concept which cements and gives sense to the whole. And into the past, borne by similar concepts such as responsibility and the duty to remember, the drive to make everything into heritage, the lifting of time limitations, and last but not least the notion of "debt." This double indebtedness, toward the past and the future, but derived from our present and weighing upon it, is another hallmark of our contemporary experience. The figure of debt is what transports us from the genocide of the Jews to the risks threatening the entire human species, from the obligation not to forget to the imperative of responsibility:[29] in order that future generations may still have the life of human beings and never forget man's inhumanity to man.

This extension of the present into the future gives rise, negatively, to catastrophism (not "rational" this time) or else, more positively, to work on uncertainty itself. The numerous fields affected by the "Probabilistic Revolution"—to use an expression adopted by the mathematician Henri Berestycki—are a sign of this.[30] Advances in computer technologies have given rise to a whole "risk technology" using virtual scenarios and simulations. In our uncertain universe, we no longer choose a single projection, through which we "foresee the future," but instead we "measure the effects of several envisageable futures on the present," such as to move forward virtually in several directions before deciding on one direction alone.[31] This is what is called a "multidirectional" or "multiple" present. From my particular perspective of the relation to time, however, does this approach not simply extend the present still further? We "start out from" the present, but never really "leave" it? It is the source of all enlightenment. And in a sense there is nothing but the present, not as infinite, but as indefinite. The managerial response to uncertainty is called "flexibility," where the idea is not so much to anticipate change as to be as flexible as possible at every moment, that is, to be able to be immediately *present* ("on the case"). It is worth noting that the centrality of uncertainty and of the present applies not only in relation to the future, but also in our approach to the past. It too can be reconstructed as multidirectional and multiple, at least up to a certain point.

So tell me now, "how do you interpret the present?" Not simply as a vast, seemingly endless expanse (which is why the past just won't go away), no, our present is not simply that. For there is a type of "time which lasts," a time of trauma, the time lived by concentration camp survivors, which resurfaces at certain moments. It is a kind of immobile, involuntary present, the present which Primo Levi identified as that of Coleridge's Ancient Mariner whenever "at an uncertain hour / That agony returns" and he then feels compelled to tell his tale.[32] In my outline of the rise of presentism in chapter 3, I identified a present that was so close to omnipresence and eternity that it could almost be assimilated to the *tota simul* by which Augustine, and before him Plotinus, defined eternity, where "Nothing passes away, but the whole is simultaneously present." I also mentioned Marinetti's *Futurist Manifesto*, which already in 1909 was proclaiming the "tragic lyricism of ubiquity and omnipresent speed." I concluded that however eternal this present might appear, it also avidly or anxiously sought to historicize itself, as though it were forced to project itself ahead, in order to turn back and see itself as already past, forgotten. Can this be interpreted as an attempt to fend off the unbearable uncertainty of events? I mentioned the regime of the contemporary event, in search of instant self-commemoration and *as* already that commemoration. But, in apparent contradiction with this regime, our dilated present, burdened with its twofold debt and twofold memory of the past and the future, is also shadowed by entropy. It is destined to be forgotten, consigned to the immediate, the instantaneous, and the ephemeral.

Such are the major traits of this manifold and multivalent present, a monstrous time. It is at once everything (there is nothing but the present) and almost nothing (reduced to the tyranny of the instant). One need only cite the famous lines from *Faust II*, "Now the spirit looks neither backwards nor forwards, the present alone is our happiness," to understand that Goethe's presentism is not, or can no longer be, ours. On the contrary, we are always looking both backwards and forwards, but without ever *leaving* this present that we have made into the limits of our world.

As we saw above, the humanists harbored a "hopeful expectation turned toward the past." Enlightenment came from the glorious antique past, to which one should aspire through imitation and example. And the present—as the endpoint of this process—was capable of raising itself to the splendor of this past, through the operation of *renovatio*. In the modern regime of historicity, by contrast, the hopeful expectation was directed toward the future as source of enlightenment. The present was considered to be inferior to the future, and time became an agent; not only was it palpably accelerating, but one must make it move faster still. The future lay in speed. Attempts were made to break time in two and insert the future directly into the present.

Today, enlightenment has its source in the present, and the present alone. To this extent—and this extent only—there is neither past nor future nor historical time, if one accepts that modern historical time was set in motion by the tension between the space of experience and the horizon of expectation. Are we to conclude that experience and expectation have moved so far apart that the tension between them has reached breaking point, that we are at a point where the two categories have come apart? Whether this is a temporary or a permanent state, the fact remains that this present is a time of memory and debt, of daily amnesia, uncertainty, and simulation. As such, we can no longer adequately describe our present—this moment of crisis of time—in the terms we have been using and developing, inspired by Arendt's insights, as a "gap" between past and future. The present can no longer be understood, or only partially, as an "odd in-between period" in historical time, "during which one becomes aware of an interval in time which is altogether determined by things that are no longer and by things that are not yet."[33] On the contrary, this presentist present seeks to be determined by nothing other than itself. Its features have been sketched above—and they are our own.

NOTES

Presentism

1. See "Sur la notion de régime d'historicité. Entretien avec François Hartog," in *Historicités*, ed. F. Dosse, P. Garcia, and C. Lacroix (Paris: La Découverte, 2009), 133–149.
2. Rem Koolhaas, "The Generic City," in *Small, Medium, Large, Extra-Large*, ed. Jennifer Sigler (New York: Monacelli, 1998), 1249.

Introduction

1. Anaximander, fr. B1: "And from what source things arise, to that [source] they return of necessity when they are destroyed; for they suffer punishment and give satisfaction to one another for injustice according to the order of time [*kata tou chronou taxin*]." Simplicius, *On Aristotle's Physics* 6r (24, 19); Theophrastus, *Doxography* 476, 24:13; Arthur Fairbanks, trans. and ed., *The First Philosophers of Greece* (London: Kegan Paul, Trench, Trübner & Co., 1898); http://history.hanover.edu/texts/presoc/anaximan.html#frag.
2. Catherine Darbo-Peschanski, *Le discours du particulier: Essai sur l'enquête*

hérodotéenne (Paris: Seuil, 1987), 72–74. For the case of Croesus, see François Hartog, "Myth Into Logos: The Case of Croesus," in *From Myth to Reason: Studies in the Development of Greek Thought*, ed. R. Buxton (Oxford: Oxford University Press, 1999), 185–195.

3. Michel Foucault, "The Order of Discourse," in *Untying the Text: A Post-Structuralist Reader*, ed. Robert Young (Boston: Routledge, 1981), 48–79.
4. Krzysztof Pomian, *L'ordre du temps* (Paris: Gallimard, 1984), xii. See also his "La crise de l'avenir," *Le Débat* 7 (1980): 5–17, reprinted in *Sur l'histoire* (Paris: Gallimard, 1999), 233–262.
5. More recently, the theme has been broached from a variety of perspectives, all of which have sought to carry weight beyond their disciplinary boundaries. See, for example, Roger Sue, *Temps et ordre social: Sociologie des temps sociaux* (Paris: Presses universitaires de France, 1994); Norbert Elias, *Time: An Essay*, trans. Edmund Jephcott (Cambridge: Blackwell, 1992); Paul Virilio, in several of his books over the last fifteen years; Günther Horst, *Zeit der Geschichte: Welterfahrung und Zeitkategorien in der Geschichtsphilosophie* (Frankfurt: Fischer Taschenbuch, 1993); Jean Chesneaux, *Habiter le temps: Passé, présent, futur—Esquisse d'un dialogue possible* (Paris: Bayard, 1996); Jean Leduc, *Les historiens et le temps: Conceptions, problématiques, écritures* (Paris: Seuil, 1999); Zaki Laïdi, *Le sacre du présent* (Paris: Flammarion, 2000); Jean-Noël Jeanneney, *L'histoire va-t-elle plus vite? Variations sur un vertige* (Paris: Gallimard, 2001); Lothar Baier, *Keine Zeit! 18 Versuche über die Beschleunigung* (Munich: Kunstmann, 2000); Étienne Klein, *Chronos: How Time Shapes Our Universe*, trans. Glenn Burney (New York: Thunder's Mouth, 2005). Having shown that "we still speak of time in the same way people did before Galileo" and that modern physics is intimately involved in questions of time, Étienne Klein ends his book on a more Epicurean note, exhorting the reader to "keep[ing] to a diet of the passing moment, trusting the flavor of the instant, the *kairos*."
6. Paul Ricoeur, *Memory, History, Forgetting*, trans. Kathleen Blamey and David Pellauer (Chicago: University of Chicago Press, 2004), xv; "Mémoire: Approches historiennes, approche philosophique," *Le Débat* 122 (2002): 42–44.
7. Michel Certeau, "History: Science and Fiction," in *The Certeau Reader*, ed. Graham Ward (Oxford: Blackwell, 2000), 48. See also Leduc, *Les historiens et le temps*.
8. Pomian, "La crise de l'avenir," 233–262. Marcel Gauchet, *La démocratie contre elle-même* (Paris: Gallimard, 2002), 345–359.

9. In the sense of the term used in *The Invention of Tradition*, ed. E. Hobsbawm and T. Ranger (Cambridge: Cambridge University Press, 1983).
10. François Furet, *The Passing of an Illusion: The Idea of Communism in the Twentieth Century* (Chicago: University of Chicago Press, 1999), 502.
11. Paul Valéry, *History and Politics*, trans. Denise Folliot and Jackson Mathews (New York: Bollingen Foundation, 1962), 28–29 (a letter that first appeared in English in 1919) and 135–136 (a conference at the Université des Annales, 1935). In another conference held in 1932 at the same institution, Valéry returned to his 1919 analysis of the disarray of "our Hamlet of Europe."
12. Stéphane Mosès, *The Angel of History*, trans. Barbara Harshaw (Stanford: Stanford University Press, 2009).
13. Stefan Zweig, *The World of Yesterday*, trans. Anthea Bell (Lincoln: University of Nebraska Press, 1943), xix.
14. Lucien Febvre, "Face au vent: Manifeste des *Annales nouvelles*" (1946), in *Combats pour l'histoire* (Paris: Armand Colin, 1992), 35, 40, and 41.
15. Lucien Febvre, "A New Kind of History" (1949), in *A New Kind of History*, trans. K. Folca, ed. Peter Burke (London: Routledge and Kegan Paul, 1973), 41: "History is a way of organizing the past so that it does not weigh too heavily on the shoulders of men.... Organizing the past in accordance with the needs of the present, that is what one could call the social function of history."
16. René Char, *Leaves of Hypnos*, trans. Cid Corman (New York: Grossman, 1973), 62. These notes, written between 1943 and 1944, were dedicated to Albert Camus.
17. Étienne Tassin, *Le trésor perdu: Hannah Arendt, l'intelligence de l'action politique* (Paris: Payot-Rivages, 1999), 32.
18. Hannah Arendt, *Between Past and Future: Eight Exercises in Political Thought* (New York: Penguin, 1993), 5.
19. Ibid., 3, 9.
20. See Hannah Arendt, *The Origins of Totalitarianism* (New York: Harcourt Brace Jovanovich, 1951).
21. Edgar Morin, Claude Lefort, and Jean-Marc Coudray, *Mai 1968: La brèche* (Paris: Fayard, 1968).
22. Olivier Rolin, *Paper Tiger*, trans. William Cloonan (Lincoln: University of Nebraska Press, 2007), 23.
23. Michel Deguy in *Au sujet de Shoah: Le film de Claude Lanzmann* (Paris: Belin, 1990), 40.

24. Yosef Hayim Yerushalmi, *Zakhor: Jewish History and Jewish Memory* (Seattle: University of Washington, 1982), xxxiii. Sylvie Anne Goldberg, *La Clepsydre: Essai sur la pluralité des temps dans le judaïsme* (Paris: Albin Michel, 2000), 52-55.

25. Charles S. Maier, "Hot Memory ... Cold Memory: On the Political Half-Life of Fascist and Communist Memory," *Tr@nsit* 22 (2002), in which the author discusses an open-air museum, which is slightly off the beaten track and not really finished. It contains communist-era statues—a case of conserving in order to destroy.

26. Renaud Dulong, *Le témoin oculaire: Les conditions sociales de l'attestation personnelle* (Paris: École des hautes études en sciences sociales, 1998); Annette Wieviorka, *The Era of the Witness*, trans. Jared Stark (Ithaca: Cornell University Press, 2006); François Hartog, "Le témoin et l'historien," *Gradhiva* 27 (2000): 1-14.

27. Kerwin L. Klein, "On the Emergence of Memory in Historical Discourse," *Representations* 69 (2000): 127-150; see also *Politiques de l'oubli, Le Genre Humain* 18 (1988). On the historian as one who both unsettles collective memory and preserves it, see Pierre Laborie, *Les Français des années troubles* (Paris: Desclée De Brouwer, 2001), 53-71; Régine Robin, *La mémoire saturée* (Paris: Stock, 2003).

28. François Hartog, "Temps et histoire: Comment écrire l'histoire de France?," *Annales* 1 (1995): 1223-1227. Zaki Laïdi has described an "autarchic present": *Le sacre du présent*, 102-129. Jérôme Baschet, wearing his two hats of medievalist and observer of the Zapatist movement, talks of a "perpetual present," in "History Facing the Perpetual Present: The Past-Future Relationships," *History Under Debate*, ed. Carlos Barros and Lawrence J. McCrank (New York: Haworth, 2004), 133-158; Marc Augé, *Le temps en ruines* (Paris: Galilée, 2003), in which Augé stresses the perpetual present of "our violent world, in which rubble does not have time to become ruins" (10). He sets this against a time of ruins, a sort of "pure, undatable time, which does not figure in our world of images, simulacra, and reconstitutions" (ibid.).

The meaning of presentism in this book is broader than the almost technical sense given it by George W. Stocking in his essay "On the Limits of 'Presentism' and 'Historicism' in the Historiography of the Behavioral Sciences" (included in his *Race, Culture, and Evolution: Essays in the History of Anthropology* [Chicago: University of Chicago Press, 1982], 2-12). A presentist approach considers the past with one eye on the present, whereas a historicist approach focuses on the past for itself alone.

29. René Rémond, *Écrire l'histoire du temps présent. En hommage à François Bédarida* (Paris: CNRS, 1993), 33. Henry Rousso, "For a History of the Present," *The Haunting Past*, trans. Ralph Schoolcraft (Philadelphia: University of Pennsylvania Press, 2002), 25–47.
30. See Olivier Dumoulin, *Le rôle social de l'historien: De la chaire au prétoire* (Paris: Albin Michel, 2003), 11–61.
31. François Hartog, "Marshall Sahlins et l'anthropologie de l'histoire," *Annales* 6 (1983): 1256–1263.
32. Reinhart Koselleck, *Futures Past: On the Semantics of Historical Time*, trans. Keith Tribe (1985; New York: Columbia University Press, 2004), 3.
33. This text first circulated as one of the working documents for the conference and was then published in *L'état des lieux en sciences sociales*, ed. A. Dutu and N. Dodille (Paris: L'Harmattan, 1993), 29. See Detienne's presentation of the volume in *Comparing the Incomparable*, trans. Janet Lloyd (Stanford: Stanford University Press, 2008), 40–56..
34. Ricoeur, *Memory, History, Forgetting*, xvi, and "Mémoire: Approches historiennes...," 60–61.
35. Jean-François Lyotard, "Les Indiens ne cueillent pas de fleurs," *Annales* 20 (1965): 65 (article on Claude Lévi-Strauss's *The Savage Mind*).
36. For example, Günter Grass, *Too Far Afield*, trans. Krishna Winston (London: Faber, 2000); Cees Nooteboom, *All Souls Day*, trans. Susan Massotty (New York: Harcourt, 2001). In a different register, Emmanuel Terray, *Ombres berlinoises: Voyage dans une autre Allemagne* (Paris: Odile Jacob, 1996); Régine Robin, *Berlin chantiers* (Paris: Stock, 2001).
37. Étienne François, "Reconstruction allemande," in *Patrimoine et passions identitaires*, ed. Jacques Le Goff (Paris: Fayard, 1998), 313 (for the quotation from Scharoun), and Gabi Dolff-Bonekämper, "Les monuments de l'histoire contemporaine à Berlin: Ruptures, contradictions et cicatrices," in *L'abus monumental*, ed. Régis Debray (Paris: Fayard, 1999), 363–370.
38. See, from a philosophical perspective, the similar conclusions of Bertrand Binoche, "Après l'histoire, l'événement," *Actuels Marx* 32 (2002): 139–155.
39. Pomian, *L'ordre du temps*, 101–163. Karl Löwith, *Weltgeschichte und Heilsgeschehen: Die theologischen Voraussetzungen der Geschichtsphilosophie* (Stuttgart: Kohlhammer, 1967).
40. Daniel 2:28–45 (King James Version).
41. Arnaldo Momigliano, "Daniel and the Greek Theory of Imperial Succession,"

in *Essays on Ancient and Modern Judaism*, trans. Maura Masella-Gayley, ed. and intro. Silvia Berti (Chicago: University of Chicago Press, 1994), chap. 3, 29–35.

42. Jacques-Bénigne Bossuet, *Discourse on Universal History*, trans. Elborg Forster (Chicago: University of Chicago Press, 1976), 4, 109.

43. Saint Augustine, *The City of God*, trans. Marcus Dods, ed. Philip Schaff (New York, Cosimo, 2007), chap. 22, 30, 5. Auguste Luneau, *L'histoire du salut chez les Pères de l'Église* (Paris: Beauchesne, 1964), 285–331.

44. Koselleck, *Futures Past*, 259–263.

45. Paul Valéry, *Reflections on the World Today*, trans. Francis Scarfe (London: Thames and Hudson, 1951), 18.

46. Ernest Labrousse, *Esquisse du mouvement des prix et des revenus en France au XVIIIe siècle* (Paris: Dalloz, 1933).

47. Fernand Braudel, "History and the Social Sciences: The Long Duration [*La longue durée*]," trans. Morton Kroll and Florence Kroll, *American Behavioral Scientist* 3.3 (1960): 4.

48. Claude Lévi-Strauss, *Race and History* (Paris: UNESCO, 1952).

49. Ibid., 13, 21–22.

50. Ibid., 25.

51. Ibid., 40–45.

52. Ibid., 49.

53. Pomian, *L'ordre du temps*, 151.

54. Francis Fukuyama, *The End of History and the Last Man* (New York: Free Press, 1992), xi and 70. Jacques Derrida's *Specters of Marx* includes an extensive critique of Fukuyama's thesis (*Specters of Marx: The State of the Debt, the Work of Mourning, and the New International*, trans. Peggy Kamuf [New York: Routledge, 1994]).

55. Robert Bonnaud, who certainly did not wait for 1989 to place—or renew—his faith in a universal history, also believes that such a history is not over! Despite this, and due to our contemporary interest in time, his work has received a lot of attention from the media and the public. From an early age he had been fascinated by temporal patterns, and tried to find what he called "global historical turning-points" by documenting synchronicities (for example, 221 B.C., which is significant for the Mediterranean world and for China). In 1989 he published *Le système de l'histoire* (Paris: Fayard) and has gone on refining and perfecting his analyses ever since, convinced that history "does not suffer from an excess of dates, but from a lack of reasoned chronology" (*Tournants*

et périodes [Paris: Kimé, 2000], 13). His research, which claims to be predictive, should enable one to define a series of "planetary curves." See, lastly, Jean Baechler's *Esquisse d'une histoire universelle* (Paris: Fayard, 2002).

56. On the notion of experience, see Reinhart Koselleck, *The Practice of Conceptual History*, trans. Todd Samuel Presner, Kerstin Behnke, and Jobst Welge (Stanford: Stanford University Press, 2002), 45–48.

57. In "Language and the Human Experience," Émile Benveniste distinguishes between "linguistic time" and "chronic time." The former is "the time of language" [*"le temps de la langue"*] through which "the human experience of time is expressed," and the latter is "a necessary condition of the life of societies" (Émile Benveniste, "Language and the Human Experience," trans. Nora McKeon, *Diogenes* 13 [51] [Sept. 1965]: 1–12). The notion of regime of historicity is relevant to both. See also Elias's remarks on the notions of "past," "present," and "future": "The concepts of *past*, *present*, and *future* include in their meaning the relationship of an experiencing person (or persons) to a sequence of changes. It is in relation to someone who experiences it that one moment of a continuous flow assumes the character of a present *vis-à-vis* others with that of a present or a future. As symbols of experienced time-units, these three terms represent not only—like 'year' or 'cause and effect'—a succession, but also the simultaneous presence of the three time-units in people's experience. One might say that past, present, and future, although three different words, form a single concept" (*Time: An Essay*, 77; see chap. 2, 41–42).

58. Koselleck, *Futures Past*, 258.

59. Ibid., 274.

1. Making History

1. Marshall Sahlins, *Islands of History* (Chicago: University of Chicago Press, 1985), 72. The lecture was first given in December 1982 to the American Anthropological Association. Sartre's question can be found in the preface to Jean-Paul Sartre, *Search for a Method*, trans. Hazel E. Barnes (New York: Knopf, 1963), xxxiv.

2. Ibid., 72.

3. Marshall Sahlins, "The Apotheosis of Captain Cook," *Between Belief and Transgression*, ed. Michael Izard and Pierre Smith, trans. John Leavitt (Chicago: University of Chicago Press, 1982), 73–102.

4. Sahlins, *Islands of History*, xiii: "With some confidence, one can even offer a structural solution to the long-standing mystery of who done it?: the identity of Cook's assailant is deducible, in Holmesian fashion, from the elementary categories." See 104–135, and, more generally, the whole book. Also note 3.
5. Claude Lévi-Strauss, *The Savage Mind*, trans. John Weightman and Doreen Weightman (Chicago: University of Chicago Press, 1966).
6. If a conjuncture is "a situation resulting from a combination of circumstances" then the structure of a conjuncture is "the practical realization of the cultural categories in a specific historical context" (Sahlins, *Islands of History*, xiv).
7. Claude Lévi-Strauss, "The Scope of Anthropology," *Current Anthropology* 7.2 (1966): 121. Georges Charbonnier, ed., *Conversations with Lévi-Strauss*, trans. John Weightman and Doreen Weightman (London: Cape, 1969), 32–42.
8. Charbonnier, *Conversations with Lévi-Strauss*, 39.
9. Claude Lévi-Strauss, "Histoire et ethnologie," *Annales* 6 (1983): 1218 (italics in the original).
10. Claude Lévi-Strauss, "Retours en arrière," *Les temps modernes* 598 (1998): 66–69. The sentence explaining the cooling-down of contemporary societies is a citation from another of Lévi-Strauss's articles, published in *L'Homme* 126–128 (1983): 9–10.
11. Claude Lévi-Strauss, "Introduction," *Structural Anthropology 1*, trans. Claire Jacobson and Brooke Grundfest Schoepf (New York: Basic Books, 1963), 18. This text first appeared in the *Revue de métaphysique et de morale* 3-4 (1949), under the title "History and Ethnology."
12. See pp. 5–6.
13. Claude Lévi-Strauss, *Race and History* (Paris: UNESCO, 1952), 24–25.
14. Ibid., 25.
15. Claude Lévi-Strauss, *Structural Anthropology 2*, trans. Monique Layton (Chicago: University of Chicago Press, 1983), 14. The social facts studied by anthropology "are manifested in societies, each of which is a total, concrete, and cohesive entity."
16. Claude Lefort, *Les formes de l'histoire* (Paris: Gallimard, 2000), 46–77. The article first appeared in the *Cahiers internationaux de sociologie* 12 (1952): 3–25. It so happens that the first article in this issue was a text by Lévi-Strauss called "The Concept of Archaism in Anthropology," included in *Structural Anthropology 1*, chap. 6.
17. Ibid., 62.

18. Ibid., 65.
19. *Histoire et structure*, special issue, *Annales* 3-4 (1971).
20. Jean-Pierre Vernant, *The Origins of Greek Thought* (Ithaca: Cornell University Press, 1982); Sahlins, *Islands of History*, 33-34.
21. François Hartog, *L'Histoire d'Homère à Augustin* (Paris: Seuil, 1999), 17-19.
22. Sahlins, *Islands of History*, 35-36.
23. Ibid., 37, 49, 53.
24. Ibid., 38-39.
25. Ibid., 41.
26. Plutarch, *Vies parallèles*, ed. François Hartog (Paris: Gallimard, 2002), 16-17.
27. Sahlins, *Islands of History*, 44-45, 47, 49.
28. Ibid., 47, 49, 54.
29. Thucydides, *The Peloponnesian War*, trans. Steven Lattimore (Indianapolis: Hackett, 1998), 1.21; François Hartog, "L'oeil de Thucydide et l'histoire 'véritable,'" *Poétique* 49 (1982): 22-30.
30. Sahlins, *Islands of History*, 55.
31. François Furet, "Quantitative History," trans. Barbara Bray, *Daedalus* 100.1 (1971): 151-167.
32. Sahlins, *Islands of History*, 58.
33. Ibid., 59.
34. Ibid., 59.
35. Michel de Certeau, *The Writing of History*, trans. Tom Conley (New York: Columbia University Press, 1988), 3.
36. Sahlins, "Apotheosis of Captain Cook," 92. Nicholas Thomas objects that, in Sahlins's historical structuralism, "the indigenous system is only historicized in its dealings with Europeans; there is no basis in this historical structuralism for theories of indigenous change or of the major transformations which made Hawaiian, Tahitian, and western Polynesian societies into systems which look quite different" (*Out of Time: History and Evolution in Anthropological Discourse* [Ann Arbor: University of Michigan Press, 1996], 7, 120). Even were this to be the case, which I am unable to judge, the analysis of the moment at which the two systems interfere retains its full heuristic value. See pp. 27-28.
37. Reinhart Koselleck, *Futures Past: On the Semantics of Historical Time*, trans. Keith Tribe (New York: Columbia University Press, 2004), 237-238.
38. Sahlins, *Islands of History*, 60-61.
39. Ibid., 70-71.

40. Sahlins, "Apotheosis of Captain Cook," 89.
41. Ibid., 85.
42. Georges Duby, *The Legend of Bouvines*, trans. Catherine Tihanyi (Cambridge: Polity Press, 1990), 6.
43. See Koselleck's remarks on event and structure, and how the two intersect, but also the hiatus between them, in his analysis of the Battle of Leuthen, from which Frederick the Great emerged victorious: Koselleck, *Futures Past*, 113.
44. Koselleck, *Futures Past*, 26-42; and pp. 53-54.
45. Johannes Fabian, *Time and the Other: How Anthropology Makes Its Object* (New York: Colombia University Press, 1983), 145.
46. Marc Abélès, "Avec le temps . . . ," *Critique* 620-621 (Jan.-Feb. 1999): 42-60; "Overcoming the great divide, in other words refusing to consign alterity to a universe indexed on tradition, bound to the past, and immobilized by its origins: that is the goal of critical anthropology. But it provides us with few tools with which to think the contemporary world beyond the simple opposition of modernity and tradition. And above all, it seems indifferent to the question which is essential to any reflection on postmodernism, that of the regime of temporality of our present" (55).
47. *Time: Histories and Ethnologies*, ed. D. Owen Hughes and T. R. Trautmann (Ann Arbor: University of Michigan Press, 1995), 12.
48. Thomas, *Out of Time*, 7, 120.
49. Ibid., 109.
50. Although the fields of inquiry, the references, and the analytic instruments used are not the same, there is nevertheless a certain similarity between Sahlins's approach, as he takes apart the opposition between event and structure, and that of Pierre Nora, in his endeavor to show that the historian of the present should move back "from the evidence of the event to the evaluation of the system" ("The Return of the Event," trans. Arthur Goldhammer, *Histories: French Constructions of the Past* [New York: New Press, 1995], 435).

2. From Odysseus's Tears to Augustine's Meditations

1. François Hartog, *Memories of Odysseus: Frontier Tales from Ancient Greece*, trans. Janet Lloyd (Chicago: University of Chicago Press, 2001), 15-39.
2. Marcel Detienne, *Comparing the Incomparable* (Stanford: Stanford University Press, 2008), 54.

3. Erich Auerbach, *Mimesis*, trans. Willard R. Trask (Princeton: Princeton University Press, 1953), 7, 17.
4. Auerbach, *Mimesis*, 12, 17-18.
5. "The difference between legend and history is in most cases easily perceived by a reasonably experienced reader" (ibid., 19).
6. Homer, *The Iliad*, trans. A. T. Murray (Cambridge: Harvard University Press, 1924) and Perseus Digital Library, 19.65-70. On *thumos* as breath, associating emotion and breathing, see Richard Broxton Onians, *The Origins of European Thought* (Cambridge: Cambridge University Press, 1988), 49-56.
7. Homer, *Iliad* 23.69-72.
8. Ibid., 22.386-391: Achilles declares that he will never forget Patroclus, not even when he is in Hades.
9. Ibid., 23.100-105.
10. Ibid., 1.68-72. Marcel Detienne, *Apollon le couteau à la main* (Paris: Gallimard, 1998).
11. Homer, *The Odyssey*, trans. A. T. Murray (Cambridge: Harvard University Press, 1919) and Perseus Digital Library, 10.492-495, 11.100-137.
12. Hesiod, *Theogony*, trans. Hugh G. Evelyn-White (Cambridge: Harvard University Press, 1914) and Perseus Digital Library, 32 and 38.
13. Homer, *Odyssey* 8.79: according to Apollo's oracle, Achilles and Odysseus are "the best of the Achaeans."
14. Ibid., 17.290-327.
15. Jean-Pierre Vernant, *L'individu, la mort, l'amour* (Paris: Gallimard, 1989), 285.
16. Pseudo-Longinus, *On the Sublime*, trans. H. L. Havell (London: Macmillan, 1890) and Project Gutenberg, 9, 12: the *Odyssey* is presented as the poem of Homer's declining years (whereas the *Iliad* was the poem of his youth). In it he at last lets his heroes cry, as though in repayment of a debt that is long overdue. The *Odyssey* would be an *epilogos* to the *Iliad*, a tale coming afterward, just like historical narrative. For years now, Homer experts have tried to put a figure on the interval between the two poems: One hundred years? Fifty years?
17. Gregory Nagy, *The Best of the Achaeans: Concepts of the Hero in Archaic Greek Poetry* (Baltimore: Johns Hopkins University Press, 1999), 21.
18. Thucydides, *The Peloponnesian War*, trans. Steven Lattimore (Indianapolis: Hackett, 1998): "The Hellenes, then, as they increasingly came to be called ... accomplished nothing together before the Trojan War" (5).
19. Homer, *Odyssey* 1.342-344: Penelope is weighed down by a loss she cannot

forget (*penthos alaston*); consumed by the pain of absence (*potheô*), she ceaselessly recalls (*memnêmenê aiei*) the hero whose fame was great over all Greece and the Argolid. On *pothos*, funeral rites, and the epic, see Jean-Pierre Vernant, *Figures, idoles, masques* (Paris: Julliard, 1990), 41–50.

20. Homer, *Odyssey* 4.93-94 and 98-107.
21. Ibid., 4.219-296.
22. Ibid., 8.73-93. On this otherwise unknown quarrel and its "relation" to "The Quarrel" (between Agamemnon and Achilles), see Nagy, *Best of the Achaeans*, 42-58.
23. Homer, *Odyssey* 8.266-366.
24. Ibid., 8.83-95 and 521-534.
25. Ibid., 8.543-544.
26. Ibid., 8.573-587. See David Bouvier, *Le sceptre et la lyre: L'Iliade ou les héros de la mémoire* (Grenoble: Jérôme Millon, 2002), 39-40.
27. Ibid., 8.487-492 (translation slightly modified).
28. Likewise, the sign of the veracity of the episode of the wooden horse is Demodocus's ability to sing it in its entirety (*katalegein*) and down to the last detail (*kata moiran*). Odysseus in this case promises to declare to all humanity that the bard must have received a divine gift of song (*Odyssey* 8.496-499). On *kata kosmon* in this passage, see George B. Walsh's remarks (with which I am only partially in agreement), *The Varieties of Enchantment: Early Greek Views of the Nature and Function of Poetry* (Chapel Hill: University of North Carolina Press, 1984), 8-9. Similarly, at Aeolus's request, Odysseus recounts the capture of Troy, at length and in detail (*Odyssey* 10.16). The first sentence of Gorgias's *Encomium of Helen* states that the *kosmos* of discourse is "truth."
29. Arendt, *Between Past and Future*, 45.
30. Homer, *Odyssey* 8.84-93 and 521-522. On these tears and the scene as a whole, see Walsh, *Varieties of Enchantment*, 3-13.
31. See p. 34-35. Ibid., 8.581-587. Alcinous talks of his lamentation (*achos*, 8.541); *achos* is also what the wife witnessing her husband's death feels (8.523), and it is also what Menelaus says he suffers from, a sorrow never to be forgotten (*achos alaston*, 4.108). We are certainly in the register of mourning and of *pothos*.
32. Ibid., 8.523-533. Book 23 mentions that when Odysseus and Penelope are at last reunited, "from his neck she could in no wise let her white arms go" (vv. 241-242).
33. Nagy (*Best of the Achaeans*, 101) comments on the strong resemblance to Hector,

and that the situation resulting from the comparison is strikingly similar to that of Andromache at the end of the *Iliou Persis* (as represented in Proclus's summary). Pietro Pucci, *Odysseus Polutropos* (Ithaca: Cornell University Press, 1987), 221–223.
34. Pucci, *Odysseus Polutropos*, 236–245.
35. Hartog, *Memories of Odysseus*, 21.
36. Homer, *Odyssey* 9.19 and 12–13.
37. Ibid., 8.579–580.
38. Michel de Certeau, *The Writing of History*, trans. Tom Conley (New York: Columbia University Press, 1988), 99–102.
39. Homer, *Odyssey* 11.42–50.
40. The "small miracle of recognition," as Ricoeur calls it, is not for him, consisting as it does of "coating with presence the otherness of that which is over and gone" (Ricoeur, *Memory, History, Forgetting*, 39).
41. Paul Ricoeur, *Time and Narrative*, trans. Kathleen Blamey and David Pellauer (Chicago: University of Chicago Press, 1990), 3:246. "Without the recourse to narration, the problem of personal identity would in fact be condemned to an antimony with no solution. . . . This dilemma disappears if we substitute for identity understood in the sense of being the same (*idem*), identity understood in the sense of oneself as self-same. The difference between *idem* and *ipse* is nothing more than the difference between a substantial or formal identity and a narrative identity. Self-sameness, 'self-constancy,' can escape the dilemma of the Same and the Other to the extent that its identity rests on a temporal structure that conforms to the model of dynamic identity arising from the poetic composition of a narrative text."
42. Homer, *Odyssey* 13.1–2.
43. Vernant, *L'individu, la mort, l'amour*, 145–146; Pietro Pucci, "The Song of the Sirens," *The Song of the Sirens: Essays on Homer* (Oxford: Rowman and Littlefield, 1998), 1–9; Charles Segal, "*Kleos* and Its Ironies," *Singers, Heroes, and Gods in the Odyssey* (Ithaca: Cornell University Press, 1994), 85–109.
44. Homer, *Odyssey* 12.189–191.
45. On "men yet to be born," see Bouvier, *Le sceptre et la lyre*, 54 and 93–97.
46. Homer, *Odyssey* 12.183–184; see Homer, *Iliad* 9.673; Pucci, *Odysseus Polutropos*, 209–213.
47. On the funerary function of the Muses and the bards, see Marcello Carastro, *La cité des mages: Penser la magie en Grèce ancienne* (Bernin: Jérôme Million, 2006).

48. Charles Segal notes that the Sirens speak the language of knowledge, but never of remembrance or memory ("*Kleos* and Its Ironies," 100–101). See also Laurence Kahn, "Ulysse ou, La ruse et la mort," *Critique* 393 (Feb. 1980): 121–134.
49. On the *Iliad*'s representation of the past as an inventory of exemplary deeds, see Bouvier, *Le sceptre et la lyre*, 351–352.
50. Herodotus, *The History of Herodotus*, trans. G. C. Macaulay (London: Macmillan, 1890) and Project Gutenberg, 1, 5.
51. Homer, *Iliad* 16.31; see Bouvier, *Le sceptre et la lyre*, 426–427, on Achilles, who puts himself "outside of human time," before he finally agrees to "reintegrate a history which passes from fathers to sons."
52. Homer, *Odyssey* 1.326–327: Phemios sings of "the woeful return from Troy which Pallas Athena laid upon them."
53. Saint Augustine, *Confessions* 11.14.17, trans. Henry Chadwick (Oxford: Penguin, 1991).
54. Ibid., 11.28.37.
55. Ibid., 11.28.38.
56. Homer, *Odyssey* 5.157–158 and 219–220.
57. Aimé Solignac, "Notes," in *Oeuvres de saint Augustin* 14: *Les Confessions* (Paris: Desclée De Brouwer, 1996), 590.
58. Ricoeur comments: "The entire province of narrative is laid out here in its potentiality, from the simple poem, to the story of an entire life, to universal history. It is with these extrapolations, which are simply suggested here, that the present work is concerned" (*Time and Narrative*, 1:22). Ricoeur could equally have begun with Odysseus.
59. Saint Augustine, *Confessions* 11.29.39.
60. Epistle of Paul to the Philippians (King James Version), 3:12–14.
61. Saint Augustine, *The City of God*, trans. Marcus Dods, ed. Philip Schaff (New York: Cosimo, 2007), 1.
62. Epistle of Paul to the Philippians 3:16 and 20.
63. Genesis 12:1–2.
64. Hartog, *Memories of Odysseus*, 20–21. Catherine Chalier, *L'histoire promise* (Paris: Cerf, 1992), 48–60.
65. Exodus 19:6.
66. Yosef Hayim Yerushalmi, *Zakhor: Jewish History and Jewish Memory* (Seattle: University of Washington, 1982), 15 and 24.
67. Michael Walzer, *Exodus and Revolution* (New York: Basic Books, 1985), 7, 12.

68. Matthew 24:34, 36, 42, and 44.
69. Oscar Cullman, *Salvation in History*, trans. Sidney G. Sowers (New York: Harper and Row, 1967), 172.
70. Ibid., 184.
71. John 5:39 and 46.
72. Luke 9:27.
73. Saint Augustine, *City of God* 22.30.5.
74. Arendt, *Between Past and Future*, 125.
75. Ibid., 127.
76. Karl Löwith, *Meaning in History: The Theological Implications of the Philosophy of History* (Chicago: University of Chicago Press, 1957), 47. See chap. 5, p. 134. Not to forget the theme of disenchantment introduced by Max Weber: see Pierre Bouretz, *Les promesses du monde: Philosophie de Max Weber* (Paris: Gallimard, 1996).

3. Chateaubriand

1. See chap. 4 and chap. 5, pp. 104–107 and 162–170.
2. Reinhart Koselleck, *The Practice of Conceptual History*, trans. Todd Samuel Presner (Stanford: Stanford University Press, 2002), 76.
3. François-René de Chateaubriand, *Memoirs*, trans. A. S. Kline, 2005–2007, "Testamentary Preface of 1st December 1833," section 4 [translation of Chateaubriand, *Mémoires d'outre-tombe* (posthumous, 1848) (Paris: Gallimard, 1951), vol. II].
4. Chateaubriand, *Memoirs*, book 6, chap. 1, section 1.
5. Chateaubriand, *An Historical, Political, and Moral Essay on Revolutions, Ancient and Modern* (1797) (London: Henry Colburn, 1815), chap. 49, 355 (henceforth *Historical Essay*). [*Translator's note* (henceforth *TN*): this is a partial translation of Chateaubriand, *Essai historique, politique et moral sur les révolutions anciennes et modernes, considérées dans leurs rapports avec la Révolution française* (1797; 1826) (Paris: Gallimard, 1978). The 1815 English translation of the *Essai* is an abridged (and unauthorized) version of the original 1797 text, as Chateaubriand complains in the foreword to his 1826 (French) edition. It contains none of the extensive notes added for this later edition. Where an English translation exists, it will be given (as *Historical Essay*), otherwise reference in the notes will be to the French 1826 edition (as *Essai*). The English translation of chapter 57 of Chateaubriand's *Essai*, "Nuit chez les sauvages de l'Amérique," translated

as "A Night Among the Savages of America," is published in his *Recollections of Italy, England, and America, with Essays on Various Subjects, in Morals and Literature* (Philadelphia: Carey, 1816), 138–145.]

6. Chateaubriand, *Travels in America and Italy* (London: Henry Colburn, 1828), 2:146. [TN: *Travels in America and Italy*, in two volumes, is the translation of Chateaubriand, *Voyage en Amérique* (1827), in *Oeuvres romanesques et voyages* (Paris: Gallimard, 1978), vol. 1.]

7. Chateaubriand, *Essai*, 224: "From a literary point of view, the *Essay* touches on everything, takes on every subject, raises a multitude of questions, stirs up a whole world of ideas, and is a mixture of all styles. I do not know if my name will come down to future generations; I do not know if posterity will hear of my works; but were my *Essay* to escape oblivion, especially in its present state, with the Critical Notes, it would be one of the most singular monuments of my life." On Chateaubriand's tendency to multiply beginnings (as he does here), see Claude Reichler, "Raison et déraison des commencements," *Revue des sciences humaines* 247 (July 1997): 175–176.

8. Chateaubriand, *Voyage en Amérique*, ed. Richard Switzer (Paris: Didier, 1964) 1:lxix.

9. François Hartog, "Confronto con gli Antichi," in *I Greci*, vol. I, *Noi e I Greci*, ed. Salvatore Settis (Turin: Einaudi, 1996), 3–37; *La querelle des Anciens et des Modernes*, ed. Anne-Marie Lecoq (Paris: Gallimard, 2001); Levent Yilmaz, *Le temps moderne: Variations sur les Anciens et les contemporains* (Paris: Gallimard, 2004).

10. Jean-Jacques Rousseau, "XIII: History of Lacedaemonia," *Political Fragments: The Collected Writings of Rousseau* 4, trans. Judith R. Bush, Roger D. Masters, Christopher Kelly, ed. Roger D. Masters and Christopher Kelly (Hanover, NH: University Press of New England, 1994), 64. On Rousseau and antiquity, see Yves Touchefeu, *L'antiquité et le christianisme dans la pensée de Jean-Jacques Rousseau* (Oxford: Voltaire Foundation, 1999).

11. Chateaubriand, *Essai*, 440.

12. "For my own part I have saved myself in solitude, far from the ocean of the world. I sometimes observe the storms with which it is agitated, like a man cast alone on a desert island, who experiences a secret pleasing melancholy, while he contemplates the waves breaking at a distance on the coast where he was wrecked" (Chateaubriand, *Historical Essay*, chap. 47, 314).

13. Jean-Jacques Rousseau, "Discourse on the Origin and the Foundations of

Inequality Among Men," *Basic Political Writings*, 2nd ed., ed. and trans. Donald A. Cress (Indianapolis: Hackett, 2011), n. X, 111–112.
14. Chateaubriand, *Historical Essay*, "Introduction," 1–2.
15. Lévi-Strauss, *Structural Anthropology 2*, 33.
16. François Hartog, "Entre les anciens et les modernes, les sauvages," *Gradhiva* 11 (1992): 23–30.
17. Chateaubriand, *Essai*, "Introduction," 40. On the "Record of a journey from Paris to Jerusalem," see Jean-Claude Berchet, "Un voyage vers soi," *Poétique* 14 (1983): 91–108; Pierre Macherey, "L'*Essai sur les révolutions*, ou le laboratoire d'un style," *Europe* 775 (1993): 29–45; Philippe Antoine, *Les récits de voyage de Chateaubriand: Contribution à l'étude d'un genre* (Paris: Honoré Champion, 1997).
18. Chateaubriand, *Essai*, 37.
19. *Recollections of Italy, England, and America*, 138.
20. Jean-Jacques Barthélemy, *Travels of Anacharsis the Younger, in Greece* (London: printed by J. D. Denwick for Vernor and Hood, Lackington, Allen and Co., Otridge and Son, T. Hurst, and T. Boosey, 1800), 2.
21. Chateaubriand, *Historical Essay*, chap. 34, 157–158, n. 2.
22. François Hartog, *The Mirror of Herodotus*, trans. Janet Lloyd (Berkeley: University of California Press, 1988).
23. On Anacharsis the Elder, see François Hartog, *Memories of Odysseus: Frontier Tales from Ancient Greece*, trans. Janet Lloyd (Chicago: University of Chicago Press, 2001), 108–115.
24. Abbé Charles Rollin, *The Ancient History of the Egyptians, Carthaginians, Assyrians, Babylonians, Medes and Persians, Macedonians and Grecians*, vol. 2 (New York: George Long, 1830), 20–21.
25. Chateaubriand, *Historical Essay*, chap. 35, 163.
26. Ibid., chap. 35, 159.
27. Ibid., chap. 35, 160.
28. Ibid., chap. 35, 168, 157 n. 2.
29. Chateaubriand, *Essai*, 193.
30. Cicero coined the canonical phrase in *De oratore* (2.9.36), but the idea of *historia magistra* actually dates from earlier: see Hartog, *L'Histoire d'Homère à Augustin*, 185–186.
31. Chateaubriand, *Historical Essay*, chap. 13, 55.
32. Koselleck, *Futures Past*, 9–25.

33. Ibid., 259–263.
34. Chateaubriand, *Historical Essay*, chap. 1, 9.
35. Homer, *Odyssey* 4.385–393.
36. Chateaubriand, *Historical Essay*, chap. 1, 9–10.
37. Ibid., chap. 13, 43.
38. Ibid., chap. 11, 202.
39. Ibid., chap. 49, 346.
40. Ibid., "Recapitulation," 394.
41. Chateaubriand, *Essai*, "Préface" (1826), 15.
42. Ibid., chap. 47, 306.
43. Ibid., chap. 42, 255.
44. François Hartog, "The Concept of Liberty in Antiquity and Modern Times: The French Revolution and Antiquity," in *Greeks and Romans in the Modern World*, ed. Roger-Pol Droit (Boulder: Social Science Monographs, 1998), 97.
45. Chateaubriand, *Historical Essay*, chap. 42, 255.
46. Ibid., chap. 42, 254–255.
47. Karl Marx, *The Eighteenth Brumaire of Louis Bonaparte*, 3rd ed., trans. Daniel de Leon (Chicago: Charles H. Kerr & Company, 1913), 9–10.
48. Chateaubriand, *Historical Essay*, chap. 42, 255. [*TN*: Translation slightly modified.]
49. Chateaubriand, *Essai*, 268 and 270.
50. Chateaubriand, *Historical Essay*, chap. 42, "Recapitulation," 397 and 398; *Essai*, 438.
51. Chateaubriand, *Essai*, 268.
52. "It is a feeling, natural on the part of the unfortunate, to aim at the illusions of happiness by the recollection of past pleasures" (Chateaubriand, *Recollections of Italy, England, and America*, 138; the chapter opens on these words).
53. Chateaubriand, *Travels in America*, 1:98, 100. At the time, parallels with antiquity did not yet appear compromised.
54. Ibid., 1:99–100.
55. Letter from Washington to the marquis de la Rouërie, who had written a letter of introduction for Chateaubriand. Quoted by Richard Switzer in *Voyage en Amérique*, 1:xxxvi.
56. Chateaubriand, *Travels in America*, 1:98, 108.
57. Ibid., 2:35; 1:201; 2:32; 1:233–234; 2:81.
58. Ibid., 2:46.

59. Chateaubriand, *Atala*, trans. James Spence Harr (New York: Cassell & Co., 1884), vii.
60. Chateaubriand, *Travels in America*, 1:145-153.
61. Chateaubriand, *Recollections of Italy, England, and America*, 196-197.
62. Ibid., 206.
63. Chateaubriand, *Travels in America*, 2:143.
64. Ibid., 2:143, 146.
65. Chateaubriand, *Essai*, 37.
66. Ibid., 42. Jean-Claude Bonnet, "Le nageur entre deux rives: La traversée comme expérience révolutionnaire," *Bulletin de la Société Chateaubriand* 32 (1989): 55-60.
67. P. Macherey, "L'*Essai sur les révolutions*, ou le laboratoire d'un style," 33.
68. Chateaubriand, *Essai*, 15.
69. Chateaubriand, *Études ou discours historiques*, in *Oeuvres complètes*, vol. 3 (Paris: Ladvocat, 1831), 1.
70. Chateaubriand, *Travels in America*, 1:195. In actual fact, as scholars have shown, the text was largely based on book summaries.
71. Chateaubriand, *Travels in America*, "Advertisement," 1:113.
72. Ibid., 1:78, 2:84.
73. Michel Butor, "Chateaubriand and Early America," in *Inventory: Essays*, ed. Richard Howard (New York: Simon and Schuster, 1968), 59-99.
74. Chateaubriand, *Recollections of Italy, England, and America*, 138: "When I travelled among the Indian tribes of Canada—when I quitted the habitations of Europeans, and found myself, for the first time, alone amid boundless forests..."
75. Chateaubriand, *Travels in America*, 1:112-113.
76. Ibid., 1:181.
77. Ibid., 1:155 and 157.
78. Ibid., 1:164.
79. Ibid., 2:47.
80. Ibid., 2:48, 93.
81. Ibid., 1:196.
82. Ibid., 2:93.
83. Ibid., 2:104 and 101 [*TN*: Translation slightly modified.]
84. Chateaubriand's depiction of Tahiti in the preface to the *Travels* already has a very "Segalenian" flavor to it: the island's customs of singing, dancing, and sensuality have all been replaced by the activity of printing bibles.

85. Chateaubriand, *Travels in America*, 2:109.
86. Ibid., 2:109.
87. Ibid., 2:117.
88. Ibid., 2:118-119.
89. Ibid., 2:121.
90. Hartog, "The Concept of Liberty in Antiquity and Modern Times," 105-108; Nicole Loraux and Pierre Vidal-Naquet, "The Formation of Bourgeois Athens," *Politics, Ancient and Modern*, trans. Janet Lloyd, ed. Pierre Vidal-Naquet (Cambridge, MA: Polity, 1995), 82-140.
91. This approach to the issue of freedom is obviously quite different from that adopted by Chateaubriand in his political writings. See Chateaubriand, *Grands écrits politiques*, ed. Jean-Paul Clément (Paris: Imprimerie nationale, 1993).
92. Jean Roussel, *Jean-Jacques Rousseau en France après la Révolution, 1795-1830* (Paris: Armand Colin, 1972), 369-380.
93. Chateaubriand, *Essai*, "Préface," 23.
94. This does not settle everything, however, since the modern conception of history as progress has yet to be harmonized with the Christian viewpoint and the teachings of the Church. A sign of this concern can be found in the care Chateaubriand takes to ensure that the most recent discoveries corroborate Old Testament chronology (Chateaubriand, *Essai*, 57, note to the 1826 edition).
95. Chateaubriand, *Memoirs*, book 62, chap. 14; and see pp. 152-153.
96. Lucien Febvre, *The Problem of Unbelief in the Sixteenth Century: The Religion of Rabelais* (1942), trans. Beatrice Gottlieb (Cambridge: Harvard University Press, 1982), 5: "The problem is to determine what set of precautions to take and what rules to follow in order to avoid the worst of all sins, the sin that cannot be forgiven—anachronism."
97. Chateaubriand, *Memoirs*, "Preface," sec. 5.
98. See Agnès Verlet, *Les vanités de Chateaubriand* (Geneva: Librairie Droz, 2001), particularly 328-329, which show how the concept of the "vanities" can shed light on the writing of the *Memoirs*.
99. Claude Reichler, "Raison et déraison des commencements," 179.
100. Chateaubriand, *Vie de Rancé*, in *Oeuvres romanesques et voyages*, 1:989.
101. Michel de Certeau, *Psychanalyse et histoire*, rev. ed. (Paris: Gallimard, 2002), 78.
102. Chateaubriand, *Vie de Rancé*, 989.
103. Chateaubriand, "General Preface" to his *Oeuvres complètes* of 1826.

104. Constantin-François Volney, *Volney's Ruins; or, Meditation on the Revolutions of Empires*, trans. Count Daru (Boston: J. Mendum, 1866). See Jean Gaulmier, *L'Idéologue Volney, 1757-1820: Contribution à l'histoire de l'orientalisme français* (1951; Geneva: Slatkine, 1980).
105. Constantin-François Volney, *Travels Through Syria and Egypt*, vol. 1, 3rd ed. (London: G. and J. Robinson, 1805), "Preface," vi–vii. It is worth noting that although Volney visited Baalbek, he never actually got as far as Palmyra.
106. Volney, *Ruins*, 24.
107. Ibid., 26.
108. Ibid., 40, 66.
109. Ibid., 66.
110. Ibid., 66.
111. Ibid., 67, 74.
112. Volney, *Lectures on History* (London: Ridgeway, 1800), vi–vii.
113. Volney, *View of the Climate and Soil of the United States of America* (London: J. Johnson, 1804), iv.
114. Chateaubriand, *Études historiques*, in *Oeuvres complètes*, vol. 1 (Paris: Firmin-Didot, 1842), 1.
115. Ibid., 2.
116. Ibid., 1.
117. Ibid., 2.
118. Ibid., 12.
119. François Furet, preface to Alexis de Tocqueville, *De la démocratie en Amérique* (Paris: Garnier-Flammarion, 1981), 41. The first part of the book was published in 1835, and the second in 1840.
120. François Mélonio, *Tocqueville and the French*, trans. Beth G. Raps (Charlottesville: University of Virginia Press, 1998), 16.
121. Alexis de Tocqueville, letter to Comte Molé, August 1835, cited in Hans J. Morgenthau, *The Purpose of American Politics* (New York: Knopf, 1963), 29.
122. Chateaubriand, unpublished letter, 11 January 1835, cited in Mélonio, *Tocqueville and the French*, 36.
123. Alexis de Tocqueville, *Democracy in America*, trans. Arthur Goldhammer (New York: Library of America, 2004), 6–7.
124. Ibid., 11.
125. Ibid., 831.

126. Ibid., 14, 3.
127. Ibid., 14-15.
128. Ibid., 17.
129. Ibid., 831.
130. Ibid., 7.

4. Memory, History, and the Present

1. See chap. 3, pp. 80-81.
2. Lorenz von Stein, cited by Reinhart Koselleck, *Futures Past: On the Semantics of Historical Time*, trans. Keith Tribe (1985; New York: Columbia University Press, 2004), 61.
3. *Les lieux de mémoire*, III: *Les France*, ed. Pierre Nora (Paris: Gallimard, 1993), 1:11-32. [TN: Nora's *Lieux de mémoire* comprises three parts, each of which contains one, three, and again three volumes respectively, published between 1984 and 1993. Partial—revised and abridged—translations into English have appeared as Pierre Nora and Lawrence Kritzman, eds., *Realms of Memory: Rethinking the French Past*, 3 vols., trans. Arthur Goldhammer (New York: Columbia University Press, 1996-1998); and as Pierre Nora and David Jordan, eds., *Rethinking France*, 4 vols., trans. Mary Trouille (Chicago: University of Chicago Press, 2001-2010). For clarity I shall retain the French title *Lieux de mémoire* in the main text while referring in the notes to the relevant English translation when available.]
4. *1789: La commémoration* (Paris: Gallimard, 1999) contains the articles published in the review *Le Débat* on the bicentenary of the French Revolution. Patrick Garcia, *Le Bicentenaire de la Révolution française: Pratiques sociales d'une commémoration* (Paris: CNRS, 2000).
5. See pp. 149-152.
6. See pp. 92-94.
7. *Les lieux de mémoire*, III.1: "Présentation."
8. Fernand Braudel, *The Identity of France*, trans. Siân Reynolds (London: Fontana, 1989-1990), 2 vols.
9. Ibid., 2:667. See pp. 13-14.
10. Of the many authors who could be cited here, I choose a historian, Eric Hobsbawm, who was an actively involved observer of his century: "Very few

people would deny that an epoch in world history ended with the collapse of the Soviet bloc and the Soviet Union, whatever we read in the events of 1989-91. A page in history has been turned" (*On History* [London: Abacus, 1998], 311).

11. Carol Gluck, "11 septembre: Guerre et télévision au xxie siècle," *Annales HSS* 1 (2003): 135-162. Carol Gluck presents a history-testimony of the "war on terror" launched by the United States by carrying out an "ethnography" of the media. She focuses on the immediate narrativization of the war, but does not examine the equally immediate self-commemoration constitutive of the event.
12. François Hartog, "Preface," *Plutarque, Vies parallèles* (Paris: Gallimard, 2002), 35-36. The phrase "entering one's future backwards" was coined by Valéry.
13. Koselleck, *Futures Past*, 33.
14. Arendt, *Between Past and Future*, 3, 9.
15. Chateaubriand, *Memoirs*, book 32, chapter 14: "The Future—The difficulty of comprehending it."
16. See pp. xiv-xviii.
17. On the longevity of *historia magistra*, see Koselleck, *Futures Past*, 26-42.
18. François Hartog, "Preface," *Plutarque, Vies parallèles*, 26-27.
19. Francois Hartog, "From Parallel to Comparison (or Life and Death of Parallel)," in *Applied Classics*, ed. Angelos Chaniotis, Annika Kuhn, and Christina Kuhn (Stuttgart: Steiner, 2009), 15-26. See also Yilmaz, *Le temps moderne*.
20. See pp. 128-136.
21. Giovanni Lista, *Le Futurisme* (Paris: Terrail, 2001), 29, 30, and 38. Umberto Boccioni, Carlo Carrà, Luigi Russolo, Giacomo Balla, and Gino Severini, "Manifesto of the Futurist Painters, 1910," *Futurist Manifestos*, trans. Robert Brian et al., ed. Umbro Apollonio (New York: Viking, 1973), 24-26.
22. Jean Fourastié, *Les trente glorieuses; ou, La Révolution invisible de 1946 à 1975* (Paris: Fayard, 1979). Fourastié makes two main points: there has been progress, but most importantly it has come to an end.
23. Émile Benveniste, *Problems in General Linguistics*, trans. Mary Elizabeth Meek (Coral Gables: University of Miami Press, 1971), 115.
24. Horace, *The Epistles of Horace*, trans. David Ferry (New York: Farrar, Strauss, and Giroux, 2001), 1.4.14-16.
25. Marcus Aurelius, *Meditations*, trans. A. S. L. Farquharson (New York: Random House Digital, 2009), 12.4.3.

26. Goethe, *Goethe's Faust*, part II, trans. Leopold J. Bernays (London: Sampson Low and A. Bielfeld, 1839), 124. See Pierre Hadot, "'Le présent seul est notre bonheur': La valeur de l'instant présent chez Goethe et dans la philosophie antique," *Diogène* 133 (1986): 71 and idem, "The Present Alone Is Our Happiness: The Value of the Present Instant in Goethe and in Ancient Philosophy," *The Present Alone Is Our Happiness: Conversations with Jeannie Carlier and Arnold I. Davidson*, trans. Marc Djaballah and Michael Chase (Stanford: Stanford University Press, 2011), 217–237 [TN: This is an interview, and a discussion of the original article].
27. Franz Rosenzweig, letter of 5 February 1917, quoted in Stéphane Mosès, *The Angel of History*, trans. Barbara Harshav (Stanford: Stanford University Press, 2009), 60.
28. Blaise Pascal, *Pascal's Pensées; or, Thoughts on Religion*, trans. Gertrude Burfurd (Mount Vernon: Peter Pauper, 1900), 17.
29. Éric Michaud, "Le présent des avant-gardes" (forthcoming in *New German Critique*).
30. André Gide, *The Immoralist*, trans. Stanley Appelbaum (Mineola: Dover, 1996), 32.
31. Lucien Febvre replied to Valéry's charges on several occasions, leaving him to his lifeless history and accusing him of knowing nothing about living history (1941). See *Combats pour l'histoire* (Paris: Armand Colin, 1992), 24, 102, and 423.
32. "Aux lecteurs," *Annales d'histoire économique et sociale* 1 (1929): "While historians apply their good old tried and tested methods to the documents of the past, an increasing number of people devote their time to examining contemporary societies and economies, often with passion; in principle there should be a common understanding between these two classes of workers, but in general they work side by side and know nothing of each other."
33. Jean-Paul Sartre, *Nausea*, trans. Lloyd Alexander (New York: New Directions, 2007), 95–96, 100.
34. Jean-Paul Sartre, "Introducing *Les Temps Modernes*," *"What Is Literature?" and Other Essays* (Cambridge: Harvard University Press, 1988), 253–254. The idea recurs in *The Words*, trans. Bernard Frechtman (New York: Braziller, 1964), 254: "I claim sincerely to be writing only for my time."
35. Jean-Paul Sartre, *The Words*, trans. Bernard Frechtman (New York: Vintage, 1981), 2.
36. Cited in Arendt, *Between Past and Future*, 8.

4. MEMORY, HISTORY, AND THE PRESENT   229

37. Claude Lévi-Strauss, *A World on the Wane* [*Tristes tropiques*], trans. John Russell (New York: Criterion, 1961), 397.
38. See pp. 14, 27–28.
39. Pierre Clastres, *Society Against the State*, trans. Robert Hurley and Abe Stein (New York: Zone, 1987); Jacques Lizot, *Tales of the Yanomami*, trans. Ernest Simon (New York: Cambridge University Press, 1985).
40. Luc Boltanski and Ève Chiapello, *The New Spirit of Capitalism*, trans. Gregory Elliott (New York: Verso, 2005).
41. Sylviane Agacinski, *Time Passing: Modernity and Nostalgia*, trans. Jody Gladding (New York: Columbia University Press, 2003), 168–172.
42. Pierre Bourdieu, *Pascalian Mediations*, trans. Richard Nice (Stanford: Stanford University Press, 2000), 222.
43. However, in his analysis of "spectacular time" as "consumable pseudo-cyclical time," Guy Debord maintains that "the past [in spectacular time] continues to dominate the present" (Debord, *Society of the Spectacle*, trans. Donald Nicholson-Smith [New York: Zone, 1999], 113).
44. T.S. Eliot, *On Poetry and Poets* (New York: Farrar, Straus, and Giroux, 2009), 72.
45. Philippe Ariès, *The Hour of Our Death*, trans. Helen Weaver (New York: Vintage, 2008), 560 [*TN*: translation slightly modified].
46. Helga Nowotny, *Time: The Modern and Postmodern Experience*, trans. Neville Plaice (Cambridge: Polity, 1996).
47. Bourdieu, *Pascalian Mediations*, 226.
48. Emmanuel Kant, *The Conflict of Faculties*, cited in Koselleck, *Futures Past*, 39. On the historicization of the event before it even occurs, one can refer (in another register) to Woody Allen's film *Bananas* (1971), in which the viewer is the witness, live, to a president's assassination.
49. Olivier Dumoulin, *Le rôle social de l'historien: De la chaire au prétoire* (Paris: Albin Michel, 2003), 27–63.
50. See pp. 180–181.
51. Jean Favier and Daniel Neirinck, "Les archives," in *L'histoire et le métier d'historien en France, 1945–1995*, ed. François Bédarida (Paris: Maison des Sciences de l'Homme, 1995), 89–110. François Hartog, "Archives: La loi, la mémoire, l'histoire," *Le Débat* 112 (2000): 45–48. For an overview of the issues involved, see Sophie Coeuré and Vincent Duclert, *Les archives* (Paris: La Découverte, 2001).
52. Standard practice is for access to documents to be immediate, but the

ordinances accompanying the 1979 law set restrictions of thirty or sixty years on certain archives (namely those containing information potentially harmful to privacy, state security, or national defense). In 1995, the Braibant Report recommended reducing these time spans to twenty-five and fifty years, respectively.

53. No one could have imagined at the time that Papon would be sent home from the Santé prison in Paris on medical grounds in September 2002. But this release, justified only by the application of a new provision in the law, caused a public outcry, showing unequivocally that Papon would remain until his dying day contemporary with his crime. As would we.

54. See pp. 200-201. Henry Rousso, "The Confusion Between Memory and History," *The Haunting Past*, trans. Ralph Schoolcraft (Philadelphia: University of Pennsylvania Press, 2001), 1-24.

55. André Fermigier, *La bataille de Paris: Des Halles à la Pyramide, chroniques d'urbanisme* (Paris: Gallimard, 1991), 54. The series of articles that Fermigier wrote for the *Nouvel Observateur* and later for *Le Monde* document the battle for the Halles, the defeat of the preservationists, and the gradual emergence of the theme of heritage.

56. Ibid., 149.

57. See the set of articles "L'utopie Beaubourg dix ans après," *Esprit* 123 (1987). Geneviève Gallot, "Le Centre Pompidou, une utopie épuisée," *Le Débat* 98 (1998): 102.

58. See pp. 150-151.

59. Mona Ozouf, in *1789: La commémoration*, 322.

60. Étienne François, "Nation retrouvée, nation à contrecoeur: L'Allemagne des commémorations," *Le Débat* 78 (1994): 62-70. *Deutsche Erinnerungsorte*, ed. E. François and H. Schulze (Munich: Beck, 2001-2002).

61. Colin Lucas, "Introduction," *Constructing the Past*, ed. Jacques Le Goff and Pierre Nora, trans. David Denby, Martin Thom, and Ian Patterson (Cambridge: Cambridge University Press, 1987), 1 [*TN*: this is a partial translation of Jacques Le Goff and Pierre Nora, eds., *Faire de l'histoire* (Paris: Gallimard, 1974)].

62. Thucydides, *Peloponnesian War*, 1.20-21.

63. Pierre Nora, "Mémoire collective," in *La nouvelle histoire*, ed. J. Le Goff, R. Chartier, and J. Revel (Paris: Retz, 1978), 400-401.

64. See Marie-Claire Lavabre, "Maurice Halbwachs et la sociologie de la mémoire," *Raison Présente* 128 (1998): 47-56.

65. Maurice Halbwachs, *The Collective Memory*, trans. Francis J. Ditter (New York: Harper and Row, 1980), 101.
66. Ibid., 80, 107.
67. Ibid., 106.
68. J. Thiénot, *Rapport sur les études historiques* (Paris: Imprimerie impériale, 1868), 356.
69. Pierre Nora, "The Return of the Event," trans. Arthur Goldhammer, *Histories: French Constructions of the Past* (New York: New Press, 1995).
70. Nora and Kritzman, eds., *Realms of Memory*, 1:1.
71. Jean-Noël Jeanneney, *L'histoire va-t-elle plus vite? Variations sur un vertige* (Paris: Gallimard, 2001). Jeanneney maintains that acceleration is "a partial reality, a useful concept, but only if we relativize it and understand that what is really new is not our civilization's increased mobility but rather the growing disparity between all the rhythms which fashion our future" (137). I will come back to this theme of disparity or dissonance.
72. See chap. 3, p. 73. Koselleck, *Futures Past*, 40–41.
73. Lothar Baier, *Keine Zeit: 18 Versuche über die Beschleunigung* (Munich: Antje Kunstmann, 2000).
74. Pierre Nora, "Pour une histoire au second degré," *Le Débat* 122 (2002): 27.
75. Pierre Nora, "Ernest Lavisse: Son rôle dans la formation du sentiment national," *Revue Historique* (July–Sept. 1962), included in *Les lieux de mémoire*, 1:247–289.
76. Ernest Renan, "Prayer on the Acropolis," *Recollections from My Youth*, 3rd ed. (London: Chapman and Hall, 1897), 61.
77. Nora, "Pour une histoire au second degré," 30.
78. Frances A. Yates, *The Art of Memory* (New York: Random House, 2011).
79. Marcel Proust, *Time Regained*, vol. 6 of *In Search of Lost Time*, trans. Andres Mayor and Terence Kilmartin, revised by D. J. Enright (New York: Random House, 2003), 502, 528, 531–532.
80. Henry Bergson, *Time and Free Will: An Essay on the Immediate Data of Consciousness*, trans. F. L. Pogson (Mineola, NY: Dover, 2001), in particular chap. 2, which analyzes the idea of duration. Péguy attended Bergson's lectures, and the "Bergsonian revolution" was central to his thinking. Bergson said of Péguy that he understood "the essence of his thinking."
81. Charles Péguy, *Clio: Dialogue de l'histoire et de l'âme païenne*, in *Oeuvres en prose complètes* 3 (Paris: Gallimard, 1992), 1176–1178. The manuscript was written

between 1912 and 1913. François Bédarida, "Histoire et mémoire chez Péguy," *Vingtième Siècle* 73 (2002): 101-110.
82. Charles Péguy, "À nos amis, à nos abonnés," in *Oeuvres en prose complètes* (Paris: Gallimard, 1988), 2:1309.
83. Péguy, *Clio*, 1205.
84. Walter Benjamin, "Theses on the Philosophy of History," *Illuminations* (New York: Random House, 2007), 253-264. On Benjamin and Péguy, Hella Tiedemann-Bartells, "La mémoire est toujours de la guerre: Benjamin et Péguy," in *W. Benjamin et Paris*, ed. H. Wismann (Paris: Cerf, 1986), 133-145. See also the edition established by Michael Löwy, *Walter Benjamin: Avertissement d'incendie. Une lecture des thèses "Sur le concept d'histoire"* (Paris: Presses universitaires de France, 2001).
85. Walter Benjamin, *The Arcades Project*, trans. Howard Eiland and Kevin McLaughlin (Cambridge: Harvard University Press, 1999), 462.
86. Hannah Arendt, "Walter Benjamin: 1892-1940," in Benjamin, *Illuminations* (New York: Random House, 2007), 1-58.
87. Ernest Lavisse, *Histoire de France contemporaine, depuis la Révolution jusqu'à la paix de 1919* (Paris: Hachette, 1922), 511, 515, and 551.
88. Nora, "Between Memory and History," *Realms of Memory*, 1:6.
89. Marc Bloch, *The Historian's Craft*, trans. Peter Putnam (Manchester: Manchester University Press, 2004), 36. For the importance of the interaction between past and present, see Olivier Dumoulin, *Marc Bloch* (Paris: Presses de Sciences Po, 2000), 264-276.
90. Marcel Gauchet, in *Les lieux de mémoire*, II.1: *La Nation* (Paris: Gallimard, 1986), 285.
91. François Furet, *Interpreting the French Revolution*, trans. Elborg Forster (Cambridge: Cambridge University Press, 1997) [*TN*: This is the translation of *Penser la Révolution française* (Paris: Gallimard, 1978)].
92. Augustin Thierry, *The Formation and Progress of the Tiers État, or Third Estate, in France*, vol. 1, trans. Francis B. Wells (London: Thomas Bosworth, 1855), 7.
93. Carine Fluckiger, "Le Moyen Âge domestiqué: Les historiens narrativistes et la couleur locale," *Équinoxes* 16 (1996): 27-37.
94. François Hartog, "L'oeil de l'historien et la voix de l'histoire," *Communications* 43 (1986): 55-69.
95. Jules Michelet, "Préface de *l'Histoire de France*," in *Oeuvres complètes* (Paris: Flammarion, 1974), 4:13ff.

96. Braudel, *Identity of France*, 1:15.
97. François Hartog, *Le XIXe siècle et l'histoire: Le cas Fustel de Coulanges* (1988; Paris: Seuil, 2001).
98. Fustel de Coulanges, *Histoire des institutions politiques de l'ancienne France* (Paris: Hachette, 1875), "Introduction," 2.
99. Braudel, *Identity of France*, 2:678-679.
100. Gabriel Monod, "Preface: *Revue Historique*," trans. Nora Beeson, in *The Varieties of History*, ed. Fritz Stern (New York: Vintage, 1973), 172-174.
101. Febvre, *Combats pour l'histoire*, "Foreword," v.
102. Nora, *Les lieux de mémoire*, II.1:327.
103. Valéry, *Reflections on the World Today*, 18 and 36.
104. Lucien Febvre, "L'histoire dans le monde en ruines," *Revue de Synthèse Historique* 30 (February 1920): 4.
105. Toward the end of his career, Marc Bloch had endeavored to define a certain French originality, through comparative analysis ("There is no such thing as French history, there is European history"). And Lucien Febvre, in his lectures at the Collège de France in 1945/6 and 1947, worked on delineating how a national consciousness had emerged (*Honneur et patrie*, ed. Thérèse Charmasson and Brigitte Mazon [Paris: Perrin, 1996]).
106. Georges Duby and Robert Mandrou, *A History of French Civilization*, trans. James Blakely Atkinson (New York: Random House, 1964). Duby nevertheless contributed to the educational publisher Hachette's History of France series, which focused on political history, and wrote the first volume, *France in the Middle Ages, 987-1460: From Hugh Capet to Joan of Arc* (Oxford: Blackwell, 1983).
107. Charles Péguy, *L'argent suite*, in *Oeuvres en prose complètes*, 3:883. Henri-Irénée Marrou, "De la logique de l'Histoire à une Éthique de l'historien," *Revue de Métaphysique et de Morale* 54 (1949): 248-272.
108. François Dosse, *Empire of Meaning: The Humanization of the Social Sciences*, trans. Hassan Melehy (Minneapolis: University of Minnesota Press, 1999).
109. Braudel, *Identity of France*, 1:23.
110. Ibid., 1:24-5.
111. *Histoire de la France*, ed. André Burguière and Jacques Revel (Paris: Seuil, 1989), "Preface," 18 and 19. The "original characteristics" are of course a discreet allusion to Marc Bloch.
112. See for example, *Passés recomposés: Champs et chantiers de l'histoire*, ed. J. Boutier and D. Julia (Paris: Autrement, 1995).

113. Christian Amalvi, "Bastille Day," in *Realms of Memory*, vol. 3, ed. Nora (1998), 117-159.
114. Péguy, *Clio*, 3:1083-1084.
115. Jean-Michel Leniaud, *L'utopie française: Essai sur le patrimoine* (Paris: Mengès, 1992), 115-150; see chap. 5.
116. Nora, *Les lieux de mémoire*, III.1:29.
117. Emmanuel Kattan, *Penser le devoir de mémoire* (Paris: Presses universitaires de France, 2002).
118. Nora, *Les lieux de mémoire*, III.1.
119. P. Nora, *Essais d'ego-histoire* (Paris: Gallimard, 1987).
120. Henry Rousso, "L'historien, lieu de mémoire, hommage à Robert Paxton," in *Vichy: L'événement, la mémoire, l'histoire* (Paris: Gallimard, 2001), 453-480, in which he shows that Paxton has become "a sort of site of memory."
121. See chap. 5, pp. 180-181.
122. Raymond Aron, *Introduction to the Philosophy of History*, trans. George J. Irwin (Boston: Beacon Press, 1961), 222: "We understand here by contingency both the possibility of conceiving the other event and the impossibility of deducing the event from the totality of the previous situation."
123. Ricoeur, *Time and Narrative*, 3:216. Bernard Lepetit, "Le présent de l'histoire," in *Les formes de l'expérience: Une autre histoire sociale* (Paris: Albin Michel, 1995), 295-298.
124. See *L'Europe entre cultures et nations*, ed. Daniel Fabre (Paris: Maison des Sciences de l'Homme, 1996), which explores how the three terms of heritage, identity, and nation operate in Europe.
125. On the relation between heritage and the present, see chap. 5, pp. 189-191.
126. Namely Beck in Germany, Blackwell in Great Britain and the USA, Critica in Spain, Laterza in Italy, and Le Seuil in France. The books were published simultaneously in the different countries. To date, nineteen titles have been published.
127. See the debate on this in several issues of *Vingtième Siècle: Revue d'histoire*: Nicolas Roussellier, 38 (1993): 106-108; Jean-Pierre Rioux, "Pour une histoire de l'Europe sans adjectif," 50 (1996): 101-110; Jean-Clément Martin, "Pour une histoire 'principielle' de l'Europe," 53 (1997): 124-128; and the collection of articles *Apprendre l'histoire de l'Europe* [Learning Europe's history], which were the proceedings of a conference aiming, in J.-P. Rioux's words, to "lay down the

scientific precautionary principles which should set limits on voluntarism," 71 (2001).

128. J. Le Goff, "Editor's Preface" to the Making of Europe series. This text figures in all the volumes of the series.

129. See the thought-provoking remarks of the medievalist Patrick J. Geary in his *The Myth of Nations: The Medieval Origins of Europe* (Princeton: Princeton University Press, 2002).

5. Heritage and the Present

1. The new department comprised Historic Monuments, the General Inventory [*l'Inventaire général*], Archaeology, and a Council on Ethnological Heritage attached to an Ethnological Task Force. It was the ethnologist Isac Chiva who proposed this organization. See Daniel Fabre, "L'ethnologie devant le monument historique," in *Domestiquer l'histoire: Ethnologie des monuments historiques*, ed. D. Fabre (Paris: Maison des Sciences de l'Homme, 2000), 8-9.

2. *L'abus monumental*, proceedings of the Heritage Debates chaired by Régis Debray, (Paris: Fayard, 1999). See in particuliar R. Debray, "Le monument ou la transmission comme tragédie," 11-32. A few years earlier, Tzvetan Todorov had published *Les abus de la mémoire* (translated as *Memory as a Remedy for Evil*, trans. Gila Walker [Kolkata: Seagull, 2010]).

3. According to a survey, carried out by the French Ministry of Culture at the end of the 1980 Heritage Year, concerning the public's perception of heritage, in 1979 heritage evoked material goods in private hands, whereas after 1980 more than a third of the French public conceived it as "national, cultural, artistic and other treasures." See Hervé Glevarec and Guy Saez, *Le patrimoine saisi par les associations* (Paris: La Documentation Française, 2002), 26.

4. Olivier Godard, "Environnement, modes de coordination et systèmes de légitimité: Analyse de la catégorie de patrimoine naturel," *Revue Économique* 41.2 (1990): 239.

5. Jean-Pierre Babelon and André Chastel, "La notion de patrimoine," *Revue de l'Art* 49 (1980): 5-32; Marc Guillaume, *La politique du patrimoine* (Paris: Galilée, 1980). Thereafter, the number of texts published on the subject increased dramatically. See particularly André Chastel, "La notion de patrimoine," in *Les lieux de mémoire*, II.2: *La Nation* (Paris: Gallimard, 1986), 405-450; Françoise

Choay, *The Invention of the Historic Monument*, trans. Lauren M. O'Connell (New York: Cambridge University Press, 2001); Roland Recht, *Penser le patrimoine: Mise en scène et mise en ordre* (Paris: Hazan, 1998); and Jean-Michel Leniaud, *Les archipels du passé: Le patrimoine et son histoire* (Paris: Fayard, 2002) (and by the same author, *L'utopie française*).

6. Krzysztof Pomian, *Sur l'histoire* (Paris: Gallimard, 1999), 215. and particularly "The Collection: Between the Visible and the Invisible" (1978), included in his *Collectors and Curiosities: Paris and Venice, 1500-1800*, trans. Elizabeth Wiles-Portier (Cambridge: Blackwell, 1990), 7-44.

7. Jean Davallon, "Le patrimoine: Une filiation inversée," *EspacesTemps* 74/75 (2000): 7-16.

8. See chap. 2, pp. 61-62.

9. Gilbert Dagron, *Emperor and Priest: The Imperial Office in Byzantium*, trans. Jean Birrell (Cambridge: Cambridge University Press, 2003), 84-85.

10. Leniaud, *Les archipels du passé*, 42. The Capetian king is conceived as the "heir to the crown of Christ."

11. Patrick J. Geary, *Furta Sacra: Thefts of Relics in the Central Middle Ages* (1978; Princeton: Princeton University Press, 1990).

12. Marc Bourdier, "Le mythe et l'industrie ou la protection du patrimoine culturel au Japon," *Genèses* 11 (1993): 82-110.

13. Nicolas Fiévé, "Architecture et patrimoine au Japon: Les mots du monument historique," in *L'abus monumental*, 333.

14. This was the title ("*Conservare o restaurare*") given by the Italian architect Camillo Boito to a text he published in 1893. In it he attempted to define an intermediary position between that of Viollet-le-Duc ("To restore a building is not to preserve it, to repair it, or rebuild it; it is to reinstate it in a condition of completeness that could never have existed at any given time" [*The Architectural Theory of Viollet-Le-Duc*, 269]), and that of Ruskin (preserving absolutely, even if the building ends up a ruin as a result). See Leniaud, *Les archipels du passé*, 186-188.

15. Masahiro Ogino, "La logique d'actualisation: Le patrimoine au Japon," *Ethnologie Française* 25 (1995): 57-63.

16. Yan Thomas notes that the terminology of ancient Roman law makes no clear distinction between persons and things. *Patrimonium* means "the legal status of *pater*," that is, a kind of social extension of his person ("Res, chose et patrimoine," *Archives de Philosophie du Droit* 25 [1980]: 422). Claudia Moatti, "La

construction du patrimoine culturel à Rome aux Ier siècle av. et Ier siècle ap. J.-C.," in *Memoria e identità: La cultura romana costruisce la sua imagine*, ed. Mario Citroni (Florence: Università degli Studi di Firenze, 2003), 79-96.

17. Raymond Chevallier, *L'artiste, le collectionneur et le faussaire: Pour une sociologie de l'art romain* (Paris: Armand Colin, 1991).
18. Christian Jacob, "Lire pour écrire: Navigations alexandrines," in *Le pouvoir des bibliothèques*, ed. M. Baratin and Ch. Jacob (Paris: Albin Michel, 1996), 47-56.
19. Just after the papacy returned to Rome. Choay, *The Invention of the Historic Monument*, 17. On Rome and its relation to time in different periods, see Claudia Moatti, *Roma* (Arles: Actes Sud, 1997).
20. Roland Mortier, *La poétique des ruines en France: Ses origines, ses variations de la Renaissance à Victor Hugo* (Geneva: Droz, 1974), 15-16, and Alain Schnapp's comments, "Vestiges, Monuments, and Ruins: East Faces West," in *The Art Historian*, ed. Michael F. Zimmerman (Williamstown, MA: Sterling and Francine Clark Art Institute, 2003), 3-24.
21. Pausanias, *Description of Greece*, trans. W. H. S. Jones (Cambridge: Harvard University Press, 1918) and Perseus Digital Library, 9.36.5.
22. Pausanias, *Description of Greece* 1.26.4; see François Hartog, *Memories of Odysseus: Frontier Tales from Ancient Greece*, trans. Janet Lloyd (Chicago: University of Chicago Press, 2001), 140-149.
23. Guizot created the post of Inspector of Historic Monuments, held first by Ludovic Vitet and then by Prosper Mérimée, from 1834 onward. The "Inspector" was the person who "listed" monuments as "historic."
24. On Pausanias, see *Pausanias: Travel and Memory in Roman Greece*, ed. S. Alcock, J. Cherry, and J. Elsner (Oxford: Oxford University Press, 2001).
25. Alois Riegl, "The Modern Cult of Monuments: Its Character and Its Origin," trans. Kurt W. Forster and Diane Ghirardo, *Oppositions Reader: Selected Essays, 1973-1984*, ed. K. Michael Hays (New York: Princeton Architectural Press, 1998), 626, 629, 624. See Daniel Fabre's remarks on Riegl in "Ancienneté, altérité, autochtonie," in *Domestiquer l'histoire: Ethnologie des monuments historiques* (Paris: Maison des Sciences de l'Homme, 2000), 196-204. Jean-Philippe Antoine, *Six rhapsodies froides sur le lieu, l'image et le souvenir* (Paris: Desclée De Brouwer, 2002), 258-289 (on A. Riegl).
26. Caesar Augustus, *Res Gestae Divi Augusti: Text, Translation, and Commentary*, trans. Alison E. Cooley (New York: Cambridge University Press, 2010), 20:1-5.

27. Robert Sablayrolles, "Espace urbain et propagande politique: L'organisation du centre de Rome par Auguste (*Res Gestae*, 19 à 21)," *Pallas* 28 (1981): 61 and 68.
28. Suetonius, "Divus Vespasianus," *The Lives of the Twelve Caesars*, trans. Alexander Thomson and T. Forester (Philadelphia: Gebbie, 1889) and Perseus Digital Library, 8.
29. Claudia Moatti, *La raison de Rome: Naissance de l'esprit critique à la fin de la République* (Paris: Seuil, 1997), 150–151.
30. Paul Veyne, *Le pain et le cirque* (Paris: Seuil, 1976), 643.
31. François Loyer, "Les échelles de la monumentalité," in *L'abus monumental*, 187.
32. This *Senatus consultum* was declared in AD 44–56, as quoted by Alain Schnapp, *The Discovery of the Past*, trans. Ian Kinnes and Gilian Varndell (New York: Abrams, 1997), 334.
33. Yan Thomas, "Les ornements, la cité, le patrimoine," in *Images romaines* (Paris: Presses de l'École normale, 2001), 263–283.
34. Ibid., 275.
35. Ibid., 283.
36. Schnapp, *Discovery of the Past*, 334.
37. Thomas, "Les ornements," 282.
38. Leniaud, *Les archipels du passé*, 69.
39. Babelon and Chastel, "La notion de patrimoine," 13, and Leniaud's remarks in *Les archipels du passé*, 67.
40. Louis Aubin Millin, *Antiquités nationales; ou, Recueil de monuments pour servir à l'histoire générale et particulière de l'Empire français, tels que tombeaux, inscriptions, statues, vitraux, fresques ... tirés des Abbayes, Monastères, Châteaux et autres lieux devenus Domaines nationaux* (Paris, 1790). See Françoise Bercé, "La conservation des monuments, une mesure d'exception," in *L'abus monumental*, 169.
41. Cicero, *The Academics*, trans. James S. Reid (London: Macmillan and Co., 1880), 1.3.9. See Moatti, *La raison de Rome*, 121ff.
42. Renaldo Weiss, *The Renaissance Discovery of Classical Antiquity* (Oxford: Blackwell, 1969).
43. Mortier, *La poétique des ruines en France*, 30.
44. Petrarch, *Lettres familières*, IV–VII, trans. A. Longpré (Paris: Les Belles Lettres, 2002), note, 473.
45. Francesco Petrarca, *Rerum familiarum, Libri I–VIII*, trans. Aldo S. Bernardo (Albany: State University of New York Press, 1975), book 6, letter 2, 294.
46. Petrarca, *Rerum Familiarium, Libri I–VIII*, 293. The letter invites one to take a

stroll, that is, to read, but also to better oneself by dwelling on the philosophical and religious reflections that frame the description, and in which Christ appears as the "Bastion of Truth." There is obviously no question of leaving this bastion.

47. C. R. Ligota, "From Philology to History: Ancient Historiography Between Humanism and Enlightenment," in *Ancient History and the Antiquarian* (London: Warburg Institute, 1995), 108.
48. Ibid. See Francisco Rico, *Le rêve de l'humanisme: De Pétrarque à Érasme*, trans. J. Tellez (Paris: Les Belles Lettres, 2002), 41.
49. Philippe Coarelli, in Poggio Bracciolini, *Les ruines de Rome, De varietate fortunae, livre I*, trans. J.-Y. Boriaud (Paris: Les Belles Lettres, 1999), xlvi.
50. Poggio, *Les ruines de Rome*, 14, 20-25, 70.
51. Riegl, "Modern Cult of Monuments," 626-628. Schnapp, *Discovery of the Past*, 122; Sabine Forero-Mendoza, *Le temps des ruines: Le goût des ruines et les formes de la conscience historique à la Renaissance* (Seyssel: Champ Vallon, 2002), 68-70.
52. Choay, *Invention of the Historic Monument*, 32-33.
53. Schnapp, *Discovery of the Past*, 123, 125.
54. Francis Haskell and Nicholas Penny, *Taste and the Antique: The Lure of Classical Sculpture, 1500-1900* (New Haven: Yale University Press, 1981), 8.
55. K. Pomian, "Musée et patrimoine," in *Patrimoines en folie*, ed. H.-P. Jeudy (Paris: Maison des Sciences de l'Homme, 1990), 186.
56. Françoise Choay, "Foreword" to Alois Riegl, *Le culte moderne des monuments, son essence et sa genèse*, trans. D. Wieczorek (Paris: Seuil, 1984), 13.
57. Montaigne, *Essays of Montaigne*, trans. Charles Cotton, ed. William Carew Hazlitt (London: Reeves and Turner/New York: Scribner's, 1902), vol. 4, chap. 9, 129.
58. Ibid., 130.
59. *The Diary of Montaigne's Journey to Italy in 1580 and 1581*, trans. E. J. Trechmann (London: Hogarth, 1929), 131-132.
60. Rico, *Le rêve de l'humanisme*, 19.
61. Alphonse Dupront, *Genèse des temps modernes* (Paris: Gallimard/Seuil, 2001), 49.
62. Dupront, *Genèse des temps modernes*, 51.
63. Goethe, "Rome, Dec. 3, 1786," *Goethe's Travels in Italy*, trans. Charles Nisbet (London: George Bell, 1885), 136.
64. François Hartog, "Faire le voyage d'Athènes: J. J. Winckelmann et sa réception

française," in *Winckelmann et le retour à l'antique. Entretiens de la Garenne-Lemot* (Nantes: 1995), 127–143. See the excellent book by Élisabeth Décultot, *Johann Joachim Winckelmann: Enquête sur la genèse de l'histoire de l'art* (Paris: Presses universitaires de France, 2000), 121–188.

65. The Gospel according to John, 1:46. These were the words of Philip to Nathanael, who at first refused to believe that Jesus of Nazareth was the Messiah.
66. Johann Joachim Winckelmann, *History of the Art of Antiquity*, trans. Harry Francis Mallgrave (Los Angeles: Getty Research Institute, 2006), 351. See also the description of the Belvedere Torso of Hercules: "I deplore the way this Hercules has been irreparably altered, after his beauty had been so well captured.... But art shows us how much we can still learn from what still remains, and with what eye the artist should consider these vestiges" (quoted in Décultot, *Johann Joachim Winckelmann*, 277).
67. R. Schneider, *Quatremère de Quincy et son intervention dans les arts* (Paris: Hachette, 1910).
68. Édouard Pommier, *L'art de la liberté* (Paris: Gallimard, 1991), 74.
69. Antoine-Chrysostome Quatremère de Quincy, *Letters to Miranda and Canova on the Abduction of Antiquities from Rome and Athens*, trans. Chris Miller and David Gilks (Los Angeles: Getty Research Institute, 2012), 94.
70. Cicero, quoted in Quatremère de Quincy, *Letters to Miranda*, 108.
71. Ibid., 101.
72. Ibid., 98.
73. On Pirro Logorio, see Schnapp, *Discovery of the Past*, 125–126.
74. Quatremère de Quincy, *Letters to Miranda*, 108.
75. Ibid., 102.
76. H. Jansen, Winckelmann's publisher and translator, quoted by Édouard Pommier, "Winckelmann et la vision de l'Antiquité dans la France des Lumières et de la Révolution," *Revue de l'art* 83 (1989): 9. Mona Ozouf, *L'homme régénéré: Essais sur la Révolution française* (Paris: Gallimard, 1989).
77. This is a chapter title in Pommier's *L'art de la liberté*, 93–166.
78. Pommier, *L'art de la liberté*, 142 and 143.
79. Ibid., 153–166.
80. Ibid., 156.
81. Ibid., 157.
82. Ibid., 160.
83. Ibid., 163.

84. Abbé Grégoire, quoted in Leniaud, *Les archipels du passé*, 87.
85. Pommier, *L'art de la liberté*, 453 and 454.
86. Quatremère de Quincy, *Considérations morales sur la destination des ouvrages de l'art* (1815) (Paris: Fayard, 1989), 48. See Schneider, *Quatremère de Quincy*, 179-197. Carine Fluckiger, "L'investissement affectif de l'objet historique (Winckelmann, Quatremère de Quincy et Augustin Thierry)," *Dénouement des Lumières et invention romantique*, ed. Giovanni Bardazzi and Alain Grosrichard (Geneva: Droz, 2003).
87. Quatremère de Quincy, *Considérations morales*, 48.
88. Dominique Poulot, "Alexandre Lenoir and the Museum of French Monuments," trans. John Goodman, *Rethinking France: Les lieux de memoire*, 4: *Histories and Memories*, ed. Pierre Nora, trans. Mary Trouille and David Jordan (Chicago: University of Chicago Press, 2010), 101-136. Dominique Poulot, *Musée, nation, patrimoine, 1789-1815* (Paris: Gallimard, 1997), 285-339.
89. Pommier, *L'art de la liberté*, 371-379.
90. Poulot, *Musée, nation, patrimoine*, 305.
91. Jules Michelet, "Dedication to M. Edgar Quinet," *The People*, trans. G. H. Smith (New York: D. Appleton and Company, 1846), 19.
92. Hartog, "Faire le voyage d'Athènes ...," 141.
93. These are François Puthod de Maisonrouge's words, quoted in Leniaud, *Les archipels du passé*, 85.
94. François-René de Chateaubriand, *The Genius of Christianity*, trans. Charles I. White (Baltimore: John Murphy and Co., 1856).
95. Ibid., 386, 383, 525.
96. Marcel Proust in a letter to Madame Strauss, quoted in Leniaud, *Les archipels du passé*, 180.
97. See pp. 104-110.
98. Barrès, quoted in J.-M. Leniaud, *Les archipels du passé*, 232.
99. Leniaud, *Les archipels du passé*, 287 and 298.
100. Willibald Sauerländer, "Erweiterung des Denkmalbegriffs?," in *Denkmal-Werte-Gesellschaft: Zur Pluralität des Denkmalbegriffs*, ed. Wilfried Lipp (New York/Frankfurt: Campus, 1993), 120-149; Robert Hewison, *The Heritage Industry. Britain in a Climate of Decline* (London: Methuen, 1987).
101. Anne Cauquelin, "Un territoire-musée," *Alliage* 21 (1994): 195-198.
102. Francoise Choay, "Foreword" to Alois Riegl, *Le culte moderne des monuments*, 9.
103. The Athens Conference was organized by the League of Nations' International

Commission for Intellectual Cooperation, together with the International Council of Museums. See p. 183.

104. Gérard Althabe, "Productions des patrimoines urbains," in *Patrimoines en folie*, 270.

105. *Le Monde*, 4 September 2002.

106. Report for the Commission on Cultural, Family, and Social Affairs, 18 April 1996.

107. The number of protected buildings increased from 24,000 in 1960 to 44,709 in 1996.

108. Daniel Fabre, "L'histoire a changé de lieux," in *Une histoire à soi*, ed. A. Bensa and D. Fabre (Paris: Maison des Sciences de l'Homme, 2001), 32 and 33.

109. Glevarec and Saez, *Le patrimoine saisi par les associations*, 129–193.

110. Ibid., 263.

111. See Isabelle Vinson, "Le concept de patrimoine international: Théorie et praxis" ["The concept of international heritage: Theory and praxis"], thesis, Paris, École des Hautes Études en Sciences Sociales, 2001.

112. Mouchir Bouchenaki and Laurent Lévi-Strauss, "La notion de monument dans les critères du Patrimoine de l'humanité de l'Unesco," in *L'abus monumental*, 121–129.

113. Koïchiro Matsuura, "Éloge du patrimoine culturel immatériel," *Le Monde*, 11 September 2002.

114. An interministerial decree of 1967 officially recognized the notion of "regional nature reserve"; see J. Davallon et al., *L'environnement entre au musée* (Lyon: Presses universitaires de Lyon, 1992), 64–66, in which Georges-Henri Rivière's pivotal role is mentioned. A law of 21 April 1906 was still in force on the "protection of natural monuments and sites of an artistic character."

115. The label "ecomuseum" was coined in 1971. See Octave Debary, *La fin du Creusot; ou, L'Art d'accommoder les restes* (Paris: CTHS, 2002).

116. Max Querrien, "Écomusées," *Milieux* 13 (1983): 24–25. A year earlier, as president of the Caisse des Monuments Historiques (a public body), Querrien had submitted a report to the minister of culture entitled "Pour une nouvelle politique du Patrimoine" ["For a New Cultural Heritage Policy"].

117. André Desvallées, "L'écomusée: Musée degré zéro ou musée hors les murs," *Terrains* 5 (1985): 84–85.

118. Max Querrien, *Les monuments historiques demain* (Paris: Direction du Patrimoine, 1987), 265 (the proceedings of a conference held in 1984). The question of

what monuments should be preserved for future generations focused initially on the gap between social demand and available resources. Then Querrien observed that following a period of major transformation, during which threats of destruction had become more common and the damage more irreversible, an awareness had emerged of the importance for the future of cultural heritage, which he interpreted as "the salutary reaction of a community which wishes to construct its future lucidly by re-establishing the link between the past, the present and the future" (7).

119. For an ethnologist's analysis, see Françoise Zonabend, *La mémoire longue* (Paris: Jean-Michel Place, 1999), 9: "In the 1970s, French society began to become aware of the incredible changes brought about by the post-War economic boom. The modernization of the countryside caused a rural exodus, and a certain way of life came to an end in both urban and rural areas: traditional solidarities, both secular and religious, were destroyed, technical and artisanal knowledge disappeared, and regional and local particularisms fell apart. The world in which we lived, which our ancestors had known, suddenly became a world we had lost."

120. This is the title of the volume edited by Alban Bensa and Daniel Fabre, *Une histoire à soi*, cited in n. 108.

Our Doubly Indebted Present

1. Chateaubriand, *Memoirs*, book 33, chapter 9.
2. Ibid., book 42, chapter 14: "The Future—The difficulty of comprehending it." See chap. 3, pp. 87–88.
3. Ibid.
4. Ibid., book 42, chapter 18: "A summary of the changes which have occurred around the globe in my lifetime."
5. Charles Péguy, *Note conjointe sur M. Descartes*, in *Oeuvres en prose complètes* (Paris: Gallimard, 1992), 3:1428.
6. Péguy, *Clio*, 1206.
7. John Gillis, "The Future of European History," *Perspectives: American Historical Association Newsletter* 34.4 (1996): 5. The newspaper *Le Monde*'s front page on Wednesday 8 August 1945 bore the title "A scientific revolution: The Americans drop their first atomic bomb on Japan" ["Une révolution scientifique. Les Américains lancent leur première bombe atomique sur le Japon"].

8. Hans Jonas, *The Imperative of Responsibility: In Search of an Ethics for the Technological Age*, trans. Hans Jonas and David Herr (Chicago: University of Chicago Press, 1984) [*TN*: originally published as Hans Jonas, *Das Prinzip Verantwortung: Versuch einer Ethik für die technologische Zivilisation* (Frankfurt am Main: Insel, 1979); French translation *Le principe responsabilité*, trans. J. Greisch (Paris: Cerf, 1990)]. The subject generates ever more books and articles. One can usefully start with the report to the French prime minister presented by Philippe Kourilsky and Geneviève Viney, *Le Principe de précaution* (Paris: Odile Jacob, 2000) (with bibliography), and *Le Principe de précaution dans la conduite des affaires humaines*, ed. Olivier Godard (Paris: MSH and INRA, 1997). See also Olivier Godard's "De l'usage du principe de précaution en univers controversé," *Futuribles* 239–240 (Feb.–March 1999): 37–60.

9. François Ewald, "The Return of Descartes' Malicious Demon: An Outline of a Philosophy of Precaution," *Embracing Risk*, ed. Tom Baker and Jonathan Simon (Chicago: University of Chicago Press, 2002), 291; Kourilsky-Viney report, 274–275.

10. Jean-Pierre Dupuy, *Pour un catastrophisme éclairé: Quand l'impossible est certain* (Paris: Seuil, 2002), 213, in which the author formulates his maxim on rational catastrophism, namely to "obtain an image of the future sufficiently catastrophic to be undesirable and yet sufficiently credible to trigger the actions which should prevent it coming about barring an accident." See Jean-Pierre Dupuy, "Rational Choice Before the Apocalypse," *Anthropoetics* 13, no. 3 (Fall 2007/Winter 2008).

11. Jonas, *The Imperative of Responsibility*, 185, 205.

12. Ernst Bloch, *The Principle of Hope*, trans. Neville Plaice, Stephen Plaice, and Paul Knight (Cambridge: MIT Press, 1995).

13. Jonas, *Imperative of Responsibility*, 12.

14. Ibid., 17 [*TN*: translation slightly modified].

15. Ibid., *Imperative of Responsibility*, 11 and 81.

16. Paul Ricoeur, *The Just*, trans. David Pellauer (Chicago: University of Chicago Press, 2000), 29. Jonas, *The Imperative of Responsibility*, 12: "our imperative extrapolates into a predictable real future as the open-ended dimension of our responsibility."

17. Hans Jonas, *Mortality and Morality: A Search for Good After Auschwitz*, ed. Lawrence Vogel (Evanston, IL: Northwestern University Press, 1996), 108.

18. Jonas adds that "With this imperative we are, strictly speaking, not responsible

to the future of individuals but to the idea of Man, which is such that it demands the presence of its embodiment in the world" (Jonas, *The Imperative of Responsibility*, 43). It is an ontological imperative.

19. Kourilsky-Viney report, 213. *Le Monde* of 25 April 2003 reported that then–president Jacques Chirac had declared his support for incorporating the precautionary principle into the Environmental Charter. The charter was to have constitutional force.

20. Ibid., 253–276.

21. The aim of sustainable development is to "satisfy the development needs ... of current generations without compromising the ability of future generations to meet their own needs" (French Environmental Code, 1995, art. 1).

22. Jean-Charles Hourcade, "Précaution et approche séquentielle de la décision face aux risques climatiques de l'effet de serre," in Godard, *Le Principe de précaution*, 293.

23. François Ewald, in O. Godard, *Le Principe de précaution*, 99–126.

24. François Ewald, "Vers un État de précaution," *Revue de Philosophie et de Sciences Sociales* 3 (2002): 221–231.

25. Ewald, "Vers un État de précaution," 111.

26. Ibid., 117.

27. Ricoeur, *The Just*, 31.

28. Yan Thomas, "La vérité, le temps, le juge et l'historien," *Le Débat* 102 (1998): 27.

29. Emmanuel Kattan, *Penser le devoir de mémoire* (Paris: Presses universitaires de France, 2002), 134–136. Then–French president Chirac, in his speech of 16 July 1995 commemorating the police raid of the Vél' d'Hiv, talked of an "everlasting debt" ("une dette imprescriptible").

30. Henri Berestycki, "La conquête du hasard," in *À la recherche du réel* (Association Droit de suite, May 2001), 22.

31. François Rachline, "Qu'arrive-t-il au présent?," in *À la recherche du réel*, 18. Rachline gives a positive if not optimistic interpretation of the crisis of the present.

32. Primo Levi, *The Drowned and the Saved*, trans. Raymond Rosenthal (New York: Vintage, 1989), 9. Lawrence Langer, *Admitting the Holocaust: Collected Essays* (Oxford: Oxford University Press, 1995).

33. See pp. 4–5.

INDEX

Abu Simbel temples, 183
Acceleration, of time, 80, 123-24, 178, 190, 231*n*71
Achilles, 215*n*8, 215*n*13; with mourning, 43-44; with perpetual present, 43-45, 54; with time, 218*n*51
Ages: of humanity, 86; of slavery, 74; of world, 12-13, 74; *see also* Middle Ages
Aging, 113-14
Alberti, Leon Battista, 164, 165-66
Alcinous (King of the Phaeacians), 42, 47, 49, 58, 216*n*31
Allen, Woody, 229*n*48
Allusion, *see* Art of allusion
Amaterasu (Japanese goddess), 154
America, 82-86; Chateaubriand and, 77-79, 97-98; ruins in, 94-95; Tocqueville and, 93-95, 98; Volney and, 90-92
Anacharsis, 70-72
Anachronism, 53, 88, 101, 224*n*96

Anaximander (Greek philosopher), 1, 205*n*1
Ancient City (Fustel de Coulanges), 134
Ancients: imitation of, 74, 92; Indians and, 78, 83-84; moderns and, 67, 76, 86-87, 107; savages and, 67-69, 76, 77; *see also* Greece; Rome
Annales (Febvre), 4, 13
"Annals of the poor," 31-32
Anthropology, 56, 69, 112, 121, 186, 195; culture and, 23; with form of temporality, 38-40; historical, 23-28, 36; history and, 9, 36
"Anti-affliction," 46, 47
Antiquities, 155-56, 162, 165, 166, 171
Antiquities (Varro), 162, 165
Apollinaire, 110
Archaic royalty, 29-32
Archival institutions, 116
Arendt, Hannah, 4-5, 49, 52, 80, 106, 129, 204

248 INDEX

Arete (excellence), 30
Ariès, Philippe, 113, 135, 138
Aristotle, 49, 56, 60
Aron, Raymond, 139, 146
Art of allusion, 50
Arts, 170; conservation of, 176; in Greece, 169, 171, 173; historians, 171; pillaging of, 175–79; in Rome, 169, 171; with time and history, 174
Assassins of Memory (Vidal-Naquet), 102
Atala (Chateaubriand), 78
Athens Charter of 1931, 182, 183
Attention, xvi, 57, 58
Auerbach, Erich, 42–43, 57–58
Augé, Marc, 208n28
Augustine (saint), xvi, 12, 56; attention and, 57, 58; distension and, 59, 60; Odysseus compared to, 55–63; with time, 57
Augustus (emperor), 158, 159
Aurelius, Marcus, 109
Autarchic present, 208n28

Bainville, Jacques, 137–38
Bananas (film), 229n48
Bankruptcy: in ancient Greece, xiv; of history, 110, 129
Bards: heroes and, 46–49, 51–52, 55, 216n28; as historians, 48; Muses inspiring, 49, 55; with past and future divinatory knowledge, 44, 55; as seers, 48
Barrès, Maurice, 135, 181
Barthélemy, Jean-Jacques, 69–70
Baschet, Jérôme, 208n28
Bastille, 142, 161
Battle of Bouvines, 37
Baudelaire, Charles, 50, 84
Benjamin, Walter, 4, 129
Benveniste, Émile, 109, 211n57
Berestycki, Henri, 202
Bergson, Henry, 122, 128, 231n80
Berlin, 7–11

Berlin Wall, 3, 102, 106, 146–47, 185, 197
Between Past and Future (Arendt), 5
The Bible, 60–61, 153, 240n65; *see also* Old Testament, time in
Biondo, Flavio, 164, 165
Biotechnologies, 6, 198
Bloch, Marc, xiv, 110, 137, 138, 233n105
Boas, Franz, 34–35
Boissy d'Anglas, François-Étienne, 174
Boito, Camillo, 236n14
Boniface IV (Pope), 160
Bonnaud, Robert, 210n55
Bossuet, Jacques-Bénigne, xvi, 11, 12
Bourdieu, Pierre, 113
Bousquet, René, 115
Braibant Report, 229n52
Braudel, Fernand, xvi, 103, 133; on capitalism, xiv; *longe durée* and, 14, 16; as prisoner of war, 140–41
Burguière, André, 141

Camus, Albert, 207n16
Capitalism, xiv
Caractères originaux de l'histoire rurale française (Bloch), 138
Cassiodorus, 160
Castel, Robert, xviii
Catastrophism, 197, 202, 244n10
Caumont, Arcisse de, 180
Certeau, Michel de, xviii, 2, 8
Change, France with societal, 243n119
Charlemagne, 160
Charles X (King of France), 92
Char, René, 4, 5
Chartier, Roger, 121
Chateaubriand, François-René de, xvii, 11, 83, 92, 101, 179, 193; on acceleration of time, 123; America and, 77–79, 97–98; *Complete Works*, 66–67, 93; *historia magistra vitae* and, 72–77; Odysseus and, 88; return of, 79; ruins and, 89–95;

savages and, 68; time and, 65–66, 79–81, 103, 106, 194; travel and, 66–72; *see also Historical Essay; Travels in America*
Chirac, Jacques, 118, 245*n*19, 245*n*29
Christianity, 179; conversions to, 29–30, 42, 169, 223*n*84; *historia magistra vitae* and, 106; orders of time and, 56, 59–63, 153–54; present and, 109–10
Christo, 159
Chronic time, 211*n*57
Chronosophy, 11, 15
Cicero, 73, 126, 162, 171, 221*n*30
Cities, 134; city-states in Greece, 28, 54; "Generic City," xix
The City of God (Augustine), 59
Clio (Péguy), 128, 142
"Cold" societies, 8, 24–26
Coleridge, Samuel Taylor, 202
Collective memory, 121–25, 187
The Collective Memory (Halbwachs), 122
Colonna, Giovanni, 163
Commemorations, 119–20, 141–43, 191
Communism, 7, 208*n*25
Communist Manifesto, 107
Comte, Auguste, 11
Condorcet, Nicolas de (marquis), xvi
Confessions (Augustine), xvi, 56
Conservation, 115, 118, 151, 157; of art, 176; France and, 161, 173–74; of monuments, 166–67; restoration and, 152, 175
Considerations on the Arts of Design (Quatremère de Quincy), 170
Constant, Benjamin, 86
Constantine the Great, 30, 153, 163, 167
Constructing the Past (Le Goff and Nora), 120–21
Conversions, to Christianity, 29–30, 42, 223*n*84
Cook, Captain James, 24, 35–36
Cooper, Fenimore, 29
Corruption, 71–72, 75, 76, 84

Cosmic myths, 31, 33
Counter-Muses, 52–53
Crimes, 7, 230*n*53; against humanity, 8, 117, 171, 200–201; against public instruction, 172
Crises: financial crisis of 2008, xiii, xiv; modern regime's, 104–7
Croesus (King of Lydia), 2
Cultures: anthropology and, 23; cultural diversity, 14, 26, 187; gaps, 14–15; Greek, 19; heritage, 172–73, 181, 184, 189
Cumulative history, 14, 26, 112
Current events, 7, 33
Customs of the American Indians Compared with the Customs of Primitive Times (Lafitau), 69
Cynics, 72
Cyriacus of Ancona, 164

Dagron, Gilbert, 153
Dangers, of imitation, 75–76
Daniel (prophet), 12
Dates, 88, 104, 105; *see also* 9/11
Death, 7, 13, 113, 138; life after, 61, 134; mourning and, 43–44, 46, 50, 53, 216*n*31; as price for listening pleasure, 53–54; with statues uprooted, 171–72
Debord, Guy, 229*n*43
Debts, xiv, 201–2, 245*n*29
The Decline of the West (Spengler), 13
Degree zero museum, 188
De la Blache, Vidal, 125
Democracy in America (Tocqueville), 94
Denon, Vivant, 178
Description of Greece (Pausanias), 156–57
Descriptio urbis Romae (Alberti), 166
Despotism, 174–75, 194
d'Estaing, Valéry Giscard, 118
Detienne, Marcel, 9, 42
Development, *see* Sustainable development; Urban development projects

Dictionary of Architecture (Quatremère de Quincy), 170
Discourse on Inequality (Rousseau), 68
Discourse on Universal History (Bossuet), 12
Disorientation, of time, 3–5, 80
Distension: Augustine and, 59, 60; Odysseus and, 57, 58
Diversity, cultural, 14, 26, 187
Divinatory knowledge, 44–45, 55
Does History Go Faster? (Jeanneney), 123
Dreams, interpretation of, 12
Dreyfus Affair, 128
Droysen, Johann Gustav, 104
Duby, Georges, 37, 138, 233n106
Dumont, Louis, 29
Dupront, Alphonse, 168
Dupuy, Jean-Pierre, 197, 199

Earth, Heaven separated from, 33, 35
Ecclesiastical history, 62
Eclair Film Studios, 182
Ecomuseums, 187–88
"Editorial" (Sartre), 111
Egypt, 90
Einaudi, Jean-Luc, 117
Eliot, T.S., 113
"The End of History" (Fukuyama), 15
Enlightenment, 170–71, 203
"Entering one's future backwards," 227n12
"Entropology," 112
Environment: heritage and natural, 151–52, 187; heritage and time of, 186–91; protection of, 115, 198–200
Epicureanism, 109
Eschaton, 109
Essay on the Acceleration of History (Halévy), 123
Essays (Montaigne), 107, 167
Estrangement, 3; historicity and, xv; from past, present, and future, xvi; self-, 50, 51–52, 55; from time, 42–43
Eternity, 202–3

Eugene IV (Pope), 165
Europe: heritage in, 152–53; identity, 148
Eusebius (bishop of Caesarea), 62
Eventfulness, 26–27
Events: current, 7, 33; from event to myth and working misunderstandings, 34–38; from myth to, 32–34; non-events-based history, 33; as repetitious for Maori, 33; requirements for appearance of, 38–39; rethinking of, 37
Evolutionism, 14
Ewald, François, 199, 200
Excellence, *see* Arete
Exemplum, 107
Existentialism, 111
Expectation, xvi, 9, 73, 119
Experience, 9, 73, 119

Fabian, Johannes, 38–39
Fabre, Daniel, 184
False evolutionism, 14
Fault lines, of present, 114–20
Faust II (Goethe), 203
Fear: of forgetting, 45; heuristics of, 198
Febvre, Lucien, 4, 13, 110, 136, 137, 139; with national consciousness of France, 233n105; on Valéry, 228n31
Fermigier, André, 230n55
Fiji, 28–32, 56; Christianity in, 29–30; as island of history, 36
Financial crisis, of 2008, xiii, xiv
The Flood (painting), 89
Forgetting, 2, 45, 46, 102, 112
Fortune, 164, 165, 168; *see also* Tukhe
Foucault, Michel, 2
Fourastié, Jean, 108, 227n22
France, 101–3, 115–16, 129, 135; with commemorations, 119–20, 141–43; conservation and, 161, 173–74; heritage in, 149–55, 161–62, 181–83, 235n3; with national consciousness, 233n105; with national history, 131–41; national unity

of, 144; with pillaging of art, 175-79; with societal changes, 243n119; universalization and, 180-85; urban development projects in, 117-19, 182; *see also* French Resistance; French Revolution
Francis I (King of France), 161
Frazer, James George, 29
Frederick the Great, 120
Freedoms, 85-86, 175
French Heritage Foundation Law, 182-83
French Resistance, 4-5
French Revolution, 11, 65, 73, 74, 102, 104, 107; cultural heritage and, 172-73; despotism and, 174-75; with heritage and present, 170-80; museums and, 175-79; Quatremère de Quincy and, 170-72
Freud, Sigmund, 6
Fukuyama, Francis, 15, 146
Furet, François, 3, 131
Fustel de Coulanges, Numa Denis, 18, 133-36, 144
Future, xv; disorientation of, 3-5, 80; divinatory knowledge of, 44-45, 55; "entering one's future backwards," 227n12; estrangement from, xvi; forgetting of, 112; gap between past and, 5, 13, 53, 74, 88, 204; *historia magistra vitae* and, 38, 72-77; *Historical Essay* and, 73; Maori and, 33, 34; past and, 105, 109, 190, 194, 201-2; with past and present as single concept, 211n57; present threatened by, xviii, 13, 191, 198
Futures Past (Koselleck), 9, 13, 17, 34, 39, 73, 104-5, 214n43
Futurism, xvii, 107-8, 113, 196, 197
Futurist Manifesto (Marinetti), 107, 108, 203

Gaps: between ancients and moderns, 87; culture, 14-15; between past and future, 5, 13, 53, 74, 88, 204; in time, 3-7, 88, 106
"Generic City," xix
Genius of Christianity (Chateaubriand), 179

German Sites of Memory, 120
Germany, 73, 120, 143; *see also* Berlin; Berlin Wall
Gide, André, 110
Gluck, Carol, 227n11
Goethe, Johann Wolfgang von, 109, 169, 203
Gracq, Julien, 105
Great Britain, 34-36
Greece: art in, 169, 171, 173; bankruptcies in ancient, xiv; city-states in, 28, 54; culture, 19; heritage in, 156-58; legacy of, 174; orders of time in, 1-2; Scythians and, 70-72; statues from, 171; tragedy, 31
Grégoire (Abbé), 175
Grey, George (Sir), 32, 33, 34
Guizot, François, 180, 237n23
Guy, Michel, 118
Gyges (King of Lydia), 2

Habitus, 31, 32
Halbwachs, Maurice, 121-22, 123, 124, 127
Halévy, Daniel, 123-24
Hartog, François, 18, 205n1, 206n26, 206n28, 209n31, 213n21, 213n26, 213n29, 214n1, 217n35, 218n64, 220n9, 221n16, 221n22, 221n23, 221n30, 222n34, 222n90, 227n12, 227n18, 227n19, 227n29, 227n51, 232n94, 233n97, 237n22, 239n64, 241n92; *see also The Mirror of Herodotus*
Hawaii, 24, 35, 36, 39
Heaven, Earth separated from, 33, 35
Hedda Gabler (Ibsen), 110
Hegel, Georg Wilhelm Friedrich, 9, 11, 27, 28, 49
Heidegger, Martin, xv, 9
Helena (Empress), 153
Hélias, Pierre-Jakez, 102
Heritage, 98, 103, 230n55; with ancients and present, 155-62; cultural, 172-73, 181, 184, 189; defined, 152; in Europe,

Heritage *(continued)*
  152–53; in France, 149–55, 161–62, 181–83, 235*n*3; with French Revolution and present, 170–80; in Greece, 156–58; history of, 151–55; identity and, 119, 151, 182; in Japan, 154–55; memory and, 11; national, 119; with natural environment, 151–52, 187; Rome and, 155–56, 158–70; with time of environment, 186–91; universalization of, 180–86; world, 6, 150, 186–87
Herodotus, 1, 12, 18, 70, 72, 157
Heroes: bards and, 46–49, 51–52, 55, 216*n*28; with perpetual present, 41–46, 54, 56, 58; *see also* Achilles; Odysseus
Heroic regimes, history and, 28–32, 36, 38
Hesiod, 44
Heuristics, of fear, 198
Hierarchy, 29, 31
Hiroshima, 124, 196
Historia magistra vitae, 38, 62–63, 72–77, 92; Christianity and, 106; defined, 105; inverted, 95, 98; new interpretation of, 190; repetition and, 91
Historians, 228*n*32; art, 171; bards as, 48; on capitalism, xiv; history and, 101, 121, 122–23, 139; as last traveler, 82; regimes of historicity constructed by, xvi, 8–9; task of, xv, xvii, 1, 16, 134–36, 144–45, 208*n*27; time and, 8, 81, 104–5; as witnesses, 115
Historical Essay (Chateaubriand), 66, 67, 68, 71, 220*n*7, 220*n*12; freedom in, 85–86; past, present, and future in, 73; time in, 79–81, 83, 90
Historical Studies (Chateaubriand), 80–81, 101
Historicity: approach, 208*n*28; connotations, xv, 9; divinatory knowledge and, 44–45; estrangement and, xv; self-estrangement and, 52; of societies, 24–28; *see also* Regimes of historicity

Historic monuments, 158, 161, 165, 180–81, 183
Histories (Herodotus), 70
History, 92; anthropology and, 9, 36; with arts and time, 174; bankruptcy of, 110, 129; "cold" societies and zero historical temperature, 24; cumulative, 14, 26, 112; ecclesiastical, 62; Germany with modern concept of, 73; global historical turning points, 210*n*55; of heritage concept, 151–55; heroic regimes and, 28–32, 36, 38; historians and, 101, 121, 122–23, 139; historical anthropology, 23–28, 36; islands of, 36, 38–39; justice and link to, 1–2; legend differentiated from, 215*n*5; memory and, 2, 6–7, 16, 102, 120–31; with modern regime's crises, 104–7; from myth to event, 32–34; national, 127–28, 131–41; non-events-based, 33; *The Odyssey* as "first" historical narrative, 45, 49; orders of time and universal, 11–15; of present time, 8; of price, 13; repetition and, 71; scientific, 121, 138; social function of, 207*n*15; stationary, 26
A History of French Civilization (Duby and Mandrou), 138
History of Art in Antiquity (Winckelmann), 169–70, 177
History of Contemporary France (Lavisse), 125–26, 129, 140, 144
History of France (Bainville), 137–38
History of France (Burguière and Revel), 141
History of France (Lavisse), 136
History of France (Michelet), 120
History of Private Life (Ariès and Duby), 138
History of the Peloponnesian War (Thucydides), 32
History of the Political Institutions of Ancient France (Fustel de Coulanges), 134
The History of the French Population and Its Attitudes to Life Since the Eighteenth Century (Ariès), 138

Hobsbawm, Eric, 226*n*10
Hocart, Arthur Maurice, 29
Holocaust, 102, 121, 202
Homecomings, 44, 45, 53, 58
Homer, xvi, 11, 71, 82, 215*n*16; with narrative devices, 50; perpetual present and, 41-46, 54, 56; *see also The Iliad*; *The Odyssey*
Hone Heke, 34, 37, 41
Horace, 72, 109
The Horse of Pride (Hélias), 102
"Hot" societies, 8, 24, 27, 112, 127
The Hour of Our Death (Ariès), 138
Humanism, 13, 159, 168-69, 175, 190
Humanity: ages of, 86; crimes against, 8, 117, 171, 200-201
Human spirit, regeneration of, 174

Ibsen, Henrik, 110
Identity: European, 148; heritage and, 119, 151, 182; with memory, heritage, and commemoration, 119; narrative, 52; personal, 217*n*41
Identity of France (Braudel), 103, 133, 140
The Iliad (Homer), 43, 45, 53, 215*n*16, 218*n*49
Imitation, 152, 171, 177, 188; of ancients, 74, 92; dangers of, 75-76; of moderns, 74; proscribed, 104
The Immoralist (Gide), 110
The Imperative of Responsibility: In Search of an Ethics for the Technological Age (Jonas), 197
"imprescriptibilité," 117, 200-1
Indians, 69, 78, 83-84
Injustice, fortune's, 165, 168
In Search of Lost Time (Proust), 128, 143
Instantaneism, 110
Institutions, archival, 116
Instruction of Year II, 173-74
Interpretation: of dreams, 12; *historia magistra* and new, 190
Iroquois, 78, 83, 84

Islands of History (Sahlins), 23-24, 28-38
Islands, of history, 36; *see also* Fiji; Hawaii; Polynesia
Israel, 60, 153
Italy, 107-8

Japan, 124, 154-55, 196
Jaucourt, Louis de, 70, 71
Jeanneney, Jean-Noël, 123, 231*n*71
Jesus Christ, 12, 61, 62, 153, 189, 240*n*65
Jetztzeit (presence of now), 129
Jews, 61; Holocaust and, 102, 121, 202; Israel and, 60, 153; with memory of past, 6-7
John the Evangelist, 169
Jonas, Hans, 196, 197-98, 199, 244*n*18
Julius II (Pope), 166
"Junkspace," xix
Justice, 201; fortune's injustice, 165, 168; history and, 1-2
Justin, 71, 72

Kamehameha (king of Hawaii), 36
Kant, Immanuel, 6, 15, 114, 198
Klein, Étienne, 206*n*5
Kleos (renown), 52, 53, 55
Knowledge, 156; of bards and historians, 48; divinatory, 44-45, 55; not knowing and, 56; sirens with language of, 218*n*48
Kohl, Helmut, 120
Koolhaas, Rem, xix
Koselleck, Reinhart, xvi, 9, 17, 39, 73, 104; see also *Futures Past*

Lafitau, Joseph-François, 68-69
Laïdi, Zaki, 208*n*28
Land treaties, 34-35
Lang, Jack, 181
Language, 24, 84, 89, 147; of knowledge and Sirens, 218*n*48; Latin, 109, 155, 162, 164; linguistic time, 211*n*57
Lanzmann, Claude, 6, 102

A Lapse of Memory (Segalen), 84
Latin, 109, 155, 162, 164
Lavisse, Ernest, 102, 125-26, 129, 136, 144
Leaves of Hypnos (Char), 4
Lectures on History (Volney), 92
Lefort, Claude, 27-28, 32, 37, 40, 42
Legacy, 172-75, 178, 198
Legends, 31, 43, 215*n*5
Le Goff, Jacques, 120-21, 147-48
Lenclud, Gérard, 9
Lenoir, Alexandre, 176-77
Leon X (Pope), 166
Letters to Miranda (Quatremère de Quincy), 170, 171
Levi, Primo, 202
Lévi-Strauss, Claude, 8, 9, 14-15, 37, 40, 67; cultural diversity and, 187; with eventfulness, 26-27; on historicity of societies, 24-26; savages and, 111-12; *see also Race and History*
Liberty, *see* Freedoms
Lieux de mémoire (Nora), 98, 102, 103, 106, 123, 126; commemorations and, 141-42; moment of, 143-48
Life, after death, 61, 134
Life of Rancé (Chateaubriand), 89
Linguistic time, 211*n*57
Listeners, 47, 50, 53-54, 121
Little Red Book (Mao), 5
Lives (Plutarch), 30, 31
Livy, Titus, 164
Logorio, Pirro, 171
Longue durée, 14, 16, 19, 103, 106
Lono (Hawaiian deity), 36
Loschi, Antonio, 164
Louis-Philippe (king of France), 180
Louis XVI (king of France), 161
Luther, Martin, 120
Lycurgus, 75

Magritte, René, 119
Majority, power of, 28

Makahiki rites, 36
Malraux, André, 111, 181, 183-84
Mandelstam, Ossip, 41
Mandrou, Robert, 138
Manifesto of the Futurist Painters, 108
Maoris, 32-35, 56, 195
Mao Tse Tung, 5
Mapping, of monuments, 165-66
Marie Louise of Austria (empress of France), xvii
Marinetti, Filippo Tommaso, 107-8, 110, 172, 203
Marrou, Henri-Irénée, 139
Marx, Karl, 6, 11, 76, 197
Mazon, Paul, 43
Media, 114-15, 124, 142-43, 227*n*11
Medieval Civilization (Le Goff), 148
Meiji Restoration, 154
Mémoires d'outre-tombe (Chateaubriand), xvii, 11, 66, 67, 106, 193-94
Memorials, 6, 85, 120, 184, 190-91
Memories of Odysseus, 18-19
Memory, 84, 98, 102; collective, 121-25, 187; commemorations and, 119-20, 141-43, 191; communism and, 208*n*25; heritage and, 11; history and, 2, 6-7, 16, 102, 120-31; Jews and past, 6-7; reconstructed, 119; site of, 6, 10, 85, 120, 125-27, 145-46, 153-54, 184; social thought and, 122; societies based on, 124; time and, xvi, 6; witness and, 7
Memory, History, Forgetting (Ricoeur), 2, 102
"Men of former times," 46, 53-55, 73-74
Men of nature, 68, 71-72, 78
Mérimée, Prosper, 157, 180
Michaud, Éric, 110
Michelet, Jules, 82, 103, 120, 121, 124; with national histories, 132-33; with thread of tradition, 132, 185
Middle Ages, 13, 132, 148, 154, 157, 168
Millin, Louis Aubin, 161
Mimesis (Auerbach), 42

Mind, 57, 97, 109
The Mirror of Herodotus (Hartog), 18
Misunderstandings: from event to myth with working, 34–38; with Maori and British, 34–35; of present, 130
Mitterand, François, 114–15, 119–20
Modern: concept of history, 73; freedoms, 85–86; with regime's crises, 104–8
Moderns: ancients and, 74, 76, 86–87, 107; ancients and sagaves, 66–67, 77; imitation and, 74
Momigliano, Arnaldo, 69
Monod, Gabriel, 135, 136, 148
Montaigne, Michel de, 107, 110, 167–68
Monuments: conservation of, 166–67; historic, 158, 161, 165, 180–81, 183; mapping of, 165–66
Moral Considerations on the Destination of Works of Art (Quatremère de Quincy), 176
Mortier, Roland, 156
Mos majorum, 62
Mourning: past and, 43–44, 46, 50, 216n31; Sirens and anti-, 53
Muses: bards inspired by, 49, 55; poets and, 48; with present, past, and future divinatory knowledge, 44; Sirens as counter-, 52–53
Museums, 118–19, 166, 171–73; with art pillaged, 175–79; Berlin Wall as object for, 185; degree zero, 188; eco-, 187–88; Versailles as, 179, 180
Musil, Robert, 123
Myths: cosmic, 31, 33; to event, 32–34; from event to myth, 34–38; Hawaii and political, 36

Nagy, Gregory, 216n33
Napoleon, xvii, 104, 107, 175
Narratives, 2; devices, 50; identity, 52; *The Odyssey* as "first" historical, 45, 49; utopian, 77

Narrator-poet, 49
Nations: consciousness of, 233n105; heritage of, 119; history of, 127–28, 131–41; society and, 130; unity of, 144
Nature: heritage and natural environment, 151–52, 187; societies compared to, 68, 70; *see also* Men of nature
Nausea (Sartre), 111
Nebuchadnezzar (King of Babylon), 12
Neufchâteau, François de, 175
New History (Le Goff, Chartier, and Revel), 121
New World, ruins in, 94–95; *see also* America
Nicholas V (pope), 166, 171
Nietzsche, Friedrich, 110
9/11, 104, 142–43, 150, 227n11
Non-events-based history, 33
Nora, Pierre, 6, 120–21; on acceleration of time, 124; commemorations and, 141–42; on heritage, 150; on historians and history, 123; with past and present, 142; with site of memory, 126–27; time and, 103; *see also Lieux de mémoire*
Nunism, 110

Oblivion, 52–55, 157, 220n7
Odysseus, xvi, 11, 18–19, 215n13; attention and, 58; Augustine compared to, 55–63; Chateaubriand and, 88; distension and, 57, 58; return of, 58; self-estrangement and, 50, 51–52; with Sirens' call to oblivion, 52–55; tears of, 46–52, 58; as witness, 48, 55
The Odyssey (Homer): as "first" historical narrative, 45, 49; with *The Iliad*, 45, 53, 215n16; narrative devices in, 50; with Odysseus's tears, 46–52, 58; past and present juxtaposed in, 54–55; perpetual present in, 41–46, 54, 56; with Sirens' call to oblivion, 52–55
Old Testament, time in, 42–43, 224n94

Omnipresent, present as, 8
On the Concept of History (Benjamin), 129
On the Inconstancy of Fortune (Poggio Bracciolini), 164
Ophüls, Marcel, 102
Opinion polls, 115
Order of Discourse (Foucault), 2
Orders of time: Christianity and, 56, 59–63, 153–54; gaps in, 3–7; historical links to, 1–2; Judaism and, 60; from the Pacific to Berlin, 7–11; regimes of historicity and, 11–19; with universal histories and, 11–15
The Order of Time (Pomian), 2
Origins of Totalitarianism (Arendt), 5
Ornamentation, *see* Urban ornamentation
Ostrogoths, 160
"Other Times, Other Customs: The Anthropology of History" (Sahlins), 23
Othon, 75

Pacific, with orders of time, 7–11
Papon, Maurice, 117, 201, 230n53
Pascal, Blaise, 109–10
Past, xv; disorientation of, 3–5, 80; divinatory knowledge of, 44–45, 55; estrangement from, xvi; future and, 105, 109, 190, 194, 201–2; gap between future and, 5, 13, 53, 74, 88, 204; *historia magistra vitae* and, 38, 72–77; Jews and memory of, 6–7; Maori and, 33, 34; mourning and, 43–44, 46, 50, 216n31; *The Odyssey* with present juxtaposed with, 54–55; present and, 121, 142, 156, 194–95, 229n43; with present and future as single concept, 211n57; with presentist and historicist approaches, 208n28; time and objectification of, 2; *see also* Memory
Patrimony, 154, 236n16; *see also* Heritage
Paul (Saint), 163
Paul III (Pope), 166
Pausanias, 156–57

Paxton, Robert, 102
Péguy, Charles, 142, 231n80; on historians, 139; on history and memory, 128–29; on present, xvii, 194
Peripety, 30–31
Perpetual present: heroes and, 41–46, 54, 56, 58; ruins and, 208n28
Perrault, Charles, 65, 107
Personal identity, 217n41
Pétain, Philippe, 102
Peter (Saint), 163
Petit-Dutaillis, Charles, 137
Petrarch, Francesco, 163, 164
Philology, 164
Pillaging, of art, 175–79
Pirenne, Henri, xiv
Pius II (Pope), 166
Pleasure, death and listening, 53–54
Plotinus, 202–3
Plutarch, 30, 31, 104
Poets, 48, 49, 53
Poggio Bracciolini, Gian Francesco, 164–65, 166
Politics, 134; of environmental protections, 198–200; Hawaiian political myths, 36; of utopia, 197
Polls, opinion, 115
Polynesia, 32, 38, 106, 195, 213n36
Pomian, Krzysztof, 2, 152
Pommier, Edouard, 172
Pompidou Center, 118
Pompidou, Georges, 117
Poor, *see* "Annals of the poor"
Poussin, Nicolas, 89
Power: antiquities and, 166; Kamehameha and, 36; of majority, 28; of seers, 55
Praesens, 109
Praesentism, 110
Precautionary principle, 196–200, 245n19
Presence of now, *see* Jetztzeit
Present: autarchic, 208n28; Christianity and, 109–10; disorientation of, 3–5, 80;

INDEX 257

divinatory knowledge of, 44-45, 55; estrangement from, xvi; eternity and, 202-3; fault lines of, 114-20; with French Revolution and heritage, 170-80; future as threat to, xviii, 13, 191, 198; with heritage and ancients, 155-62; *Historical Essay* and, 73; history of present time, 8; misunderstandings of, 130; *The Odyssey* with past juxtaposed with, 54-55; as omnipresent, 8; past and, 121, 142, 156, 194-95, 229*n*43; with past and future as single concept, 211*n*57; perpetual, 41-46, 54, 56, 58, 208*n*28; presentism distinct from, xvii-xviii; Sirens as muses of antimourning in, 53

Presentism, 196; defined, 8, 18; "Generic City" and, xix; present distinct from, xvii-xviii; with presentist approach, 208*n*28; with regimes of historicity, xv; reign of, 193-204; rise of, 107-14

Preservation, restoration or, 155, 158

Price: history of, 13; listening pleasure with death as, 53-54

Primitive societies, 27, 32

Principles: of eventfulness, 27; precautionary, 196-200, 245*n*19

Prisoners: Papon and release, 230*n*53; of war, 140-41

Proscription, of imitation, 104

Protection, of environment, 115, 198-200

Proteus of Egypt, 73-74

Proust, Marcel, 127-28, 143, 180

Pucci, Pietro, 50

Quatremère de Quincy, Antoine-Chrysostome, 170-72, 175, 176, 178
La Querelle des Anciens et des Modernes, 107
Querrien, Max, 187-88, 242*n*118

Race and History (Lévi-Strauss), 14, 26, 27, 187
Raphael, 166-67

Rational catastrophism, 197, 244*n*10
Recognition, 39, 42, 45, 51, 54, 217*n*40
Recollection, 127-29, 222*n*52
Reconstruction, 5, 37, 119, 154
Record of a Journey from Paris to Jerusalem (Chateaubriand), 83
Reflections on Imitation (Winckelmann), 177
Reflections on the World Today (Valéry), 3
Regeneration, 172, 174-75
Regimes: connotations, xv; heroic, 28-32, 36, 38; modern regime's crises, 104-7
Regimes of historicity: defined, xvi-xvii, 9, 15-17; gaps in time with, 3-7; heroic, 29; historians constructing, xvi, 8-9; orders of time and, 11-19; from the Pacific to Berlin, 7-11; presentism and, xv; relevancy of, 38; universal histories and, 11-15
Relativity, 14, 26, 27
Relics, 153, 154, 167
Renaissance, 157; historic monument and, 158; humanists and, 159, 168-69, 190; in Rome, 156, 162-68
Renovatio: defined, 168, 196; Enlightenment and, 203; of Rome, 163-65, 171, 190, 196
Renown, *see Kleos*
Repetition, 73-74, 137; *historia magistra* and, 91; history and, 71; Maori with events as, 33
Res Gestae (Augustus), 158
Responsibility, 197, 198, 199-201, 244*n*16
Restitution, 164, 175
Restoration, 176, 190; conservation and, 152, 175; Meiji, 154; preservation or, 155, 158; of Rome, 159, 165-66
Returns, 6, 99, 218*n*52; of Chateaubriand, 79; homecomings, 44, 45, 53, 58; to life of savage, 77, 111-12; of Odysseus, 58
Revel, Jacques, 121, 141
Revue Historique, 135
Rico, Francisco, 168
Ricoeur, Paul, 2, 60, 102, 217*n*40, 218*n*58;

Ricoeur, Paul *(continued)*
 on historicity, 9; narrative identity and, 52; on responsibility, 198, 200, 244n16; *see also* Forgetting; History; Memory; *Time and Narrative*
Riegl, Alois, 157–58
Risk technology, 202
Rites, of Makahiki, 36
Rodin, Auguste, 180
Roland, Jean-Marie, 173
Rolin, Olivier, 5
Rollin, Charles, 71, 72
Roma instaurata (Rome Restored) (Biondo), 165
Rome: art in, 169, 171; heritage and, 155–56, 158–70; as home of antiquity, 171; Latin and, 164; Renaissance and, 156, 162–68; *renovatio* of, 163–65, 171, 190, 196; restoration of, 159, 165–66; ruins of, 165, 166–68; statues and, 169–70; as tomb, 168
Rome Restored, see Roma instaurata
Rosenzweig, Franz, 4, 109
Rousseau, Jean-Jacques, 24, 55, 67–68, 71, 76, 86
Rousso, Henry, 102
Royalty, archaic, 29–32
Ruins: in America, 94–95; Chateaubriand and, 89–95; Indian, 83; perpetual present and, 208n28; of Rome, 165, 166–68
Ruins; or, Meditation on the Revolutions of Empires (Volney), 90–91, 130
Rule, *see* Transfer of rule

Sahlins, Marshall, 8, 9; with anthropology and forms of temporality, 38–40; from event to myth and working misunderstandings, 34–38; heroic regime and, 28–32, 36, 38; with historical anthropology, 23–28, 36; from myth to event, 32–34; *see also Islands of History*

Saint Augustine and Aristotle, 60
Sartre, Jean-Paul, 23, 111
The Savage Mind (Lévi-Strauss), 24
Savages, 70, 77–79; ancients, and moderns and, 32, 66–69, 76; freedom of, 85–86; as interpretive vantage point, 86; as men of nature, 68, 71–72; return to the life of, 77, 111–12; time and, 82–84
"savage thought," 112
Scharoun, Hans, 10
Scholem, Gershom, 4
Scientific history, 121, 138
Scott, Walter, 132
Scythians, 70–72, 76, 86
The Scythians (Voltaire), 70
Seers, 74; bards as, 48; power of, 55; with present, past, and future divinatory knowledge, 44–45, 55; as voyeurs, 48
Segal, Charles, 218n48
Segalen, Victor, 56, 84
Self-estrangement, 50, 51–52, 55
Semiophores, 152, 154, 162, 175, 189
Shoah (film), 6, 102
Simiand, François, 130, 146
Simultaneism, 110
Sirens: call to oblivion, 52–55; as counter-Muses, 52–53; with language of knowledge, 218n48; in present as muses of anti-mourning, 53
Site: defined, 126; of memory, 6, 10, 85, 120, 125–27, 145–46, 153–54, 184
Sixtus IV (pope), 166
Slavery, ages of, 74
Social function, of history, 207n15
Social space, 185
The Social Contract (Rousseau), 68
Social thought, 122
"Société 'sans histoire' et historicité" ("Societies 'without history' and historicity") (Lefort), 27
Societies, 228n32; changes in French,

243n119; "cold," 8, 24–26; historicity of, 24–28; "hot," 8, 24, 27, 112, 127; memory-based, 124; nations and, 130; nature compared to, 68, 70; primitive, 27, 32; social forms, 31

"Societies 'without history' and historicity"; see "*Société 'sans histoire' et historicité*"

Solon, xiv

Some Ideas on the Arts, on the Need to Support Them, on the Institutions Which Can Ensure Their Progress, and on Various Institutions Necessary for Their Teaching, 174

The Sorrow and the Pity (Ophüls), 102

Space: "junkspace," xix; social, 185

Sparta, 76, 78

Spengler, Oswald, 11, 13

Stationary history, 26

Statues: communist-era, 208n25; death and uprooting of, 171–72; in dreams, 12; Greek, 171; Roman, 169–70

Stocking, George W., 208n28

Stoicism, 109

Strabo, 72

Structuralism, 24, 28, 38, 213n36

Suetonius, 158, 163

Supplement to the Voyage of Cook (Sahlins), 24

Sustainable development, 186–87, 199, 200, 245n21

The Swan (Baudelaire), 50

Syria, 90

Le système de l'histoire (Bonnaud), 210n55

Tableau de la géographie de la France (Vidal de la Blache), 125

Tacitus, 74–75, 79, 89

Tahiti, 223n84

Tane (separator of Earth and Heaven), 35

Tears, of Odysseus, 46–52, 58

Technology, 6, 197, 198, 202

Temporality, anthropology and, 38–40

Testament, 4–5, 75, 174–75

Thakombau (Fijian leader), 29, 42

Theodoric (Ostrogoth king), 160

Theory, of relativity, 14, 26

Thermidorian Reaction, 75

Thiénot, J., 122

Thierry, Augustin, 101, 132, 136

Thomas, Nicholas, 39

Thomas, Yan, 159–60, 166, 201

Thread of tradition, 132, 185

Threat, of future, xviii, 13, 191, 198

Thucydides, 32, 33, 121, 142

Time, 23, 69, 110, 128, 143; acceleration of, 80, 123–24, 178, 190, 231n71; Achilles with, 218n51; with arts and history, 174; attention and, 57; Augustine with, 57; Chateaubriand and, 65–66, 79–81, 103, 106, 194; chronic and linguistic, 211n57; disorientation of, 3–5, 80; of environment with heritage, 186–91; estrangement from, 42–43; experience of, 79–81; gaps in, 3–7, 88, 106; historians and, 8, 81, 104–5; in *Historical Essay*, 79–81, 83, 90; history of present, 8; Indians and, 83; memory and, xvi, 6; mind and, 57; Nora and, 103, 124; in Old Testament, 42–43, 224n94; with past objectified, 2; of ruins, 208n28; savages and, 83–84; with temporality and anthropology, 38–40; in three modes, xvi; of traveling, 81–89; unanchored, 78–79; *see also* Future; Orders of time; Past; Present; Presentism

Time and Narrative (Ricoeur), 2, 217

Time: Histories and Ethnologies, 39

Tocqueville, Alexis de, 93–95, 98

Tomb, Rome as, 168; *see also Mémoires d'outre-tombe*

Tonga, 30

Tourism, 113, 167, 188–89

Touvier, Paul, 117

Toxaris, 70

Toynbee, Arnold J., 11
Tradition, 132, 185
Tragedy, 31, 49, 76
Trajan's Column, 160
Transfer of rule, 13, 164
Travel: Chateaubriand and, 66–72; historians as last travelers, 82; time of, 81–89
Travel Diary (Montaigne), 167
Travels in America (Chateaubriand), 66, 67–68; ancients and savages in, 77; freedom in, 85–86; time of traveling and time in, 81–89; unanchored time in, 78–79
Travels of Anacharsis the Younger in Greece (Barthélemy), 70
Treaties, land, 34–35
"trente glorieuses," 108
Tristes tropiques (Lévi-Strauss), 67, 111
Tukhe (Fortune), 30

Unanchored time, 78–79
Unemployment, xiii, 112, 113
UNESCO, 14, 15, 26, 150, 186–87
Unity, national, 144
Untimely Meditations (Nietzsche), 110
Uprisings, of Hone Heke, 34
Urban development projects, 117–19, 182
Urban ornamentation, 159–60, 166
Utopia, 77, 197

Valéry, Paul, 3, 13, 104, 110, 137, 207*n*11; Febvre on, 228*n*31; with future, 227*n*12
Valla, Lorenzo, 164
Varro, Marcus Terentius, 162, 163, 165, 190
Venice Charter of 1964, 182, 183
Versailles, 179, 180
Vespasian, 158

Veyne, Paul, 159
Vichy France: Old Guard and New Order, 1940–1944 (Paxton), 102
The Vichy Syndrome: History and Memory in France Since 1944 (Rousso), 102
Vico, Giambattista, 29, 38, 41, 133
Vidal-Naquet, Pierre, 102
Viewing from afar, 37, 55, 68, 77
View of the Climate and Soil of the United States of America (Volney), 92
Viollet-le-Duc, 180, 236*n*14
Volney, Constantin-François, 90–92, 130, 225*n*105
Voltaire, 11, 70
Von Stein, Lorenz, 101
Voyeurs, seers as, 48

Walzer, Michael, 60
War, prisoner of, 140–41
Washington, George, 78
Weber, Max, xvi
Winckelmann, Johann Joachim, 169–70, 171, 177–78
Witnesses, 7, 48, 55, 115, 229*n*48
World, 3, 4; ages of, 12–13, 74; heritage, 6, 150, 186–87; New, 94–95
The World of Yesterday (Zweig), 4

Yerushalmi, Yosef, 6–7

Zakhor (Yerushalmi), 6–7
Zalmoxis, 70
Zero: "cold" societies and historical temperature of, 24; degree zero museum, 188; growth, 5
Zweig, Stefan, 4

European Perspectives
A Series in Social Thought and Cultural Criticism
Lawrence D. Kritzman, Editor

Gilles Deleuze, *The Logic of Sense*
Julia Kristeva, *Strangers to Ourselves*
Theodor W. Adorno, *Notes to Literature*, vols. 1 and 2
Richard Wolin, ed., *The Heidegger Controversy*
Antonio Gramsci, *Prison Notebooks*, vols. 1, 2, and 3
Jacques LeGoff, *History and Memory*
Alain Finkielkraut, *Remembering in Vain: The Klaus Barbie Trial and Crimes Against Humanity*
Julia Kristeva, *Nations Without Nationalism*
Pierre Bourdieu, *The Field of Cultural Production*
Pierre Vidal-Naquet, *Assassins of Memory: Essays on the Denial of the Holocaust*
Hugo Ball, *Critique of the German Intelligentsia*
Gilles Deleuze, *Logic and Sense*
Gilles Deleuze and Félix Guattari, *What Is Philosophy?*
Karl Heinz Bohrer, *Suddenness: On the Moment of Aesthetic Appearance*
Julia Kristeva, *Time and Sense: Proust and the Experience of Literature*
Alain Finkielkraut, *The Defeat of the Mind*
Julia Kristeva, *New Maladies of the Soul*
Elisabeth Badinter, *XY: On Masculine Identity*
Karl Löwith, *Martin Heidegger and European Nihilism*
Gilles Deleuze, *Negotiations, 1972–1990*
Pierre Vidal-Naquet, *The Jews: History, Memory, and the Present*
Norbert Elias, *The Germans*
Louis Althusser, *Writings on Psychoanalysis: Freud and Lacan*
Elisabeth Roudinesco, *Jacques Lacan: His Life and Work*
Ross Guberman, *Julia Kristeva Interviews*
Kelly Oliver, *The Portable Kristeva*
Pierre Nora, *Realms of Memory: The Construction of the French Past*
Vol. 1: *Conflicts and Divisions*
Vol. 2: *Traditions*
Vol. 3: *Symbols*
Claudine Fabre-Vassas, *The Singular Beast: Jews, Christians, and the Pig*
Paul Ricoeur, *Critique and Conviction: Conversations with François Azouvi and Marc de Launay*
Theodor W. Adorno, *Critical Models: Interventions and Catchwords*
Alain Corbin, *Village Bells: Sound and Meaning in the Nineteenth-Century French Countryside*
Zygmunt Bauman, *Globalization: The Human Consequences*
Emmanuel Levinas, *Entre Nous: Essays on Thinking-of-the-Other*
Jean-Louis Flandrin and Massimo Montanari, *Food: A Culinary History*
Tahar Ben Jelloun, *French Hospitality: Racism and North African Immigrants*

Emmanuel Levinas, *Alterity and Transcendence*
Sylviane Agacinski, *Parity of the Sexes*
Alain Finkielkraut, *In the Name of Humanity: Reflections on the Twentieth Century*
Julia Kristeva, *The Sense and Non-Sense of Revolt: The Powers and Limits of Psychoanalysis*
Régis Debray, *Transmitting Culture*
Catherine Clément and Julia Kristeva, *The Feminine and the Sacred*
Alain Corbin, *The Life of an Unknown: The Rediscovered World of a Clog Maker in Nineteenth-Century France*
Michel Pastoureau, *The Devil's Cloth: A History of Stripes and Striped Fabric*
Julia Kristeva, *Hannah Arendt*
Carlo Ginzburg, *Wooden Eyes: Nine Reflections on Distance*
Elisabeth Roudinesco, *Why Psychoanalysis?*
Alain Cabantous, *Blasphemy: Impious Speech in the West from the Seventeenth to the Nineteenth Century*
Luce Irigaray, *Between East and West: From Singularity to Community*
Julia Kristeva, *Melanie Klein*
Gilles Deleuze, *Dialogues II*
Julia Kristeva, *Intimate Revolt: The Powers and Limits of Psychoanalysis*, vol. 2
Claudia Benthien, *Skin: On the Cultural Border Between Self and the World*
Sylviane Agacinski, *Time Passing: Modernity and Nostalgia*
Emmanuel Todd, *After the Empire: The Breakdown of the American Order*
Hélène Cixous, *Portrait of Jacques Derrida as a Young Jewish Saint*
Gilles Deleuze, *Difference and Repetition*
Gianni Vattimo, *Nihilism and Emancipation: Ethics, Politics, and Law*
Julia Kristeva, *Colette*
Steve Redhead, ed., *The Paul Virilio Reader*
Roland Barthes, *The Neutral: Lecture Course at the Collège de France (1977–1978)*
Gianni Vattimo, *Dialogue with Nietzsche*
Gilles Deleuze, *Nietzsche and Philosophy*
Hélène Cixous, *Dream I Tell You*
Jacques Derrida, *Geneses, Genealogies, Genres, and Genius: The Secrets of the Archive*
Jean Starobinski, *Enchantment: The Seductress in Opera*
Julia Kristeva, *This Incredible Need to Believe*
Marta Segarra, ed., *The Portable Cixous*
François Dosse, *Gilles Deleuze and Félix Guattari: Intersecting Lives*
Julia Kristeva, *Hatred and Forgiveness*
Antoine de Baecque, *History/Cinema*
François Noudelmann, *The Philosopher's Touch: Sartre, Nietzsche, and Barthes at the Piano*
Roland Barthes, *How to Live Together: Novelistic Simulations of Some Everyday Spaces*
Georges Vigarello, *The Metamorphoses of Fat: A History of Obesity*
Eelco Runia, *Moved by the Past: Discontinuity and Historical Mutation*

GPSR Authorized Representative: Easy Access System Europe, Mustamäe tee 50, 10621 Tallinn, Estonia, gpsr.requests@easproject.com

www.ingramcontent.com/pod-product-compliance
Lightning Source LLC
Chambersburg PA
CBHW051352290426
44108CB00015B/1979